D1474160

Amirs, Admirals & Desert Sailors

Amirs, Admirals & Desert Sailors

bahrain, the u.s. navy, and the arabian gulf

david f. winkler

NAVAL INSTITUTE PRESS
ANNAPOLIS, MARYLAND

Naval Institute Press
291 Wood Road
Annapolis, MD 21402

Library of Congress Cataloging-in-Publication Data

Winkler, David F. (David Frank), 1958–
  Amirs, admirals, and desert sailors : Bahrain, the U.S. Navy, and the
Arabian Gulf / David F. Winkler.
     p. cm.
  Includes bibliographical references and index.
  ISBN-13: 978-1-59114-962-0 (alk. paper)
  ISBN-10: 1-59114-962-2 (alk. paper)
  1. Bahrain—Military relations—United States. 2. United
States—Military relations—Bahrain. 3. United States. Navy—Foreign
service—Bahrain. 4. Persian Gulf Region—Strategic aspects. I. Title.

VA667.B34W55 2007
359'.03—dc22

                                                  2006033360

Printed in the United States of America on acid-free paper ∞

14 13 12 11 10 09 08 07   9 8 7 6 5 4 3 2
First printing

Book design: David Alcorn, Alcorn Publication Design

Dedicated to the memory of
Vice Adm. Marmaduke Gresham Bayne and
Yousuf Ahmed Al Shirawi

Contents

Foreword

After I arrived in Bahrain, I instantly became impressed with the relationship between Bahrain and the U.S. Navy—a relationship dating back over a half a century that is truly remarkable on what it has produced and how it has worked to enhance America's and Bahrain's standing in the region. And it has struck me that this has been delivered to the United States of America and to the government of Bahrain not by grand design, but by the good offices, the good will, the professionalism, the humanity, and the generosity of the amirs and the admirals who have resided there before me.

And I dare say that many of the Bahraini leaders and American naval commanders produced this great outcome that we enjoy today at their professional peril. For former commanders of the U.S. Navy's Middle East Force, it is clear to me that over the years they probably didn't get a lot of support. In the days before Central Command, the command was overlooked by both the Atlantic and Pacific Fleets—somehow the command here in the Middle East was a necessary inconvenience, a temporary condition. Even today the U.S. Navy has a Euro-Pacific-centric focus, although that has shifted some since 11 September 2001.

I'm struck by the obvious incredible disconnect between what's so obvious when one lives in Bahrain—how vital the region is to the security not only to the United States but to our significant allies throughout the western world. Yet it is the strategic partnership that has grown up between Bahrain and the U.S. Navy that has given the region the opportunity for long-term stability and prosperity. It is a partnership that has become critical for global security in the ongoing war against terrorists.

America has been blessed because of the admirals who learned about the importance of the region. They are a great group of unsung heroes. I admire every one of them and you will learn to admire them as you hear about each one in Bahrain. They all left a lasting legacy and it inspired me to do my best to maintain their legacy.

Meanwhile Bahrain suffered tremendous political ramifications for standing by the U.S. Navy. The amirs who accepted the Navy here knew it was a bold and courageous stand but they knew it necessary for the long haul. Some cynics would say they were just trying to protect their small island emirate from less than friendly neighbors, but I give them the benefit of the doubt and say they had a strategic vision and they were willing to take the risk. And they took the risk and today they are revered by their friends in the region for having asserted that leadership.

When the history books are written, and this is a history book, you really have to give the Bahrainis a lot of credit. Because they had the bold vision with the courage to carry through, the Bahrainis have succeeded in making their island a strategic center. Indeed they have a greater appreciation for the strategic role of the U.S. Navy in the Gulf than we do in the States. There is no question that the late Shaikh Essa bin Salman Al Khalifa, by sustaining support for the U.S. Navy, has contributed hugely to the stability in the region.

Today His Highness King Hamad bin Essa Al Khalifa continues to support our objectives in the region. Because of the Bahraini-American partnership and cooperation between the United States and other states throughout the Gulf, the region is prospering. Granted much work needs to be completed to transform a post-Saddam Iraq, but the threat that regime posed to the region is gone. Of course, over the long-term the Bahrainis are more concerned about Iran, given the territorial claims the government in Tehran has made on Bahrain.

Indeed, the late Shaikh Essa once told me, "Your men and women, the ships and aircraft of the Fifth Fleet, are a mountain of fire that separates us from the Iranians and that presence of naval forces is what has given us peace and prosperity."

Shaikh Essa's observation is intuitive in that he recognizes that it is the Desert Sailors who over the decades have delivered. While the personal efforts of amirs and admirals deserve recognition, it is the daily efforts of hundreds of thousands of Sailors and Marines over a period of five decades operating in one of the harshest environments on the planet that truly earns tribute. Without them this story could not have come about.

To tell this story I thank Director of Naval History Dr. William S. Dudley for providing the resources of his Naval Reserve Combat Documentation Detachment 206 with Commanders David F. Winkler and James A. Wombwell. As detailed by the bibliography, these two officers conducted an immense amount of research in Bahrain and the United States to capture over fifty years of U.S. Navy–Bahraini relations. With this collected material, Commander Winkler then wrote a history for the staff of U.S. Navy Fifth Fleet and submitted his narrative in 2001.

With the ongoing war in Iraq, I felt it appropriate that a broader audience have access to Commander Winkler's work. Therefore, I am most appreciative to Commander Winkler's boss, Vice Adm. Robert F. Dunn, USN (Ret.), President of the Naval Historical Foundation, for allowing for him to rewrite and update the narrative on Foundation time.

Commander Winkler had the assistance of many outstanding individuals sharing the same passion for the subject matter as I do. I second his thanks to those Bahrainis and Americans who helped to make *Amirs, Admirals, and Desert Sailors* a reality.

Charles W. Moore Jr.
Vice Admiral
U.S. Navy (Ret.)

Operation Desert Fox

O n 16 December 1998, while embarked on the aircraft carrier USS *Enterprise* (CVN 65), Rear Adm. J. Cutler Dawson wore two hats. As Commander Cruiser Destroyer Group 12, he served as the administrative caretaker for ships assigned to the *Enterprise* Battle Group, which had departed from the U.S. east coast a month earlier. As Commander Task Force 50 (CTF 50), he commanded the naval strike forces in the Arabian Gulf* and he reported directly to Fifth Fleet Commander Vice Adm. Charles W. Moore. Moore was also dual-hatted, serving also as Commander U.S. Naval Forces Central Command (COMUSNAVCENT). As such he was the Navy's component commander in U.S. Central Command (USCENTCOM), a unified command headquartered at McDill Air Force Base in Tampa, Florida. However, unlike his Army and Air Force component counterparts, Moore was actually based in the Middle East—at a small U.S. Navy facility located at Bahrain, an archipelago located off the coast of Saudi Arabia, approximately two-thirds the distance from the northwestern edge by Kuwait and the Strait of Hormuz.[1]

At 1645, Dawson received a phone call from Moore. The Fifth Fleet Commander told him that the president had approved the execute order. Operation Desert Fox was "a go." At the time the battle group was making its final preparations for the attack. Assigned cruisers, destroyers, and submarines carrying Tomahawk cruise missiles maneuvered toward preplanned launch points. Seven decks below in *Enterprise*'s magazines, ordnance teams assembled an assortment of smart munitions to be carried into battle. As plane crews scrambled over F-14 Tomcats, F/A-18 Hornets, EA-6B Prowlers, and S-3A Vikings, Dawson occasionally made notations in his wheelbook: "I talked to the CAG at 1700 and he said he was ready to go and off to take a nap. By 1730, all of our Tomahawk firing units had received their indigos and marked it down so that they were all going to be executable."

Below, on the mess decks on the "Big E," the crew was excited yet anxious. Many wondered if this was for real. Saddam had taken the United States to the

---

* The Arabian Gulf is the designation given by the U.S. military for the body of water that is most commonly knnown as the Persian Gulf.

brink before, only to back down. Others asked themselves, "Did I do every-thing I could possibly have done to make tonight's mission a success?" Naval aviation can be unforgiving in peacetime, as demonstrated a month earlier when four crewmembers of an EA-6B Prowler died in a horrible flightdeck mishap. Now naval aviators, both male and for the first time female, would be risking their lives against enemy fire in the service of their country.

However, if ever there was a carrier ready to go into combat, it was *Enterprise*. Under the command of Capt. Marty Chanik, the ship's crew, the embarked Carrier Air Wing 3, and the Cruiser Destroyer Group 12 staff had molded themselves into "Team Enterprise" over the previous six months of pre-deployment workups. And although the men and women of *Enterprise* served in one of the oldest combatant ships in the fleet, in some ways the big ship had transformed herself into the Navy's most mod-ern and capable.

Equipped with "IT-21" technology, Dawson's flagship matched most shore-based command centers in being able to receive, transmit, and inter-nally disseminate tidbits of data. Using the Secure Internet (SIPRNET), video-teleconferencing, and other communications capabilities, Dawson's staff could receive, analyze, and evaluate information from sources rang-ing from the full spectrum of national security sensors to international news media. The latter sources were useful as one intelligence specialist noted that BBC World News Service often provided more in-depth political military coverage than some of the classified agency reports! *Enterprise,* in turn, quickly pushed information down to the embarked air squadrons and out to the ships of the battle group.

With such a capable platform at his disposal, Admiral Moore was able to convince his superiors to use tactical naval aviation during the first night of Desert Fox to complement previously planned Tomahawk strikes. Sur-prise was the top priority for planners at U.S. Central Command and Joint Task Force Southwest Asia (JTF-SWA). Planners understood that with the departure of United Nations Special Commission (UNSCOM) inspec-tors, Saddam's forces could expect a strike from American and British air-craft based in Saudi Arabia and Kuwait. Forewarned by his intelligence of a ground-based air assault, Saddam's commanders could quickly disperse and hide potential targets. Consequently, no land-based aircraft would fly the first night. The initial plan called for massive Tomahawk missile strikes instead. Moore, however, convinced planners that naval aviation could add to the blow, catching many more targets off guard.

With the sun set, Dawson and others on his staff kept an eye tuned to CNN. Reports airing on CNN of pending strikes concerned him, especially an interview with retired Marine Gen. Neal Dawson, prompting Dawson to write that Neal "was perhaps being too descriptive of what was going to happen later that night. I realized the Iraqis might be watching the same analysis and might be taking advantage of that."

At 2015, Moore again called Dawson to say that the president would take one last look at 2100 and that Dawson would know by 2200 if the strikes were to be scrubbed. With no follow-up call, the Battle Group Commander went up to the bridge and chatted with the Deputy Carrier Air Wing Commander.

Down in the Carrier's Intelligence Center (CVIC), Cdr. Susan Chiaraville oversaw a flurry of activity as her intelligence officers and petty officers manning the Strike Intelligence Analysis and Mission Planning cells briefed aircrews about potential threats and the latest updates on targets. Over in the CVIC's Multi-Sensor Interpretation section, Intelligence Specialist First Class (IS1) Jules Casuga reviewed the most recent satellite photography of an Iraqi surface-to-air missile (SAM) site and saw that the Iraqis had disassembled the launchers and hid them along a nearby line of trees. With SAM sites a priority target that night, Casuga immediately shared his analysis with his colleagues and within fifteen minutes was spreading the photo evidence before the aircrew slated to go after that site.

Armed with the latest intelligence, the aircrews made their way from the various squadron ready rooms to their aircraft positioned on the flight deck. With his ready room located below the hangar deck, Cdr. Jay Sherman, executive officer of the EA-6B Prowler squadron (VAQ-130) had to pass through the aft mess deck en route to his plane. *Enterprise* crewmembers overwhelmed the veteran electronic countermeasures officer as they wished him and his squadron comrades well and to fly safe. One of those squadron comrades was Lt. Tiffany "Rocko" Styles. She had recently joined Sherman's aircrew, her prior aircrew having perished during the previously mentioned flightdeck tragedy. Had she not been grounded with a head cold, she would have been one of the fatalities. A competent electronic countermeasures officer, Styles would be one of a handful of female naval aviators to make history that night as the first female naval aviators to fly in combat.

Lt. Kendra "Yukon" Williams also flew an F/A-18 as part of the first strike that night. Although she was on her first deployment, her squadron commander, Cdr. Kevin Miller, had confidence in her and the other new pilots assigned to VFA-105. "She was a nugget, a rookie if you will, but at that point she had more than one hundred career traps and a full set of workups," noted Commander Miller.

As with Sherman, Williams recalled ten guys wishing her well and shaking her hands as she made her way toward her F/A-18 Hornet. Once in her cockpit, she repeatedly went over her checklist, wondering in the back of her mind if they really were going to go through with this.

Sitting in his EA-6B cockpit, Sherman wagered $10 with his pilot on whether the mission would be scrubbed. He had just completed double-checking everything when he suddenly noted a fireball go off and then another one on the horizon. The first blow against Saddam came from beneath the surface as the attack submarine USS *Miami* (SSN 755) fired off a salvo of Tomahawks at 2307. USS *Gettysburg* (CG 64) began firing her Tomahawks shortly thereafter. Confident in the abilities of his crew, Capt. Jake Shuford still sat at the edge of his seat as the first missile blasted out of its vertical launch cell. Once the booster fell away and the missile went into the cruise mode, whoops could be heard throughout the Aegis cruiser.

Back on *Enterprise,* Dawson would note in his wheelbook: "It was quite a sight to see the [USS] *Fletcher,* which was not far from *Enterprise,* firing their first salvo—and we then knew there was not going to be any walking back from the events of that night." Above Dawson, dozens of aircraft maintenance personnel climbed onto "Vulture's Row" to gaze at the spectacle of Tomahawks being fired by eight warships and the pending launch of aircraft several decks below. On the flightdeck Petty Officer First Class John Cessna recalled, "It was probably as much excitement as I've seen working in one place," as he watched the Tomahawks go off and spotted aircraft for launch.

With dozens of Tomahawks in the air en route to Iraq, Captain Chanik at 2345 gave the order to launch. A Navy photographer captured Chanik in action just as the two forward cats launched aircraft into the night sky. Transmitted electronically through the Fifth Fleet Public Affairs Office, the image actually appeared in late edition papers on the American West Coast on 16 December.

During the midnight hour, the *Enterprise* launched "two packages" of aircraft that had a time-over-target differential of ten minutes. Petty Officer Cessna recalled that the launch had been conducted without a hitch. The Air Boss, Cdr. Joe Flynn, later reflected that the ship's catapult officers or "shooters" were not particularly experienced. On that night, however, they performed magnificently and worked beautifully with the deck crew. Together they had risen to a higher level than ever before. Once the last aircraft was airborne, the aircraft handlers filtered into ready rooms and other spaces to watch CNN reporters in Baghdad speculate about an attack.

Airborne, Kendra Williams in her F/A-18 joined up with her flight lead, took on fuel from an S-3 Viking, and headed toward the beach. As the strike aircraft made landfall, Lt. Dave Deboskey piloting an F-14 Tomcat observed that it was very quiet over Iraq. He saw very little antiair artillery (AAA) fire or surface-to-air missiles (SAMs). Lt. Col. Steve Pomeroy, commanding officer of VMFA-312, leading a flight of Marine F/A-18 Hornets, also was surprised by the lack of hostile fire.

The American naval aviators had clearly caught Iraqi defenses with their guard down. Now the challenge was to *keep* their guard down. To deter the hostile fire-control radars from attempting to light off and lock on, the EA-6Bs Prowlers launched antiradiation missiles at predetermined points. Once Sherman's Prowler reached its launch point, the pilot hit the fire key. Sherman recalled, "It scared the devil out of me." The HARM missile's straight initial trajectory amazed him as the booster shot out yellow sparks. For a few seconds, the missile's flight totally absorbed the attention of the Prowler's aircrew until a Hornet pilot reported some AAA fire and Sherman suddenly remembered "this was a war and people are trying to kill us here."

In seemingly no time, the F/A-18s and F-14s were approaching their objectives. Assigned to destroy the radar for a SAM site, Lieutenant Williams recalled, "All of a sudden we were over the target and the training kicked in and the ordnance came off my jet. It really didn't seem real until I actually saw the impact on the ground." Her squadron skipper recalled: "Yukon did a *magnificent* job finding her target and hitting it." Flying an F/A-18 in VFA-37, Lt. Karl Kottke went after another SAM radar site. As he made his approach, his Forward Looking Infra Red (FLIR) equipment failed; however, the skilled pilot switched to his air-to-ground radar and was able to find the target on the basis of its previously known GPS coordinates. He dropped his bombs on those coordinates not knowing if he hit the target. Video taken by another pilot later proved that Kottke's pair of GBU-12s were dead-on. On board the *Enterprise,* crewmembers watched CNN coverage of the attack unfold as Tomahawk missiles struck key targets in and around Baghdad.

Having discharged their ordnance, the two strike packages returned over the *Enterprise* almost simultaneously, and the challenging task of conducting a night landing was at hand. The first aircraft hit the arresting gear at about 0130. For Williams the adrenaline kept flowing, and she concentrated and easily made her trap. Others had to fight off fatigue at that early morning hour. The final plane landed about 0245.

With aircraft from the first two strikes safely returned, there was a bit of celebration. Air Boss Flynn observed: "You'd be surprised what a lift those guys [working on the deck] get out of seeing a jet come back with slim wings, no bombs. They were high-fiving each other down there." For the ordnance personnel, the empty bomb pylons served as a double bonus. . . . They did not have to unload, transfer down seven decks, disassemble, and stow tons of explosives. To Commander Sherman's amazement, his maintenance crew had a HARM missile painted on the fuselage of his Prowler seemingly within thirty seconds of his disembarking the cockpit.

Still, a great challenge remained for the *Enterprise*'s air department. As the nearly three dozen aircraft from the first two strikes were recovered, the handlers had no choice but to stack them up forward of the island. Flynn recalled, "Everything went forward . . . it was just a mess up there." All of the returning aircraft then had to be rearmed, refueled, and moved into a position for the next strike. He said it was an "amazing synergy of performance" as the flight deck crew, ordnance handlers, and squadron aircraft handlers worked together to get off the "second event." Although the third strike got off at 0415, about thirty minutes behind schedule, given the challenge that his air department surmounted, Flynn was amazed that it went off at all.

In the early morning hours in Iraq, American munitions again found their marks. As the third strike cleared the beach, light began to glimmer on the eastern horizon. By the time the returning planes reached *Enterprise,* the pilots could maneuver toward the flightdeck in the early morning light.

Over the next three nights, *Enterprise*'s aircraft would fly farther and deeper into Iraq to strike at additional targets. In sum, the aircraft of Carrier Air Wing THREE flew 281 sorties against forty targets over the four nights of Operation Desert Fox. They would, however, not be alone over the Iraqi skies as U.S. and Royal Air Force aircraft based in Saudi Arabia and Kuwait joined in on the air assault. On the fourth night, aircraft from the USS *Carl Vinson* (CVN 70) augmented the attack from the sea. Unlike what happened on the first night, the Iraqi air defenses were no longer napping and the attackers suddenly found that the airspace over their targets was now "lit up like Christmas trees." Still, the Iraqi air defenses failed to claim any of the intruding aircraft.

How far Desert Fox set back Saddam's weapons of mass destruction program could not be gauged using bomb damage assessment photographs alone. With the invasion of Iraq and the collapse of his regime, the efficacy of the strikes can be more accurately determined through interviews with former Iraqi officials.

Unfortunately, having withstood the four-day pummeling, Saddam could proceed without being under the microscope of the United Nations inspectors, who had been withdrawn by Richard Butler after he had determined that Iraq was not serious about complying with several standing UN resolutions. While American bombs may have undermined Iraq's weapons of mass destruction (WMD) infrastructure, the regime's scientists and engineers remained at the dictator's disposal to resume work.

In retrospect, Desert Fox actually prolonged the ongoing confrontation—a confrontation that the Bush administration determined needed to be concluded in the wake of the terrorist attacks of 11 September 2001.

Although it did not end the confrontation, Desert Fox—especially the first night of Desert Fox—demonstrated the striking power of naval forces. Working together independently, Navy submarines, surface combatants, and an aircraft carrier struck hard at the enemy. Reflecting on the role of naval aviation, Capt. Robert Nelson, the Deputy Air Wing commander, stated, "That's what you dream of—one air wing off of one carrier with no external support assets—just us against the bad guys."

Nelson's statement regarding external support assets was a bit off the mark, however. The Fifth Fleet staff, based in Bahrain, played an important part in the decision-making role, and other support components based there also contributed to keeping the fleet operational during Operation Desert Fox and subsequent Operations Enduring Freedom and Iraqi Freedom. How the United States obtained the privilege of operating out of Bahrain is a remarkable story—one that spans decades.

CHAPTER ONE

Background to a Relationship

The year 1783 is significant in world history. The Treaty of Paris
concluded the war between Great Britain and her former American
colonies, and the United States of America had finally achieved
British recognition of independence. This independent United States grew
in the nineteenth century, expanding from the Atlantic to the Pacific to
become a major continental power. At the dawn of the twentieth century,
the United States fought a war with Spain and rose within the ranks of
the world's global powers. By the end of World War II, this nation's economic, military, and cultural influences allowed it to achieve a new status: "superpower."

Yet 1783 is also significant for events occurring in another region of
the world. For centuries, different peoples contested for rule of the Bahrain
Archipelago. In the sixteenth century, Portugal held control. After an invasion in 1602, it was the Persians. During the eighteenth century, control of
the islands shifted among Arabs from the nearby mainland, Omanis, and
Persians. In 1755, Persian forces under Shaikh Nasr Al Mazkoor of Bushire
took seemingly firm control of the archipelago. In 1783, however, after a
series of battles as grand in scale as those in the American Revolution,
Arabs from the mainland seized the islands, forcing its former Persian rulers to flee. With the exception of one decade, Persia would continue to lay
claim to Bahrain, threatening the ruling Al Khalifa family.[1]

The Al Khalifa family traces it roots to Shaikh Khalifa bin Mohammed,
who lived with his tribe in the Najid, an area in the central Arabian
Peninsula. Khalifa moved his tribe northeast to present-day Kuwait.
After Khalifa died in about 1747, the tribe, led by his son, Mohammed,
moved once again and established a base at Az Zubarah on Qatar's west-
ern shore in 1763. Five years later, the Al Khalifas fortified the base and
were able to dominate much of the territory that is today's modern Qatar.
When Mohammed died in 1776, rule passed to his son, Khalifa. Because Az
Zubarah was a center of the pearl trade, its growth did not go unnoticed.
In 1782, following the premature death of Khalifa during his pilgrimage to
Mecca, Shaikh Nasr ordered attacks on shipping transiting to and from Az
Zubarah. A year later, the Shaikh's forces laid siege to the port. But Khalifa's

brother, Shaikh Ahmed bin Mohammed Al Khalifa, rallied his family's forces to break the siege and drive off the Persian forces.

Reinforced by a coalition of related Arab tribes, including the Al Sabahs of Kuwait, the Khalifas, led by Shaikh Ahmed "the Conqueror," seized Bahrain, driving Shaikh Nasr back to Bushire. Shaikh Ahmed became the first Al Khalifa ruler of Bahrain, ruling until his death in 1796. Shaikh Ahmed's sons, Salman and Abdulla, agreed to share power as the archipelago's resources and trade potential attracted many of the Al Khalifas to resettle there, joining a diverse population that had been in place for centuries.[2]

The Al Khalifas deftly maintained their independence during the first half of the nineteenth century. After fending off an Omani invasion attempt in 1799, they were forced to retreat to Az Zubarah briefly in 1801 after Omani forces occupied Bahrain, but in 1802, with the assistance of Arab kinsmen, the Al Khalifas expelled the Omani garrison.[3]

Throughout the early nineteenth century, Bahrain prospered while the ruling family maneuvered and occasionally acknowledged the authority of various regional powers, primarily the Persians and the Ottoman Turks. In 1819, the Sultan of Muscat and Oman, Saiyid Sa'id, lobbied hard to obtain British support for another Omani attempt to invade Bahrain; however, an envoy from the two ruling Al Khalifa brothers induced the British representative in the region, Maj. Gen. William Keir, to sign a general treaty that fended off the Omani move. Signed by Shaikh Salman and Shaikh Abdulla in February 1820, the agreement committed the Bahrainis to counter piracy and promote peace. A separate arrangement provided for the Bahrainis to pay a tribute to Oman.[4]

Still, the Omani sultan continued to harbor designs for Bahrain. A leadership crisis occasioned by the death of Salman in 1825 offered an opportunity for Omani intervention, however, the naming of Salman's son, Khalifah, to serve as co-ruler with his uncle Abdulla staved that off. Finally, in August 1828, Oman declared war and a fleet sailed from Muscat to join with forces from Abu Dhabi to attack Bahrain. This fleet commenced a blockade of the Bahraini port of Manama in late October and began bombarding the city on 5 November. Meanwhile, troops were landed on Sitrah to the south of Manama for an overland assault on the port. The invasion would be thwarted. At a site called Jufair, Bahraini forces overwhelmed troops allied with the Omanis, reportedly killing five hundred of the invaders. Barely escaping with his life, the Omani sultan regrouped and continued the blockade, but an outbreak of cholera forced him to call off the campaign.[5]

Five years after Oman's failed campaign against Bahrain, two strange warships arrived off Muscat. The sloop of war USS *Peacock* and the schooner

USS *Boxer* dropped anchor to deliver "Special Agent" Edmund Roberts, who sought to negotiate a commercial treaty. Sultan Saiyid Sa'id welcomed the American envoy and on 21 September 1833, a treaty was signed, establishing the first diplomatic ties between a country on the Arabian Peninsula and the young republic on the opposite side of the globe.[6]

With the death of Shaikh Khalifah bin Salman in 1834, sole rule of Bahrain passed to Shaikh Abdulla. The elder Al Khalifa struggled to govern while putting down revolts in Qatar. A five-year revolt against Al Khalifa rule on that peninsula led by the tenacious Isa bin Tarif hurt the Bahraini economy. Diplomacy brought the struggle to an end. After Shaikh Abdulla signed an agreement of friendship with the Egyptians in 1839, he concluded an arrangement with Shaikh Khalifa of Abu Dhabi to persuade Isa bin Tarif to cease hostilities.[7]

Over time Shaikh Abdulla had built up a number of domestic foes. Led by his grandnephew, Mohammad bin Khalifah Al Khalifa, they forced the elder Al Khalifa to step down in April 1843. Exiled, Shaikh Abdulla attempted to make his grandnephew's rule uncomfortable through raids against Bahraini shipping. In early 1847, he even convinced his former enemy, Isa bin Tarif, to resume his campaign in Qatar, a campaign that cost the rebel leader his life. Shaikh Abdulla next attempted to elicit Persian and then Omani aid to recapture his former land before passing away in 1849. However his son, Mohammad bin Abdulla, kept his father's dream alive from a base he established at Dammam on the Arabian coast.[8]

Over the next decade, Mohammad bin Khalifah acknowledged both Persian and Ottoman claims of sovereignty and then appealed to one side for protection whenever the other side wanted to assert its claim. He also exploited opportunities to raid shipping in the Gulf and to tax British Indian traders on Bahrain.

To counter Ottoman claims on Bahrain as well as the imperial aims of Great Britain and Tsarist Russia, Persia sought outside assistance. In the autumn of 1855, a Persian charge' d'affaires approached the U.S. minister at Constantinople with a proposed seventeen-article treaty. Included were provisions for U.S. Navy protection of Persian merchant shipping, a commitment for American defense of Persian coasts, and naval assistance to "subjugate such of its islands and ports as show insubordination and refuse to pay revenue."[9]

The United States had neither the resources nor the desire to become militarily engaged in the region. Persia settled on signing a strictly commercial accord with the growing Atlantic power on 13 December 1856.

Great Britain, the maritime superpower of the nineteenth century, was not amused with Persia's courting of the United States, its pro-Russian leanings during the Crimean War, and its capture of the Afghani city of Herat. After a diplomatic breakdown, the British launched a Persian Expeditionary Force in November 1856. British and Indian troops landed and routed the Persian army in several engagements, leading to the signing of a peace treaty on 4 March 1857.[10]

With the British settling scores on the northern side of the Gulf, the focus turned to all of the maritime extracurricular activities around Bahrain. A British squadron arrived off Muharraq Island in May 1861 and seized two of Bahrain's finest war dhows. Consequently the British offered "the Treaty of Perpetual Peace and Friendship" with Shaikh Mohammad bin Khalifah Al Khalifa to end the shipping raids in exchange for British maritime protection. Mindful of threats from Persia and from the Ottoman Empire, as well as demands for tribute by Saudi amirs, the Bahraini leader saw the benefits of such an arrangement and signed the accord on 31 May 1861. Subsequently, Shaikh Mohammad enlisted the support of the British to arrange for Mohammad bin Abdulla's expulsion from Dammam.

Stability was short-lived. The 1860s represented a period of continuing struggle for the Al Khalifas and the people of Bahrain. Although not to be compared with the scale of the conflict that occurred on the North American continent, the power struggles of this period would have repercussions into the twenty-first century. When Bahrain fell to Shaikh Ahmed "the Conqueror" in 1783, family elements continued to maintain holdings in the western port of Az Zubarah. However, during the early nineteenth century the Al Thani family on Qatar's east coast gained power and moved to control the whole peninsula. Reacting in October 1867, the Al Khalifas sent forces to attack the Al Thani–dominated ports of Doha and Al Wakrah.

Although the British were appalled by the Bahraini action, the Bahraini amir felt completely justified in handling what he considered an internal matter. Around the Gulf, various Arab tribes watched to see if the British would react; however, with no Royal Navy ships in the region, continued maritime peace was uncertain. Seeking revenge, in June 1868, the Al Thanis put a fleet to sea to attack Bahrain. Shaikh Mohammad bin Khalifah sent his navy to intercept the attackers. In the ensuing engagement, the two sides between them reportedly lost sixty ships and approximately one thousand Sailors.

Despite this obvious case of self-defense, the sea battle only further angered the British against the Bahraini leadership. Arriving at Manama with a flotilla of warships on 6 September 1868, the British inflicted retribution on Shaikh Ali bin Khalifah, brother of Shaikh Mohammad who had left for Kuwait. The next day, the British destroyed the Bahraini fort at Qalaat Abu Mahir and burned the Bahraini fleet.

The Royal Navy then steamed to Doha to forge a peaceful settlement with the Al Thanis. They arranged a deal that acknowledged the dominant position of the Al Thanis, but still had the leading Qatari families paying tribute to the small Al Khalifa enclave at Az Zubarah.[11]

Banned from returning to Bahrain, Shaikh Mohammad resettled at the Arabian coastal town of Qatif where he allied himself with his once bitter foe Nasr bin Mubarak, a renegade Al Khalifa shaikh, and another long-time nemesis, second cousin Mohammad bin Abdulla Al Khalifa. In 1869, four years after the assassination of President Abraham Lincoln, Mohammad bin Khalifah returned to Bahrain with a small force of Bedouins and stormed Rifaa Palace during which his brother Ali was killed. As the Bedouins proceeded to plunder through Manama, Mohammad bin Khalifah appointed his second cousin Mohammad bin Abdulla to command the army. However, this trust was misplaced—the new army commander promptly seized power. Needless to say, this course of events displeased the British.[12]

In November, the British dispatched warships to Bahrain with a consul embarked to bring some stability to the situation. One popular historical treatise argues that the slain Shaikh Ali's son, the twenty-two-year-old Shaikh Isa bin Ali Al Khalifa, had much popular sympathy but was powerless in view that "his enemies had garrisoned all the forts and strong points on the islands." The narrative then describes how a small naval flotilla arrived off Muharraq out of sight of land. Then, on the night of 19 November 1869, a landing party captured the fortress of Abu Mahur after a fierce but brief struggle. The other forts succumbed to artillery fire with little loss of life and "Shaikh Isa bin Ali was, according to the record, 'installed as ruler without interference on the part of the British Resident, amid every sign of popular rejoicing.'" The two Mohammads were exiled, while Nasr bin Mubarak escaped to remain a threat to Bahrain for years to come.[13]

The installation of Isa bin Ali Al Khalifa in 1869 marked a turning point in Bahrain's history. He ruled until 1923 and brought stability. Furthermore, with the appointment of his eldest son Shaikh Hamad as the heir apparent, he established a method of leadership transition that continues and has spared the archipelago the succession struggles it saw earlier in the nineteenth century. Over the long term, his steady rule earned him and Bahrain considerable respect. King Adul-Aziz ibn Adul Rahman Al Saud once remarked, "Shaikh Isa was the father not only of the Gulf, but also to the whole of Arabia. We Arabs, especially we in our house, looked upon him with the greatest affection."[14]

However, in the short term, the Al Khalifa foothold on Qatar came to an end in the 1870s. The Al Trani allied themselves with the Turks and seized most of the peninsula in 1871. With the recognition of Turkish sovereignty in 1872, the payment of tribute to the Al Khalifas at Az Zubarah ceased. Six years later, under the pretext that pirates loyal to the Al Khalifas were attacking shipping, the Al Thanis, joined by Nasr bin Mubarak, assaulted and destroyed Az Zubarah. The Al Khalifas, however, retained a presence on most of the islands in between. Consequently, the sixteen Hawar Islands would continue to be a contentious issue until an International Court of Justice ruling in March 2001.

Given the geopolitical situation, Shaikh Isa signed additional agreements with the British in 1880 and 1892, formalizing a relationship lasting well into the twentieth century where Bahrain became a "protected state" under which the British assumed responsibility for the archipelagos' defense and obtained a substantial say in its external affairs. The ruling Al Khalifa family maintained control over Bahrain's internal affairs, although they employed British nationals in various capacities. The most notable of these British nationals was Charles D. Belgrave, who served the ruling family as a financial adviser, as chief of constabulary, and in other capacities from 1926 to 1957.[15]

Oxford-educated, Belgrave came from a distinguished English family. His great-grandfather, James Richard Dacres, commanded the frigate HMS *Guerriere* during the War of 1812. On 30 August 1812, Captain Isaac Hull and the USS *Constitution* met with and sank Dacres' frigate, and Belgrave's great-grandfather became a prisoner of war. With this lineage, it seemed only fitting that Belgrave himself would one day engage with American naval officers.[16]

Belgrave learned Arabic while serving with the British Camel Corps in Egypt during World War I. After the war he served with the Colonial Service in Tanganyika in east Africa. While in London on leave, Belgrave noticed a posting in *The Times* for a position in an eastern state. After correspondence and interviews, Belgrave and his new bride found themselves heading to Bahrain. There Belgrave met Shaikh Hamad bin Isa Al Khalifa.

Shaikh Hamad had assumed control as Regent in 1923 after his father, Shaikh Isa, retired from active control of affairs after ruling for fifty-five years. After taking control, Shaikh Hamad traveled to England. Impressed by what he saw and determined to implement reforms that would bring about modernization at home, the new ruler sought to employ an Englishman as an adviser. Prior to that, he had sought the council of Clive Daly, the British political agent in Bahrain. Daly, however, worked for the British government, and his views were clearly biased. Shaikh Hamed wanted an advisor who worked exclusively for him. Belgrave would become that man.[17]

Manama, the seat of government at the north end of the main island, hosted two outstanding natural harbors: Bahrain harbor, which faced north and was shallow, and a second to the northeast, where a waterway between Manama and the sandy island of Muharraq formed a deep-water anchorage. The location of these harbors made Bahrain a strategic base for British operations. In 1914, Bahrain acted as a staging point for the British Expeditionary Force that would serve in the Mesopotamian Campaign. In 1935, the British had to abandon their naval base at Hemjam on the Persian coast. Consequently, the Royal Navy eyed Bahrain as an ideal location to establish a facility.

After innumerable discussions among the Bahraini, Royal Navy, and British government representatives, Shaikh Hamad approved a site at Jufair. That news of the base agreement didn't seem to bother the local residents. One Bahraini observed to Belgrave, "The price of eggs will surely go up." Asked what eggs had to do with a navy base, he responded, "When English men-of-war are here, they buy up all the eggs and we get a very high price for them."[18]

Thus the British started construction on a facility adjacent to the deep water between Manama and Muharraq. Established on 13 April 1935, HMS Jufair became a major anchorage for Royal Navy ships operating in the Gulf. With the Royal Navy ensconced at HMS Jufair, Belgrave wryly observed, "the price of eggs did go up." Previously, in 1932, an aerodrome on Muharraq Island opened to commercial and military aviation.[19]

Separated by oceans and continents, the two peoples sharing an affinity for the year 1783 came into little contact during the nineteenth century. When the USS *Ticonderoga* passed through the Strait of Hormuz into the Gulf in 1879, she was the first American warship to visit the region, but she did not make a port call to Bahrain. Other Americans would have to travel to the region to establish ties with the Bahraini people.[20]

For example, in November 1892, the Rev. Samuel Zwemer, a missionary with the Dutch Reformed Church, arrived with medicines that could treat certain ailments. Winning friends, the Reverend Zwemer returned in 1893 and established a dispensary. On occasion, missionary doctors would visit to treat serious cases. The visits were helpful, but Zwemer sought permanent medical assistance and received it in 1900 with the arrival of a husband-wife doctor team. Impressed with their work, Shaikh Isa allowed the mission to obtain land to build a two-story structure. Named the Mason Memorial Hospital (for the New York family that donated construction funds), this institution served the Bahraini's healthcare needs for the next sixty years. Replaced with new buildings in 1962, the hospital was renamed the American Mission Hospital.[21]

In the 1930s, American oilmen also became involved in Bahrain. During the previous decade, a New Zealander, Frank Holmes, had formed a consortium of British businessmen and mining engineers and had won a concession in 1925 from Shaikh Hamad. Under-capitalized by the British, the concession seemed doomed to failure, until Standard Oil of California (SoCal) expressed an interest. British resistance to a direct American corporate presence in the region led to the chartering, on 11 January 1929, of the Bahrain Petroleum Company Limited (Bapco), at Ottawa, Canada, a commonwealth country. It was a subterfuge: Bapco was a wholly owned subsidiary of SoCal. With the concession transferred to this new entity, drilling began and on 1 June 1932, oil began flowing—the first successful strike in the lower Gulf region. Two years later, Bahrain began to export oil, with the departure of SoCal tanker *El Segundo* for Yokohama.

In June 1935, officials from SoCal and the Texas Corporation joined together to form the California Texas Oil Company (CalTex). In October, this new company's subsidiary, Bapco, broke ground for a new refinery.[22]

Writing twenty-five years later, Charles Belgrave still seemed bitter that British oil companies were unwilling to take a risk, subsequently allowing the Americans to move into Bahrain. Yet Belgrave thought very highly of the Americans. Expecting them to behave like cowboys, Belgrave observed, "They *were* a tough lot, but they must have been carefully picked, for they behaved extremely well."[23]

A year after war broke out in Europe, the Italians, as Germany's Axis partner, targeted Bahrain for air attack. In October 1940, aircraft departed from the Dodecanese Islands in the Aegean Sea to conduct a night raid on the Bapco refinery. Lit up like a Christmas tree, the refinery must have been an inviting target. However, the Italian flight commander may have received poor targeting intelligence, because he was told to drop his bombs between two waste gas flares. Little did he know that one of the flares had been moved outside of the refinery's perimeter before the attack. Hence the Italian bombs fell harmlessly onto an adjacent petroleum coke pile.[24]

A greater threat appeared two years later as General Erwin Rommel's Afrika Korps drove into Egypt. Contingency plans were made to plug and destroy the oil facilities to prevent them from being exploited by the Germans if Rommel broke through. However, Gen. Bernard Montgomery's decisive victory at El Alamein helped secure the Gulf region for the remainder of the war.[25]

The British and Russians also saw a threat to regional security a year earlier when Reza Shah Pahlavi refused to expel German advisers in the wake of the May 1941 German onslaught on the Soviet Union. With a secure supply route from the Gulf to the Soviet Union vital for the British-Soviet alliance, the two countries occupied the Persian state. After Reza Shah Pahlavi abdicated, his son Mohammad Reza Hah Pahlavi signed the Anglo-Russian-Persian Treaty of January 1942, thus legitimizing the joint occupation of his country.

A month earlier, the Japanese attack at Pearl Harbor had brought the United States into the war. Soon American lend-lease support for the Soviet war effort brought a substantial American military presence to the Gulf for the first time. With Liberty and Victory ships unloading war supplies at Iranian ports, U.S. Army Transportation Corps trucks began the long over-land run north to the Soviet border. By the end of the war, American forces presented a dominant presence in the southern half of Iran.[26]

On the other side of the Gulf, the war also affected Bahrain. Because of the difficulty of moving Middle East oil through the Mediterranean or around Africa to western Europe, the British limited oil production in the region to only enough to supply military operations in the vicinity. Some oil fields actually shut down. In contrast to the other Arab shaikdoms—most of which had oil production curtailed—Bahrain kept producing oil at pre-war levels and actually expanded its refining capacity as oil was pumped to the island from Saudi Arabia via an underwater pipeline.

American interest in Bahraini production capabilities began shortly after the United States entered the conflict, when the Office of Petroleum Coordinator asked Bapco to submit a proposal to add a 100-octane aviation fuel facility to their refinery. Harold Ickes, who served as the coordinator, also proposed to increase refining capability throughout the region. Superiors deferred his proposal as long as the military situation remained uncertain. However, as sea lanes of communication were reopened in the Mediterranean and western Pacific, demand for Middle East oil increased.

Back in the United States, the Army-Navy Petroleum Board—an agency of the Joint Chiefs of Staff—authorized the Petroleum Administrator for War (formerly the Office of Petroleum Coordinator) to reach an agreement with Bapco to fund the construction of additional facilities, including the avia-tion fuel refining plant. The actual contract was let by the Defense Supplies Corporation, a subsidiary of the Reconstruction Finance Corporation. Military oversight for this construction activity would be indirect. The War Department assumed jurisdiction over the American construction workers on Bahrain. A substantial number of these men did not reach Bahrain until early 1944. The project was fraught with challenges. An insufficient work force, delays in material deliveries, lack of motor transport, and competition for native unskilled labor by the Royal Air Force for airbase construction, all conspired to set back production schedules. The aviation fuel plant opened in 1945, and the first shipment of 100-octane gasoline was sent in July. By the end of the war, these new facilities were providing the U.S. Navy with tens of thousands of barrels of high-octane aviation gasoline, Navy diesel, and Navy specialized fuel oils. To inspect the quality of the fuel, the Navy stationed some personnel from the Inspector of Naval Material's Office at the Bapco facilities. In addition, the Air Transport Command stationed a few hundred men at the greatly expanded airfield at Muharraq.[27]

Oil was not the only Bahraini contribution to the war effort. General Rommel's Afrika Corps destroyed millions of British jerrycans and oil drums during its push into Egypt. A lack of containers to carry the oil needed to fuel tanks, trucks, and planes threatened to stall British and American counteroffensives. The Americans built three plants for British use at Abadan, Iran, and production of jerrycans, thirty-six-imperial gallon, and U.S. fifty-five-gallon drums began during 1943. Looking for backup facilities closer to the Burma theater, the War Department contracted with Bapco to operate two production lines. The War Department provided the manufacturing machinery and, after assembly, production began on 1 August 1944. By the end of the year, 41,307 barrels had been accepted. With better supervision and additional pieces of equipment, production increased to an average of more than 40,000 barrels a month. By 1 May 1945, total output had reached 188,346 barrels. The barrels were shipped to theaters throughout the Middle East and Southeast Asia and contributed to allied success. With the war over, the Army's Jersey City Quartermaster Depot negotiated the sale of the plants to Bapco.[28]

With the investment of U.S. Government dollars and the influx of American civilian and military personnel, the United States proposed the establishment of a U.S. Consulate. The British refused. Instead, on 2 September 1944, the United States opened a consulate in Dhahran. Under State Department guidance, the consulate would informally provide coverage for Bahrain.[29]

Despite the military activity and the influx of foreign resources, Bahrainis faced some hardships during World War II. There was, for example, food rationing. Bahraini native Hamza Kaedi recalled that when he was a young boy, certain foods, such as bread, were scarce; for a period, however, there was an overabundance of cheese. Bapco's head chef ordered thirty tuns or casks of cheese from the home office in New York. The New York office misread *tuns* as *tons*! Bahrain became the Kraft Cheese Company's best overseas customer.[30]

Shaikh Hamad bin Isa Al Khalifa strongly supported the allied effort against the Axis and contributed to war funds as well as to a special fund to purchase Spitfire aircraft. With his death in February 1942, the new ruler, Shaikh Salman bin Hamad Al Khalifa, continued Bahrain's strong support for the allied war effort. At the end of the war, Shaikh Salman celebrated the allied victory by hosting a dinner for four hundred British, American, Indian, and Iraqi soldiers and Sailors.[31]

When World War II ended with the allied defeat of Italy, Germany, and finally Japan, Bahrain retained its status with the British as a "protected state." However, the United States had created a positive reputation on the archipelago through the establishment of a missionary hospital and the ownership of oil producing and refining facilities that generated an improved standard of living for the native population. Because of the region's contributions to the allied war effort, Bahrain's strategic importance gained recognition by leaders in Washington, especially in the Navy, and became a topic for debate in the ensuing years. The two countries, sharing a common affinity for the year 1783, would be drawn closer together.

CHAPTER TWO

The Arrival of the U.S. Navy

S oon after World War II, a series of events occurred that set the stage for the Cold War. While historians continue to debate just when it was that the Cold War began, the situation in Iran certainly contributed to the downturn in relations between the Soviet Union and her wartime allies. According to the January 1942 Anglo-Soviet-Iranian Treaty, allied occupation of Iran was supposed to end within six months of the cessation of hostilities. With the Japanese surrender on the deck of the USS *Missouri* (BB 63) on 2 September 1945, the departure date was set for 2 March 1946.

Yet on 4 March 1946, American Vice Council Robert Rossow Jr. observed Soviet forces moving south through one of Iran's northern provinces. One day later, Winston Churchill made his famous "Iron Curtain" speech at Fulton, Missouri. On 6 March, the State Department announced plans to return the remains of a deceased Turkish ambassador using the *Missouri*. Finally, at the end of March, Stalin decided to withdraw his forces.

During the crisis, American military planners examined what immediate military options could be taken if the Soviets decided to remain or even push southward to the Gulf. With American forces rapidly demobilizing, there were few assets that could be diverted into the region. What would be the consequences? When asked later that year by the State Department for an analysis of American "strategic interests in Iran," a Joint Chiefs of Staff (JCS) Joint Strategic Survey Committee (JSSC) determined that the United States and its allies could fight the Soviets for two years without Middle East oil. In such a military confrontation, the committee foresaw the United States denying the Soviets access to the wells for as long as possible, and then recapturing them later in the war to augment domestic sources. At the same time, the Joint War Plans Committee (JWPC) of the JCS explored warfighting options against the Soviet Union in various geographical regions, under the code name "Pincher." The JWPC foresaw offensive action in Europe, defensive action in the Far East, and concluded, as did the JSSC, that the Gulf area would initially succumb to the Soviet forces. Navy planners on the JWPC, acknowledging the difficulty of defending the whole area, pointed out that it might be easier to hold Bahrain as a base to serve as a staging area to recapture adjacent areas. Air Force and Army officers resisted the concept. For the time being, the United States remained unwilling to make a major military commitment to the region.[1]

However, given the perceived Soviet threat, the Navy forged ahead under the assumption that the JWPC would eventually agree on the need for contingency plans covering the Gulf. For Navy leaders, the need was obvious. While the United States had been the world's leading exporter of oil for decades, diminishing reserves were forcing American leaders to reexamine their export policies, especially after the expanding economy created unexpected demands for fuel and led to a domestic oil shortage in the winter of 1947. The shortfall was such that, to meet domestic needs, the Navy provided from its strategic reserves one million barrels of oil to heat east coast cities.

With its reserves being rapidly depleted, the Navy stepped up its purchases from overseas sources. American warships serving in the Mediterranean and in the Pacific depended almost exclusively on petroleum from the Gulf, especially the special and diesel fuels refined in Saudi and Bahraini refineries. In addition, with jet aircraft coming into the inventory, the Navy predicted a dramatic increase in fuel consumption rates. The Chief of Naval Operations (CNO), Fleet Adm. Chester W. Nimitz, clearly understood the Navy's vulnerability regarding fuel, especially fuel from the Middle East. In July 1947, he issued a "Tentative Assignment of Forces for Emergency Operations," designed to ensure global sea lines of communication. The Commander in Chief, Northeastern Atlantic and Mediterranean (CINCNELM) and the Commander in Chief, Pacific (CINCPAC), were given joint responsibility for preparing forces to occupy and defend Bahrain.[2]

Given an apparent green light by Nimitz, Adm. Richard L. Conolly, upon assuming the duties as CINCNELM on 1 November 1947, sought to improve the Navy's ability to operate and fight in the Gulf. Having already toured Saudi Arabia and Bahrain the previous May during his first official visit to the region, Conolly reacted with interest to a report submitted by Capt. Thomas Kelly, a logistician, who had visited the region in September. Impressed with the area's resources and disturbed by its vulnerabilities, Kelly urged Conolly to deploy carrier task groups to the Gulf for climate familiarization and also to initiate plans to defend the region. In December 1947, after Nimitz read Kelly's report, he added a reinforced Marine battalion to Conolly's forces in the Mediterranean to cover a Middle East contingency. One month later, Nimitz expanded Conolly's area of responsibility to include the Arabian Sea and Ceylon.[3]

As for Kelly's recommendation on climate familiarization, Nimitz's staff had already begun planning for a ten-ship task force to be sent into the Gulf in August 1948 to test equipment and personnel, conduct port visits, and collect hydrographic and photographic information on the region. Contingencies caused the plan to be modified, but 1948 marks the appearance of American warships into the Gulf at unprecedented levels.[4] For Admiral Conolly, the decision to deploy warships to the Gulf reflected his belief in the value of forward deployment. In an oral history conducted by Columbia University in 1960, Conolly commented: "If the situation grew tense, and you sent forces into the area, it was a menacing gesture; whereas if you had forces already there, and reinforced them, it could not be so considered, although it would have more actual deterrent effect on the opposition than sending a force on an emergency basis."[5]

The *Essex*-class carrier USS *Valley Forge* (CV 45) and her escorts entered the Gulf in March 1948. Although the ship did not call at Bahrain, the task group commander, Rear Adm. Harold Martin, apparently visited with American oilmen and Bahrainis. He came away from these meetings extremely impressed with the high esteem that the Bahrainis held for these American foreigners. He anticipated that this good will would be helpful in gaining support for building a regional defensive infrastructure.[6]

Two months later, the USS *Rendova* (CVE 114) and USS *Charles H. Roan* (DD 853) arrived in the Gulf and conducted an exhausting fifty-two-hour visit to Bahrain. Commencing on 19 May, this port call represented the first time an American aircraft carrier had visited the archipelago. The visitors pursued an aggressive itinerary prepared by Lt. Cdr. E. B. House, the CNO's representative at Bahrain, and Lt. Cdr. C. C. Porter, the Resident Inspector of Naval Material. Prior to *Rendova*'s arrival, three fighters and four torpedo bombers were allowed to land at the airport on Muharraq Island. During the visit, these planes conducted flight operations, taking overhead photographs of Bahrain for later presentation. Because of the lack of camels [wooden floats] available to cushion the carrier against the Bapco Sitra Pier, the *Rendova* opted to Mediterranean moor, with her stern facing the pier. This made refueling a bit awkward.

The carrier's commanding officer spent his first day calling on local officials and receiving return calls. At 1630, His Highness Shaikh Salman bin Hamad Al Khalifa arrived for a two-hour tour. Reporting afterward, the executive officer noted that drinking water from the ship's electric coolers "proved to be the prize indulgence of the royal retinue." Most appreciative of the tour, on the following evening the Shaikh hosted a dinner for 120 guests, including forty-five officers from the visiting U.S. Navy ships. In a report submitted at the conclusion of the *Rendova*'s cruise, the executive officer wrote, "The Dinner was undoubtedly the highlight of the visit if not the entire cruise. It would take many words to describe the colorful occasion, which was at once restful and ceremonial."

The XO described the evening as "delightfully cool and dry," noting that the "open air courtyard of the Shaikh's summer palace, lighted by many colored and white lights, presented a picturesque and enchanting scene." He added, "The floor was covered with Persian rugs over matting on which the one hundred and twenty chairs were arranged in the shape of an elongated rectangle." At one end the shaikh, flanked by the British political resident and *Rendova*'s commanding officer, sat where they could observe all of the guests. The attendants wore "very bright and colorful red robes trimmed in gold," and they performed their services "with a flourish befitting their position as members of the shaikh's royal household." After about an hour of amiable chatting between servings of juices and coffee, "the entire party moved to an adjoining courtyard where the dinner was waiting." Once again the guests sat down cross-legged on rugs laid out in another elongated triangle. "The food for the entire meal was placed upon the inner rectangle of white cloth." The XO counted twelve roasted sheep on large metal plates and huge plates of rice, relish, roast chicken, and fruits. Servants walked on the white cloth and "tore the meat from the sheep with their bare hands, piling it on the guests' plates in enormous quantities whether it was requested or not." He concluded that "the Arabs believe that if a guest 'cleans' his plate they have failed as hosts."

After rising from dinner, the entire group reassembled in the first courtyard "where more coffee, fruit juice, tea, and ice cream were served." Then the servants "liberally sprinkled the hands of all the guests with rose water." For a final touch "a servant went from guest to guest with an incense burner permitting each guest to smell the aroma of the incense." At about 2230, the visitors departed and "His Highness personally bade farewell to each of his guests in a most gracious and sincere manner."[7]

The graciousness of Shaikh Salman was exceptional, considering the fact that a few days earlier the United States became the first nation to recognize the State of Israel. The behavior of the Bahraini people was also civil. Charles Belgrave had feared riots. However, not all of the shaikh's countrymen were as willing to overlook the recent events. Of sixty invitations sent out to prominent Arabs to attend a reception aboard *Rendova*, only fifteen recipients accepted. The others wrote a joint note of regret, citing the American policy toward Israel and the Palestinians.[8]

American activity in the Gulf continued after *Rendova*'s departure with the arrival of the seaplane tender USS *Greenwich Bay* (AVP 41). The dispatch of the *Greenwich Bay* to the region marked a furthering commitment by the CNO. From 19 July to 12 August 1948, she plied the waters of the Gulf "for the purpose of obtaining information concerning necessary alterations required by that type during the hot season prior to maintaining one AVP in that area on rotational basis for duty as station ship Persian Gulf." Capt. Whitmore Butts' report back to the Bureau of Ships told of the crew sleeping topside and eating on the fantail. Officers "stuck it out in the wardroom" with one meal served when the room temperature hovered at 114 degrees. He also noted a litany of effects the heat and humidity had on mechanical and electronic equipment and presented a long list of recommended ship alterations, including extensive air conditioning and painting the ship white. During her Gulf cruise, *Greenwich Bay* visited Bahrain for the first time.[9]

Shortly after *Greenwich Bay* departed, Vice Adm. D. B. Duncan, Commander Second Task Fleet, arrived in the Gulf with Task Force 128, consisting of the flagship USS *Pocono* (AGS 16), USS *Siboney* (CVE 112), USS *Carpellotti* (APD 136), USS *Massey* (DD 778), and USS *Zellars* (DD 777). During the two-week visit, calls were made to ports including Bahrain. Specially equipped photo planes from the *Siboney* conducted extensive photo mapping of the region.

Admiral Conolly stopped in Bahrain in early September as part of an inspection tour of the region. No doubt the topic of a rotating station ship must have been on the agenda. It is possible that on this trip, Conolly may have committed a major *faux pas*. Belgrave recalled a visiting American admiral around this time period coming forward to meet Shaikh Salman. The shaikh then called his teenage son to come forward. As the son reached out to shake the admiral's hand, the admiral promptly took his cover off and handed his hat to the young man as well as the hats of the two officers beside him. There was a gasp among all of the other visitors in the room, and the son stood in confusion. The shaikh defused the situation by calmly telling his son to put the hats somewhere. However, the next American flag party to call on the shaikh must have been surprised when two palace servants, wearing daggers and slung swords, forcibly grabbed the officers' hats before they were allowed to enter the shaikh's reception room.[10]

In October 1948, Hydrographic Survey Group 1, composed of USS *Maury* (AGS 16), USS *Dutton* (AGSc 8), USS *John Blish* (AGSc 10), and USS *Littlehales* (AGSc 7), arrived to map the Gulf's waters. This group remained in the Gulf until April 1949. Unfortunately, the survey's progress was not up to expectations: the four ships spent only 272 days on station (combined) during the six-month period. The obstacles encountered, including weather, logistic support, and upkeep, forewarned the naval leadership of future challenges in operating in the Gulf. *Maury,* along with USS

Allegheny (ATA 170) and USS *Stallion* (ATA 193), returned in 1950 to continue the survey work.[11]

Another *Essex*-class aircraft carrier, the USS *Tarawa* (CV 40), and her escorts USS *Hawkins* (DD 873) and USS *Dennis J. Buckley* (DD 808), also visited the Gulf in January 1949. They reportedly called at Bahrain.[12]

Meanwhile, Navy fleet oilers and chartered tankers operated in the Gulf to obtain fuel products. For example, during *Rendova*'s visit, fleet oilers USS *Caloosahatchee* (AO 98), USS *Waccamaw* (AO 109), and USS *Chemung* (AO 30), along with tankers USS *Mission Los Angeles* (AO 117) and USS *Schuylkill* (AO 76), were present. With as many as two dozen ships entering or leaving the Gulf during a given month, Admiral Conolly tightened operational control by establishing Task Force 126. Stood up on 20 January 1948, the force consisted mainly of oilers and tankers operating in the Gulf. Admiral Conolly assigned the Senior Officer Present Afloat (SOPA) as task force commander. Later, on 29 October, he subdivided Task Force 126 into Task Group 126.1, Middle East Force (MEF) Administration (ashore); Task Group 126.2, the aforementioned Hydrographic Survey Group; and Task Group 126.3, Tanker Group. With this move, he also made Cdr. Robert C. Woolverton the force's permanent commander. In December 1948, Capt. William V. O'Regan relieved Woolverton and assumed administrative command of the organization. Admiral Conolly relinquished operational control of the now-named Persian Gulf Forces to O'Regan on 26 June 1949. Capt. K. G. Hensel relieved O'Regan on 12 August 1949.

Because this new command's scope of operations envisioned activities outside the Gulf, four days after Hensel assumed command, Persian Gulf Forces was renamed Middle East Force. As Commander Middle East Force (COMIDEASTFOR), Hensel used as his command flagship *Greenwich Bay,* which returned to the Gulf in June after being reconfigured for better hot weather endurance. Previously O'Regan had flown his flag from *Maury* and USS *Duxbury Bay* (AVP 38), another airplane tender. The *Duxbury Bay* and USS *Valcour* (AVP 55) were scheduled to be hot weather configured. When *Valcour* relieved the *Greenwich Bay,* the three AVPs completed the first cycle of a COMIDEASTFOR flagship rotation that would continue nearly uninterrupted for the next sixteen years.[13] To support Navy operations in the region, the Navy established a ship-to-shore high frequency (HF) circuit at Asmara, Eritrea, and at the U.S. Air Force Base at Dhahran, Saudi Arabia.[14]

Anticipating that the Gulf would become a major operating area for the U.S. Navy, Fleet Admiral Nimitz and Admiral Conolly stepped up the Navy's presence there considerably during 1948 and 1949. Two carrier and two escort carrier task forces steamed into Gulf waters, while other ships performed hydrographic survey and logistic support duties. War plans were developed that would commit U.S. Marines to the region to defend against and delay any Soviet onslaughts. Finally, a command structure was formalized, creating the position of Commander Middle East Force, a position that would endure for decades to come. During those decades, three modified seaplane tenders would rotate in and out to serve as his flagship.

However, the Navy's vision of the Gulf as a major theater of operations faded as other demands took priority during an era of shrinking defense budgets that led, eventually, to the cancellation of an aircraft carrier and "the Revolt of the Admirals." On 24 January 1950, the Joint Chiefs of Staff eliminated the Marine battalion deployment to the Gulf when they modified the current war plan code named "Off Tackle." Then, in June 1950, the North Koreans invaded South Korea and the United States was forced to deploy its limited naval forces to the Far East. For the next twenty years, the United States would look to the British to serve as the guardians of the Gulf.[15]

CHAPTER THREE

Middle East Force: The Early Years

W
ith the Soviet detonation of an atomic bomb, the triumph of Communist forces in Mainland China, and the outbreak of war on the Korean peninsula, the Cold War entered a new phase. Rather than a direct military confrontation between the two major protagonists, the Cold War developed into a struggle along the periphery as the United States sought to contain the expansion of Communism. The strategy of containment was first publicly espoused by Ambassador George F. Kennan in an article entitled "Sources of Soviet Conduct" in the July 1947 edition of *Foreign Affairs*. Two months earlier, speaking at the U.S. Naval Academy, Kennan compared the struggle "to a sort of long-range fencing match" and concluded that "it may be the strength and health of our respective systems which is decisive and will determine the issue. This may be done—and probably will be done—without war."[1]

Containment had political, military, and economic components. In western Europe, a political-military alliance was created in 1949 with the formation of the North Atlantic Treaty Organization (NATO). In the Far East, the United States set up security arrangements with Australia, New Zealand, Japan, and the Philippines. Military force might deter external attack, but strong economic growth was vital to stem internal Communist movements. For example, the Marshall Plan pumped millions of dollars into the European economy to help restore pre-war industries. In this bipolar world, the Middle East's role proved to be pivotal. Throughout the Cold War, America's European and Asian allies, along with the United States itself, became increasingly dependent on oil pumped from the Gulf region.

In addition to sustaining economic growth, Middle East oil fueled U.S. Navy warships, allowing the United States to maintain its supremacy at sea. For the United States to be a credible ally to its overseas partners, supremacy at sea was essential. During the Korean War, this supremacy allowed UN forces to inject and sustain combat forces, conduct air strikes and shore bombardment, and deny enemy forces means to resupply.

As noted earlier, U.S. naval forces overseas during the post-war period depended on Middle East oil. In 1949, 158 U.S. Navy fleet oilers and tankers called at Bahrain and at Ras Tanura, Saudi Arabia, to obtain fuel for the fleet. With the outbreak of war in Korea, the amount of oil flowing to the fleet increased. During the first four months of the war, sixty-four government-owned or -operated tankers were called to Bahrain or Ras Tanura for loading. By the end of the year, a tanker a day was departing from the Gulf to support the war effort. Retired Rear Adm. Ernest M. Eller, who served at the time as Commander Middle East Force, recalled that the Navy had activated every "rust-bucket" it could find.[2]

Countries of the region also joined to defend against the Soviet threat. In 1955, Iraq, Turkey, Britain, Iran, and Pakistan united to form the Baghdad Pact. The United States, although not a member, did support the member states with armaments, training, and participation in exercises. In 1958, revolutionaries overthrew the government of Iraq, killing King Faisal, and promptly withdrew Iraq from the pact. The remaining countries continued the alliance for another twenty years, as the Central Treaty Organization (CENTO).

The Iraqi situation showed that the emerging Cold War was but one major story during this era. The 1950s and 1960s also marked the end of colonial rule throughout substantial sections of Asia and Africa. Britain had already pulled out of India, in 1947. Meanwhile, the French were struggling to maintain control in Southeast Asia. In the Middle East, there was a rise in Arab nationalism. Then Capt. Ernest M. Eller, soon to be promoted and en route to assume command of Middle East Force in August 1950, gained an appreciation of the problem during a layover in Egypt. Speaking with the locals, he learned of resentment with the British resulting from political difficulties and mistrust. Soon after Eller's stopover, sporadic fighting broke out as the British reinforced garrisons along the Suez Canal. In 1952, Egypt's King Farouk left in exile after a military coup. Two years later, Col. Gamal Abdul Nasser became the premier. In July 1956, after the withdrawal of British forces, he nationalized the canal. This action provoked British and French demands to internationalize the waterway's administration. At the end of October, the British, French, and Israelis conspired to seize the canal through military force. Without American support, the seizure attempt failed, and the incident further fueled Arab resentment against the West. In the Middle East, the United States would have to be sensitive to the rise of Arab nationalism.[3]

Clearly, when operating in the region, the Americans had an advantage over the Europeans, because the United States had never aspired to impose its will on the region as a colonial ruler. Eller recalled a friendly visit with Prince Monsour of Saudi Arabia during which the prince expressed how much he had been impressed with the visit of an American aircraft carrier: "We hope that you will keep your Navy strong, not only to protect America, but the rest of the world. Ships like the *Valley Forge* show that the United States has reached a peak in material achievement never before approached by any nation. It is a good thing for the world that the one to do this is the United States because she devotes these achievements to the welfare of the world, to help all nations and not just herself. I am glad it is not another nation, for you alone will use your strength at sea for peace and not for imperialism."[4]

The three seaplane tenders serving as flagships on a rotating basis in the Gulf certainly could not be construed as instruments of gunboat diplomacy. Rear Admiral Eller later recalled that the mission of the command "was to show the flag, to make the people of the countries aware that the United States was interested in them, and to be a small evidence of the United States strength that would show them the free world's interest in maintaining freedom around the world."[5]

Eller relieved Capt. W. T. Rassieur on 18 August 1950 as COMIDEASTFOR. The change of command ceremony took place on board *Greenwich Bay* during a port visit to Bombay. In a 1979 interview, Eller described the ship that served as his flagship for a part of his tour as comparable to a destroyer escort in length. He added: "The *Greenwich Bay* had air conditioning to a degree. You couldn't have enough air conditioning against the heat there. She was painted white to reflect the sun's heat. This helped, and we had ample awnings, which we used a great deal, and all the time for receptions on board."[6]

The three sister flagships traced their roots to the Lake Washington Shipyard in Haughton, Washington. These *Barnegat*-class tenders were launched during World War II. Commissioned before the end of the war, both *Greenwich Bay* and *Duxbury Bay* saw some wartime service. They continued on duty in the Pacific after the war although the *Greenwich Bay* returned to the United States for a time to serve as an escort ship for the presidential yacht *Williamsburg*. Because of other priorities, *Valcour* was not commissioned until 1946; she then was assigned to the east coast. *Valcour* received extensive remodeling after a tragic collision with a collier in Hampton Roads in May 1950 engulfed the ship in flames and killed eleven crewmembers. Yard workers installed extensive air-conditioning and removed the 5-inch forward gun mount, giving the ship a unique silhouette.[7]

The three ships shared the same dimensions and characteristics: they each displaced 1,776 tons, were 310 feet 9 inches long, and had beams of 42 feet 2 inches and a mean draft of 11 feet 11 inches. They could achieve a speed of 18 knots (14 knots in later years), and the crew size averaged three hundred. As for sea-keeping abilities, retired Yeoman Chief Jim Lee, serving aboard *Greenwich Bay* in 1955, recalled: "Returning to the States in the Atlantic Ocean, we encountered a storm that made it extremely difficult to stay on course. I was in the ship's office trying to type the plan of the day on a manual Royal typewriter. The seas were so rough that I could only type when the ship rolled to starboard. I became ill three times and had to give up on the plan of the day. With the ship pitching and yawing, I bounced all the way back to my bunk aft. Got into my bunk and held onto the chains for my dear life. How the people on watch in the engine room and on the bridge were able to carry out their tasks, I'll never know."[8]

These ships were almost always commanded by an aviator. Amazingly, a tour as skipper of one of these AVPs met the requirement of having a deep-draft command prior to being assigned command of an aircraft carrier.

Later command histories complained that these small AVPs could not provide the spaces needed to support a flag officer and his staff. In 1960, the COMIDEASTFOR command history lamented that the main staff office was contained in a space measuring 15.5 feet by 20 feet, hosting eight desks and ten staff. Other grievances included the following:

- The lack of display space. Maps or charts could not be posted for display of current information.
- Bunkrooms for staff officers were too crowded with no space allotted for a year's worth of clothing. Few officers had their own desks.
- No room to expand communications and living spaces, should emergency operations necessitate the augmentation of the staff.[9]

If you wanted to go to sea and see the world, then duty aboard one of the three rotating flagships would have fulfilled your desires. Because it took nearly a month to steam to and from the Middle East, each ship deployed every year for six months. Once back at their homeport of Norfolk, they performed additional duties with the Atlantic Fleet as required. Maintaining them proved especially challenging.

Perhaps there was no greater challenge than that met by the *Duxbury Bay* in the wake of the May 1950 *Valcour* tragedy. With *Valcour* facing massive repairs, the *Duxbury Bay* took the damaged ship's place in the cycle. Instead of a six-month turnaround, *Duxbury Bay*'s commanding officer, Capt. Paul T. Blackburn Jr., had to ready his ship in just two months. Not surprisingly, morale plummeted for many crewmembers looking forward to holidays with families stateside. Fortunately, Captain Blackburn worked closely with his type commander to institute an aggressive personnel transfer program and replaced all but two crewmembers not desiring to go.

Readying a ship that had just endured six months of constant steaming proved to be far more difficult. During a two-week availability, the USS *Cadmus* (AR 14) attempted to perform repairs and maintenance normally conducted in a navy yard overhaul. The stopgap measures were inadequate. A board of Inspection and Survey (INSURV) reported that, despite *Cadmus'* efforts, the *Duxbury Bay* was not ready for sea. Moved to the Newport News Shipyard, the ship spent twenty-two days receiving necessary repairs. "The yard made very satisfactory progress in all respects and the ship's force accomplished a few minor miracles in repair, assembly and installation of machinery and hull components." After departing the yard, the *Duxbury Bay* had a day-and-a-half shakedown cruise and then spent seven days provisioning for deployment.[10]

Departing on 17 September 1951, the *Duxbury Bay* steamed across the Atlantic, calling at Gibraltar, Naples, Port Said, and Massawa, Eritrea. At Massawa, the *Duxbury Bay* met with the *Greenwich Bay* and picked up the Commander Middle East Force, Rear Adm. Rufus E. Rose, and his staff of four officers, and assumed duties as flagship. The *Duxbury Bay* then proceeded into the Gulf after stopping in Aden. For the next two-and-a-half months, the ship conducted a dozen port calls along the southern edge of the Gulf from Oman to Kuwait. Three calls, each of about a week's duration, were to Bahrain.[11]

In his annual history report, Captain Blackburn summarized logistics, weather, and navigation as major problems for ships deployed to the Gulf. He had left Norfolk expecting to be re-provisioned in November. However, dock strikes on the U.S. east coast delayed the departure of contract cargo ships. Consequently, 117 days passed before food from the United States arrived. When the SS *Steel Voyager* arrived on 30 December with provisions, only one side of bacon remained in the reefer and the crew had just enough food to sustain two meals. In the interim, *Duxbury Bay*'s supply officer had been able to obtain limited amounts of meat and vegetables from oil companies in Kuwait, Saudi Arabia, and Bahrain.

Regarding the weather, Captain Blackburn explained that Gulf weather in November and December could be unpredictable. For example, when low-pressure systems entered the Gulf, they gave rise to the Shamal or northwest winds: "These winds arise suddenly and without prior warning, they usually last from 4 to 12 hours depending on the rate of movement of the system, bringing clouds of fine dust out of the desert. This dust is often mistaken for fog at night when the winds usually abate. The dust is a very serious operating problem. Visibility is usually restricted to 2 to 3 miles. Radar performance is restricted in the low lying dust clouds and when there are high type dust clouds, radar performance is unusually good to excellent."[12]

Captain Blackburn noted that the dust provided the ship with a permanent housecleaning problem and accelerated the wear on machinery. The winds averaged 10 to 15 knots but at times could reach 55 knots. The staff on board *Duxbury Bay* tracked reports from around the region to offer some clue of oncoming weather, but weather forecasting in the Gulf was considered "uncertain at best."

Navigation was also problematic. Dust clouds obliterated the morning and evening horizon, making celestial navigation difficult, and the dust storms often hid landmarks and downgraded radar navigation. The Gulf was also filled with poorly charted coral reefs.[13]

After three months in the Gulf, *Duxbury Bay* headed out across the Arabian Sea to visit Karachi, Pakistan; Bombay, India; and Columbo, Ceylon. Reaching Massawa on 4 March 1952, the *Duxbury Bay* turned over Rear Admiral Rose and his staff to the newly refurbished *Valcour* and returned through the Suez Canal, visiting ports in Greece and France. Once back in Norfolk, the *Duxbury Bay* entered the Norfolk Naval Shipyard for an extended availability to install air-conditioning units, add insulation, remove the 5-inch gun mount, and perform other alterations.[14]

Other command histories and personal recollections echoed this operating pattern and the challenges of steaming in the Gulf. Retired Yeoman Chief Lee recalled similar problems with logistics during his tour on *Greenwich Bay*. Running the ship's office, Lee was especially frustrated with the unpredictability of the mail. Regarding provisions, he remembered that on one occasion: "We ordered 200 pounds of hamburger meat, no response; then another 200 pounds, still no response; then another 200 pounds—finally all 600 pounds came in at once. It is amazing how many ways you can prepare hamburger meat."[15]

Eller's relief, and Rear Admiral Rose's predecessor, Rear Adm. Harry D. Felt, also recalled dissatisfaction with the logistics. "So-called fresh, maybe frozen—I don't remember—came by commercial ship out of New Jersey after stopping God knows how many times on the way to the Persian Gulf, so when our stuff arrived it wasn't very fresh."[16]

Captain Blackburn's report discussed weather in November and December. Rear Admiral Felt, however, experienced the full brunt of the Gulf's heat. During what he described as one of the worst summers that had been experienced in the Gulf, with 112 degrees Fahrenheit along with high humidity, and water temperatures approaching similar heights, swim call could hardly serve as a relief. Adm. Noel A. M. Gayler, who commanded *Greenwich Bay* in 1956, remembered that one time alongside the dock at the Saudi oil port of Ra's Renora, the water temperature was 103 degrees Fahrenheit. He noted that the Bureau of Ship's tables stopped at 90 degrees. "And, of course, that hot salt water just ate up unprotected steel like sugar in a cup of coffee."[17] Felt maintained an 0600 to 1300 work routine that minimized topside exposure to the crew during the extreme afternoon heat. Retired Yeoman Chief Lee remembered having to run across *Greenwich Bay*'s topside decks to avoid suffering burns on the feet.[18]

Rear Admiral Felt was the first flag officer to be assigned as Commander Middle East Force. Admiral Conolly had lobbied back in 1948 to post a flag officer to serve as a point man to represent U.S. interests in the region. Relieving Captain Eller on 21 April 1950, Felt pursued his diplomatic chores with gusto. As with his captain predecessors and most of his rear admiral successors for the next few years, the Middle East tour was a six-month unaccompanied stint.

During Felt's tour, the Navy implemented a policy of "chopping" two destroyers from Sixth Fleet on a rotating basis to transit the Suez Canal to augment the COMIDEASTFOR flagship and conduct "show the flag" visits to ports in the region. Gayler, the former skipper of *Greenwich Bay,* noted that the destroyers were much worse off than the flagship. "They were not suitable[;] they weren't specially rigged for it like we were."[19] In contrast to the rotating seaplane tenders, the destroyers deployed out of the Sixth Fleet spent only one or two months east of Suez.

On 16 April 1956, as a result of increasing tensions in the region, the Navy ordered the number of destroyers sent into the region to be doubled to four. The destroyers rotated in pairs and, except for a period in late 1956 and 1957, a pair of destroyers passed through the Suez Canal every fifteen days. During this time, COMIDEASTFOR was directed to keep at least one destroyer in the Red Sea and in the Gulf at all times. On 12 January 1958, the CNO scaled back the number of destroyers in the region to two, and eventually the requirement for a full-time destroyer presence in the Gulf was rescinded.[20]

In the wake of Colonel Nasser's nationalization of the British-controlled Universal Suez Canal Company in late July 1956, Capt. William P. Mack, Commander Destroyer Squadron 22, took two of his destroyers through the Suez Canal to augment COMIDEASTFOR. En route, he received a confidential message from the Office of Naval Intelligence asking him to evaluate whether the Egyptians were capable of managing the canal. On the north-south leg they had a Dutch pilot, and Mack pumped him for information on maintenance organization and capabilities. Arriving in Bahrain, he was tasked with determining whether there were any British garrison movements toward the canal area. After a few weeks of observing our British allies, Mack took his destroyers back through the canal. This time he worked with an Egyptian pilot. After clearing Port Suez, Mack sent in a report stating he believed the Egyptians would have no trouble piloting ships and maintaining the canal.[21]

Nasser's action rankled the British and the French, who hated to relinquish control of a strategic waterway that carried much of Europe's oil. Working in collusion with Israel, the French and the British planned a military operation to seize the canal. On 29 October 1956, the Israeli army swept into the Sinai. The British and French then issued ultimatums to the warring Egyptians and Israelis to keep military forces away from the canal. When Nasser rejected the ultimatum, Britain and France began to bomb Egyptian forces and then send in ground forces.

Washington was aghast. In the final week of his reelection campaign, President Eisenhower had been blindsided by the Anglo-French-Israeli action and had to react to the Soviet's brutal crushing of the revolt in Hungary. Through the United Nations, the United States played hardball with its cross-Atlantic allies. A ceasefire was obtained, and the French and British withdrew to leave the canal in Egyptian hands. The United States pledged to assist in salvage efforts to reopen the waterway. In the interim, the U.S. Navy had two destroyers stranded on the other side with the *Greenwich Bay*.[22]

For Gayler and his crew aboard *Greenwich Bay*, the blocking of the canal must have been demoralizing, especially since the *Duxbury Bay* had already passed Gibraltar en route to relieve them. Instead, Gayler and his crew were ordered to stand by to assist with the evacuation of American citizens should violence erupt in the region. There were some serious demonstrations in Bahrain during which no Americans were hurt.

Fortunately for *Greenwich Bay*, relief came in the form of a destroyer tender, USS *Prairie* (AD 15). The *Prairie* had been sent to Bahrain to investigate damage to the destroyer USS *Compton* (DD 705), which had lost a screw to one of the Gulf's notorious coral heads. Relieved, the *Greenwich Bay* then escorted the maimed destroyer home as she worked her way around the Horn of Africa on one shaft. Gayler wanted to visit Brazil instead of West Africa. Therefore, he rigged his aircraft refueling equipment to conduct a replenishment at sea, so that he could provide *Compton* with enough fuel to make it across the South Atlantic. The *Valcour* relieved the *Prairie* the following March.[23]

On 22 May 1957, the canal was reopened and *McNair* (DD 679) passed through to join the Middle East Force. Up on the destroyer's bridge, newly minted Ens. James M. Jeffords observed the passage and noted that the Office of Naval Intelligence (ONI) had clandestinely placed a team on board to photograph Egyptian military facilities. Commenting on clumsy photo-collection efforts nearly a half-century later, the Vermont senator recalled that the Egyptian pilot would call over to the ONI cameramen to point out better angles to capture their targets.[24]

Few ships in American naval history can compare to the three Middle East Force flagships regarding the hosting of foreign dignitaries. For example, in February 1953, *Duxbury Bay* embarked Ethiopian emperor Haile Selasse and transported him to French Somaliland. The ship was rewarded for its hospitality with two thousand pounds of the finest Ethiopian coffee. *Greenwich Bay*'s ship's history shows this tender also hosted the Ethiopian emperor as well as the shah of Iran, King Ibu Saud of Saudi Arabia, and the shaikh of Kuwait. All of them hosted the shaikh of Bahrain as well as local political and military leaders throughout the Gulf, Arabian Sea, and Indian Ocean.[25]

The flagship and the destroyers assigned to COMIDEASTFOR also worked with other navies in the region in various exercises. In 1956, COMIDEASTFOR began a series of annual bilateral exercises with the Imperial Iranian Navy. The shah viewed the activities from the bridge of the COMIDEASTFOR flagship. Two years later the MIDLINK exercises began. Although not a member of CENTO, the United States usually participated in this annual multilateral exercise, often augmenting its forces in the region. In 1959, the Navy sent a destroyer and a submarine into the Gulf and, in 1963, the carrier USS *Essex* (CVS 9), seven destroyers, two submarines, and four maritime patrol aircraft teamed up with navies from the region.[26]

Over the years, the three flagships also performed numerous search and rescue and humanitarian missions. The crew of the *Greenwich Bay* reacted quickly when, in June 1950, an Air France plane crashed as it approached the Bahrain airfield. Boats from the tender were the first to arrive at the scene and were able to retrieve nine survivors who were clinging onto a wing of the fallen DC-4.

In 1955, *Valcour* crewmembers boarded the blazing and abandoned Italian tanker *Argea Prima*. Although the tanker was laden with seventy-two thousand barrels of crude oil, *Valcour*'s firefighters extinguished the inferno and prevented a major environmental disaster from occurring in the Gulf. The Italian crew was able to re-board and get the ship under way again.

In 1957, the *Duxbury Bay* provided aid to Ceylon in the wake of devastating floods. With COMIDEASTFOR embarked, the flagship rushed food, supplies, and medical personnel to the disaster area and coordinated the activities of the USS *Princeton* (CVS 37), her aircraft, and Navy destroyers that had been assigned to the region to help. The Navy's actions saved thousands of lives through the prevention of mass epidemics.[27]

On 18 January 1962, *Duxbury Bay* and the destroyer USS *Soley* (DD 707) came to the assistance the Danish tanker *Prima Maersk*. The tanker had suffered an engine room flash fire and one of the crewmembers had been badly burned. *Duxbury Bay*'s doctor provided the initial treatment, and the victim was offloaded to the *Soley* for rapid transit to Bahrain, some three hundred miles away. Just over a year later, in February 1963, when a lighthouse crew fell ill on Little Quim Island near the mouth of the Gulf, the *Duxbury Bay* again was first on the scene with medical assistance.[28]

Not all responses to distress were entered into the official records. Framarz Bradran, a prominent Manama carpet merchant, recalled that in the 1950s, his father, mother, and brother were crossing the Gulf to Iran when their dhow's engine failed. They floated helplessly for two days, running out of food and water. On the third day, with the sun rising, his father said a prayer for help. Soon, an American warship came over the horizon and came to their rescue. Besides towing them back into port, the crew provided medical treatment, clothes, and plenty of food.[29]

Finally, each of the ships participated in "people-to-people" and "project handclasp" programs. They distributed textbooks, medicine, clothing, and other needed items. Under these programs, Sailors also went ashore to provide entertainment, play local teams in various athletic competitions, and help construct orphanages and schools. In 1958, in Bahrain, the Americans established a fund to support the American Missionary Hospital. Each of the flagships supported the fund. In addition to monetary contributions, American Sailors pitched in with volunteer working parties and blood bank donations.[30]

By the early 1960s, part of the turnover process between outgoing and incoming flagships including "the passing of the sack." The outgoing crew packed assorted items into a big canvas bag marked "the sack." With the two ships moored alongside each other, the outgoing captain, dressed in Arab clothing, reached over from the wing of his bridge with "the sack" in his left hand and his right hand extended. The incoming skipper, dressed in his normal uniform, reached out from his bridge wing to grab the sack with his left hand and then extended his right hand to perform a handshake for both ships' photographers.[31]

In 1966, this tradition ceased. The costs of maintaining three World War II vintage seaplane tenders as rotating flagships began to mount. After cost analysis, the Navy determined that it would be less expensive to port one of the ships permanently in the Middle East and to decommission the other two. An agreement was reached with the British and with the Bahraini government to homeport the *Valcour* at HMS Jufair. (Of the three, *Valcour* was determined to be in the best material condition.)

Prior to assuming permanent duties as flagship, the *Valcour* underwent a restricted overhaul at the Philadelphia Naval Shipyard. Yard workers performed extensive work, adding additional antennas, transmitters, receivers, and cryptographic equipment. Regrettably, as her 1966 command history lamented, "Very little funding was made available for tending to the ship's machinery and hull." Once out of the yard, *Valcour* returned to Norfolk and moored alongside the soon-to-be-decommissioned *Duxbury Bay*.

Because *Valcour* would not return stateside for several years, over the next month there was a mass movement of "repair parts, equipment, consumables, and pure junk" from the *Duxbury Bay*. "Anything that anybody thought to be any good for any purpose was placed on board almost anywhere in anticipation that part or "stuff" might be used or needed say any ole time!"[32]

The ship's history continued to tell the tale: "On 18 April 1966, amid the normal confusion of a deploying ship, crying children, weeping wives, and a very brassy Anchors Aweigh supplied by the COMCRUDESFLOT FOUR band, USS *Valcour* backed away from her berth and commenced the month-long track to Port Suez via Barcelona, Beirut, Port Said and the Suez Canal."[33]

With the new communication suite, the Navy redesignated the *Valcour* from being a seaplane tender (AVP) to command ship (AGF). Consequently, her hull number was changed from AVP 55 to AGF 1. After receiving "the sack" from the *Greenwich Bay* at Port Said, *Valcour* made her way to her new homeport. The selection of Bahrain as a homeport was logical given the U.S. Navy's good relations with the British at HMS Jufair and with the shaikh. Besides, the Navy had maintained a small, but growing, presence at HMS Jufair since 1948.

Born in 1938, Hamza A. M. Kaedi was just twelve years old when approached by a family friend who worked at HMS Jufair about a position as office boy. In 1948, after receiving Bahraini permission, the British granted an office for a small American shore detachment. Now the small lad sat before an American junior officer who pummeled him with questions:

"Can you speak English?"

"A little, sir."

"If I say, 'Get me coffee or tea?' "

"Yes, I understand this."

"If I say, 'Get me that book?' "

"Yes, I understand this."

"And if I ask you to clean the office?"

"This would be no problem—I can do this."

Hamza Kaedi got the job.[34]

With the outbreak of the Korean War, the small detachment's mission was to track the arrivals and departures of tankers, route them to their destinations, and make radio reports to higher authorities. This Naval Control of Shipping Office (NCSO) became a component command of the Middle East Force.

Hamza Kaedi remembers most of the American Sailors as friendly. He recalled one radioman who was particularly gregarious. Bill Plackett had just graduated from boot camp and Radioman A school when he received orders to U.S. Naval Control of Shipping Office, Bahrain. The future Master Chief Petty Officer of the Navy (MCPON) described his first impression of the Middle East when landing at the U.S. Air Force Base at Dhahran and stepping out at two in the morning into the Saudi heat: "Literally a blast furnace when you opened the door." He thought, "What in the world has happened to me?"[35]

When Plackett arrived at HMS Jufair, there were two officers and seven enlisted assigned. With the exception of three officers assigned to the Inspector of Navy Material office located at the Bapco refinery, these men represented the entire U.S. presence in Bahrain. MCPON Plackett recalled that five of the seven were radiomen, while the other two were a yeoman and a quartermaster. He noted: "This place was McHale's Navy upside down and inside out. The uniform of the day was teeshirt, shorts, black shoes, white socks, no hat. It was not really as strict a military outfit as you would think, except when the admiral was around. If he was around, why, things were pretty squared away."[36]

MCPON Plackett discussed watchstanding. "We'd do different schemes, but for the most part we'd stand twelve-hour watches." Occasionally, he would stand a twenty-four-hour watch. In a one-in-four rotation, this gave him three days off to do other things. Often there was boredom. But when merchant ships were in, "Why, they'd come up on a net and you'd start working them, and they'd be looking for loading instructions, and we always disseminated all the loading instructions to them. In many cases we would refile their movement reports for them." Plackett noted that he used to do a lot of continuous-wave (CW) Morse code radio transmissions with these ships.

He also worked closely with the Navy Communications Station at Asmara, and there also was a voice net that served as more of a harbor net for contact with the flagships. Of course, Plackett maintained constant communications with the flagship using CW. "Within the radioman rating, you got to be known by your fist, and you had certain characteristics—everybody did—of the way that they would send Morse code." Because of these characteristics, Plackett became familiar with his counterparts. "You knew when a guy would come up on the net, you knew who he was, you knew what his capabilities were, and you could go out and 'swing out' as much as you wanted to." Having mastered the speed key, Plackett could continuously swing out 30 to 35 words per minute.[37]

In addition to the flagship, the Navy provided Commander Middle East Force with an R-4D aircraft beginning in the early 1950s to enhance his ability to move about the region. For Plackett, the old Super DC-3 equivalent proved to be the ticket to exciting adventures, after he learned how to operate the aircraft's radios and qualified to fly as a backup radioman. Stowed away aboard the aircraft, Plackett visited Pakistan, India, Ceylon, Iraq, and other parts of the region. Occasionally, he joined the crew for a flight to Naples, where once a quarter the plane underwent ten-day maintenance periods.

As for living in Bahrain, Plackett arrived just after the Suez crisis, "So our movements were pretty well curtailed during the first three or four months I was there." Eventually, the buddy system was employed and the Sailors got more freedom to roam. Of course, Plackett and his fellow Sailors lived out on the economy, bunking together in a flat they called the "Navy house." MCPON Plackett recalled striking up warm relations with the local neighbors, and he enjoyed playing with the Arab kids. For additional recreation, the detachment challenged visiting ships and oil company workers to games of softball.[38]

Plackett's duties were not limited to those of his rate. The detachment served as a liaison between the flagship and the local government, and its members would have to go over to the airport to clear arriving shipments through customs. By this time, Hamza Kaedi, now in his late teens, had become an integral component of the NCSO operation. His duties included smoothing relations with local officials and building ties between the Americans and local political and business leaders. Learning to drive the detachment's Willy's Jeep, Kaedi soon found himself tapped to become the admiral's driver whenever the flagship pulled into port and dropped the hook at her assigned anchorage. When the COMIDEASTFOR staff signaled the admiral's departure from the flagship, Kaedi donned his chauffeur outfit and drove to the end of the British jetty to await the arrival of the admiral's barge. After 1962, with the completion of the Mina Sulman pier, Kaedi merely had to drive up to the docked flagship. Kaedi recalled that the NCSO XO would conduct a weekly inspection of his haircut and clothes to see that all was proper.[39]

Calling on the amir became an integral part of the agenda for each of the Middle East Force commanders. When Captain Eller called on Shaikh Salman bin Hamad Al Khalifa, he was escorted by Charles Belgrave, who served as a translator. Eller came away impressed: "I think Shaikh Khalifa was the most progressive and enlightened and philosophic of the shaikhs I met. He had a good face and a good heart. He tried to live up to his responsibilities. He said that, in a sense, it was like being in biblical times when the priest was the father of the people and he felt he was."[40]

Eller remembered that during his calls he would be anointed with oil. After the incense, there would be a coffee ceremony. "One of the servants hauls a large coffee pot off about a yard away, they just flicks it, and hits the coffee cup every time." Eller was amazed with the precision. "He'd fill it up to a quarter of an inch of the brim with a single flick and not spill a drop." Eller then explained that the servant would keep filling the cup until you could drink no more. At that point you would wiggle your hand. "If the shaikh is ready for you to go, he wiggles his cup and you go."[41]

On calls, Captain Eller always tried to find out about the amir's interests. "His interests were people most of all, then world conditions." Having never left Bahrain, Shaikh Salman told Eller, "A man can travel all over the world by reading—I've been everywhere in the wonderful world of books."

Captain Eller concluded that the amir had the respect of his people. The shaikh had audiences after the first break-of-day prayer. "Anyone with a problem could come see him." Having lost his father at age three, Hamza Kaedi was one of those who sought the shaikh's help. With his salary as an office boy not covering family expenses, Shaikh Salman saw that he received the funds needed to get by.[42]

Of course when a call was made, there was an expectation that it would be returned. Charles Belgrave arranged with Captain Eller to have the amir return calls at Belgrave's office. Eller's relief, Rear Admiral Felt, would have none of that, though. After calling on the shaikh, Belgrave explained the arrangement and Felt responded, "If there is to be a return call it will be made under the American flag in my flagship."[43]

After a few days of negotiations through flag lieutenants, Belgrave sent a message stating that the shaikh gets seasick. With the water in Bahrain harbor plate-glass flat, Felt was hardly satisfied with that explanation. Finally, the shaikh's brother made the return call, and the protocol requirement was fulfilled.

Later, when he escorted Felt on another call on the shaikh, Belgrave again became insistent that the return call be made at his office. Consequently, Felt decided to address the question to the Shaikh Salman directly. "Gee, I would hope that you could return my call?" The amir looked at Belgrave and then at Felt. His eyes sparkled.

"I'd like to do that."

"That's fine, when?"

"Right now!"

And so the call was returned.[44]

Belgrave's unaccommodating behavior toward Felt can be understood in the context of an earlier experience. In January 1950, the flagship of the British East India Squadron was at anchor and the commander in chief, Adm. Charles Woodhouse, hosted a reception. On the boat heading to the flagship, Belgrave observed that the sea "was calmer than I had ever known it, strangely calm in fact." Upon reaching the flagship, he noted a Marine band playing and some one hundred guests drinking cocktails, chatting with ship's officers under canvas awnings. Signal flags were draped from above for décor. Belgrave recounted: "Without any warning, a terrific gale lashed the ship, ripping the canvas which enclosed the deck, tearing the flags into tatters and whirling the band music off the stands into the sea like a giant paper chase. Dresses were torn, women's hair stood up on end and soon waves were splashing on the sides of the deck."[45]

Advancing in age, Belgrave obviously did not care for ship visits.

In the late 1950s, with British and Bahraini permission, the U.S. presence at HMS Jufair was increased by the addition of a small planning cell at NCSO. At that time, the Navy also decided to extend the tenure of the flag officer to one year to provide more continuity. Because CNO policy stated overseas tours for longer than six months could be accompanied, quarters ashore for the force commander became a necessity.

Rear Adm. Jack P. Monroe was the first flag officer to spend more than a year in the region. The Suez Canal crisis occurred on his watch. Monroe and his successors rented quarters near the American Mission Hospital. Then, under Rear Adm. J. R. "Bucky" Lee, the Navy approved the leasing of a set of permanent quarters for the flag officer and his family closer to HMS *Jufair*. Lee never moved into the leased quarters, but they were ready for occupancy when Rear Adm. Andrew M. Jackson Jr. and his wife arrived in late 1960.

The Jacksons found that the home had three small bedrooms and two baths, a tiny den, a small living room, a kitchen, and a dining room that could seat twelve to fourteen people. There was also a large entrance hall that would serve the Jacksons well for receptions. The two Filipino stewards lived in a small house in the back. Some furniture had been rented. A Navy civilian worker acquired additional furniture in England and had it shipped to the Gulf. Jackson did not consider the house sumptuous, but it was comfortable and better than what had been previously rented. The home the Jacksons settled into would serve as the home to COMIDEASTFOR for many commanders to come.

Writing in the Naval Institute *Proceedings* in May 1966, Katharine Ainsworth "Kit" Semmes, wife of Rear Adm. Benedict J. Semmes, commented that the house, on the outskirts of Manama, was rented from Hussein Yateem. Rear Admiral Semmes later recalled that Mr. Yateem was a rich Arab merchant who made his fortune in the 1930s by selling Cokes and cigarettes to visiting Sailors. Both the admiral and his wife found the home satisfactory except that Mrs. Semmes complained that there was not enough water pressure to operate the washing machine. Consequently, she decided it was cheaper and easier to send the laundry out "to be pounded on the rocks by the Indian *dhobis* and spread out on the sand to dry." In addition to the two Filipino servants, Mr. Yateem hired an Omani to live in a garage apartment to serve as a maintenance man. This servant would climb the date palms located in the back to harvest the sweet delicacies.[46]

Over the years, the Navy fostered good relations with Bahrain's ruling family. This was illustrated shortly after Rear Admiral Jackson and his wife arrived when Shaikh Mohammed bin Salman Al Khalifa, one of the ruler's three sons, hosted a holiday season dinner for about seventeen American naval officers and their wives. Representing the first time American ladies were invited to dinner at a ruler's son's palace, the dinner was unprecedented. Shaikh Mohammed served young camel meat, considered a delicacy, and this also enhanced the great appreciation felt by the visiting guests.[47]

The friendship would continue after the passing of His Highness Shaikh Salman bin Hamad Al Khalifa in 1961. Shaikh Salman's eldest son, Isa, assumed the role as Bahrain's ruler, and the kindliness extended toward Americans by the ruling family continued. Kit Semmes, in her *Proceedings* article, recounted joining with the wife of an oil executive for a morning visit with Shaikha Hessa, the new ruler's wife. With serving women bringing in juices, fruits, and pistachio nuts, the three women engaged in light, friendly conversation. Mrs. Semmes also wrote about a short-notice invitation to have dinner with Shaikh Isa. Arriving at the Ruler's Palace, she and her husband stepped out onto a red carpet and entered a large reception room. With His Highness sitting on the far end, they were announced. The two Americans then walked across the room to pay their respects, with the other guests looking on. When all of the guests had arrived, they entered a dining room and sat around a table large enough to seat more than one hundred people. The table was literally covered with food—roasted sheep, chickens, saffron rice, beans, watermelons, mangoes, and salads. After dinner, they returned to the reception room, where they enjoyed coffee and conversation. Incense was then passed around, marking the end of the party.[48]

Rear Admirals Jackson and Semmes both commanded the Middle East Force during a time of transition. Ever since its inception, COMIDEASTFOR had come under the cognizance of Commander in Chief, U.S. Naval Forces Eastern Atlantic and Mediterranean (CINCNELM), set up in November 1947 as a specified command under direct JCS supervision. By 1960, changes in the Unified Command Plan had CINCNELM as the naval component commander for the Commander in Chief, European Command (USCINCEUR) and also as the specified commander for Middle East contingencies. For this role, CINCNELM had bestowed upon himself the title Commander in Chief, Specified Command, Middle East (CINCSPECOMME). Army Chief of Staff Gen. Lyman L. Lemnitzer and Air Force Chief of Staff Gen. Thomas D. White opposed this organizational arrangement. As a specified commander, CINCNELM, who was a subordinate to USCINCEUR, could command his superior's forces in a Middle East contingency. The Army and Air Force Chiefs argued that the Middle East responsibilities should be handled by USCINCEUR.

In February 1960, Secretary of Defense Thomas S. Gates acted on the advice of Joint Chiefs Chairman Gen. Nathan F. Twining, USAF, and proposed an interim solution. CINCNELM was to be called USCINCNAVEUR when acting in his component capacity in Europe. However, CINCNELM retained his specified commander role in the Middle East. When acting in this role, it would be under his title as CINCNELM. The USSPECOMME title was to be dispensed with.[49]

This arrangement would be relatively short-lived. With a new president, a new secretary of defense, a new chairman of the Joint Chiefs, and a crisis in the Congo, the command structure warranted further review. Supported by Secretary of Defense Robert S. McNamara, over the opposition of CNO Adm. Arleigh A. Burke and Marine Corps Commandant Gen. David M. Shoup, United States Strike Command (USSTRICOM) was activated on 1 January 1962, assuming operational command of U.S.-based units of the Continental Army Command (CONARC) and the Tactical Air Command (TAC). Based in Florida, this new unified command had the mission of readying forces for deployment to unified commands overseas. With USSTRICOM established, the Army and Air Force Chiefs of Staff now argued that it could assume the planning and force employment missions for the Middle East. The new CNO, Adm. George W. Anderson Jr., and General Shoup again rose in opposition but were again overruled by Secretary McNamara. On 30 November 1963, Gen. Paul Adams, who commanded STRICOM, assumed responsibility for planning and operations in the Middle East, sub-Saharan Africa, and Southern Asia. Because this Army general was dubbed CINCSTRIKE, some State Department officials felt the term might elicit a negative reaction overseas. Consequently, Adams received the title "Commander in Chief, Middle East, Southern Asia, and Africa South of the Sahara" (USCINCMEAFSA). He toured the region in November 1963. With the disestablishment of CINCNELM on 1 December 1963, USCINCMEAFSA assumed operational command of the Middle East Force.[50]

Yet COMIDEASTFOR continued to depend on CINCUSNAVEUR for assets and logistical support. CINCUSNAVEUR also continued as COMIDEASTFOR's administrative boss and coordinated plans to meet Middle East contingencies. This function was assumed by CINCLANTFLT in December 1966 when the Atlantic Fleet commander was designated Commander-in-Chief, U.S. Navy Middle East, Southern Asia, and Africa South of the Sahara (CINCUSNAVMEAFSA). These shifting command arrangements were a precursor for one of the more interesting turf wars in American military history.[51]

CHAPTER FOUR

The British Withdrawal

Briefly in October 1962, the world held its breath as the United States and the Soviet Union brought both sides to the brink of nuclear warfare during the Cuban Missile crisis. Although the Soviets eventually removed the missiles they had placed in Cuba, the two sides proceeded to increase their atomic stockpiles, placing thousands of warheads on the tips of land-based and sea-based ballistic missiles. With the two major powers facing possible annihilation through direct military confrontation, the struggle between their ideologies intensified along the periphery of the Eurasian landmass. Communist-backed insurgencies, called "national wars of liberation," challenged governments throughout Asia, Africa, and even South America. During the late 1950s, Great Britain and the United States successfully helped governments in Malaysia and the Philippines to quell insurgencies. During the 1960s, the United States became deeply involved in supporting South Vietnam in its struggle against a North Vietnamese–directed insurgency that had strong backing from the Soviets and Communist Chinese.

In the Middle East, an area of the world dominated by Islam, a Communist ideology stressing atheism had little appeal. That said, Soviet aid in the form of arms was certainly welcomed by countries such as Egypt and Iraq that had strong disagreements with the West. For the most part, the United States maintained good relations with most nations in the region. Its reputation as a non-colonial power was enhanced by the low-key, friendship-building approach employed by COMIDEASTFOR. However, with the creation of the State of Israel, the Soviets attempted to use Arab opposition to the Israelis as a wedge to disrupt Arab-American relations. In the wake of Israeli military triumphs in June 1967 and the subsequent closure of the Suez Canal, the Soviets saw opportunities to expand their influence in the region. Immediately after the fighting ended, the Soviet Union broke its diplomatic ties to Israel and offered aid to many Arab nations. Soviet warships, a constant presence in the Mediterranean since 1964, began to appear east of Suez.[1]

In addition, Great Britain's announcement in 1968 that it would withdraw its military forces from the region promised to create a vacuum, which the Soviets aspired to fill. For years, while the United States shored up the defenses of NATO and countries on the Pacific Rim, and fought Communist forces in Southeast Asia, the British and French provided a Western sea power presence in areas bordering the Indian Ocean, the Arabian Sea, and the Gulf. Indeed, the British stepped up their naval presence in the region after the Suez Canal fiasco of 1956. A 1957 White Paper noted that the Royal Navy lacked the ability to put ashore quickly "small numbers of high-quality light infantry" backed up by ground attack aircraft. Consequently, the British converted the aircraft carrier HMS *Bulwark* into a commando carrier to embark a helicopter squadron and a six-hundred-man Royal Marine detachment. Departing for the Middle East in the spring of 1960, the carrier was followed by an amphibious warfare squadron consisting of a small headquarters ship, three LSTs, and three LCTs.

The arrival of these forces proved fortuitous. Kuwait, as did Bahrain, had a "protected state" status. With both sides desiring complete independence, the British and the Kuwaitis signed a Treaty of Friendship on 19 June 1961 granting the Arab state complete control over its foreign and internal affairs. Within a week, however, Iraq's leader Karim Kassem laid claim on Kuwait. The small Kuwaiti armed forces could hardly withstand an attack from the massive, Soviet-equipped Iraqi forces. On 29 June, with reports filtering in of Iraqi army movements to the Kuwaiti border, the British moved their amphibious forces toward the northwestern end of the Gulf. The Kuwaitis requested outside help the next day, and on 1 July the British began flying in Royal Marines from HMS *Bulwark* and landing troops and tanks from the amphibious ships. When Kuwait's only airfield had been secured, additional troops were flown in, including two battalions of infantry based in Bahrain. Two British aircraft carriers also entered the area to provide additional air cover.

Shortly thereafter, Kassem declared he would not use aggression against Kuwait, but he did maintain his claim. When the crisis was defused, the British withdrew after reinforcements from the Arab League countries of Saudi Arabia, Jordan, Sudan, Tunisia, and Egypt arrived to ensure Kuwaiti territorial integrity.[2]

The British forces that remained at HMS Jufair also helped deter Iraqi aggression. Rear Admiral Semmes recalled seeing a few LSTs and minesweepers, as well as a British army regiment stationed at the Bahraini base. As for the Americans, their presence grew somewhat in the mid-1960s with the homeporting of *Valcour* at HMS Jufair. The permanent arrival of *Valcour* led to an increase in the shore staff consisting of a supply department to augment the planning staff and communications personnel assigned to the

Naval Control of Shipping Office. In summary, the homeporting of *Valcour* in Bahrain meant that eighteen additional service personnel and their families joined the fifteen American families already on the island.[3]

Because of the influx of families arriving from the United States, Hamza Kaedi's role increased substantially. His title became "director of personnel services." In reality, he was "jack of all trades." Working around the clock, he helped Sailors and their families settle into the region. He met incoming flights, inspected prospective rental homes, negotiated for services, and acted as a chauffeur for the admiral. When the Suez Canal closed in the wake of the June 1967 Arab-Israeli war, supplies for the little Navy outpost at HMS Jufair were flown in by Air Force cargo planes. Kaedi quickly learned how to operate a forklift, thus ensuring the quick offloading and distribution of needed material.

The period in the aftermath of the June 1967 war proved tense for the Middle East Force Commander, Rear Adm. Walter S. Small, and for the Sailors and their dependents stationed in Bahrain. Besides the *Valcour*, Small had four destroyers under his operational control, with the fourth destroyer arriving through the Suez Canal shortly before the outbreak of hostilities. He recalled, "When hostilities commenced, I collected all ships at the southern end of the Red Sea and established a patrol across the Bab el Mandeb." Fuel was scarce, and Emperor Haile Selassie sold his reserves to keep the American flotilla steaming.[4]

With false reports from Radio Cairo accusing the Americans of complicity with the Israelis, anti-American demonstrations erupted throughout the region. Mob violence in the Dharhan area caused several hundred thousand dollars' worth of damage to U.S. property. There were also demonstrations in Manama. The shaikh ensured, however, that the demonstrations were controlled, and he offered free transportation to the battle zone to those who were particularly outraged and desired to fight the Israelis. Throughout this period, the American residents of Bahrain restricted their movements, and everyone remained safe. One Sailor did have his car incinerated. To obtain supplies and other services in town, Kaedi drove his own vehicle into the demonstration areas. While Kaedi survived unscathed, his six year-old daughter was attacked by classmates and badly beaten and scarred. The Navy arranged for her to be flown to Iran for proper rehabilitation.[5]

In the wake of the June 1967 war, the British also maintained a low-key albeit growing presence as HMS Jufair absorbed forces from Aden. As a result of British Defense Minister Dennis Healy's February 1966 announcement of reductions in British defense commitments outside Europe, the Royal Navy base at Aden, long a key installation within the British Empire, was slated for closure in 1968.[6]

The British announcement caused concern in the Gulf, where the British had maintained a presence for centuries and, as illustrated by the Kuwaiti case, had proved a stabilizing force. To counter rumors of additional withdrawals, British envoy Goronwy Roberts left London on 30 October 1967 for a tour of the Gulf. Visiting leaders in Bahrain, Qatar, Kuwait, the Trucial states, and Iran, Roberts emphasized that "Britain will stay in the Persian Gulf as long as necessary to maintain peace and stability."[7]

That length turned out to be two months. Facing a huge deficit, the Labour government of Harold Wilson had the choice between cutting back social programs and abrogating defense responsibilities. To gain acceptance of some social service cuts, on 4 January 1968 the British cabinet agreed to a complete withdrawal of British forces east of Suez, to be completed by March 1971. While Roberts was dispatched to the Gulf to inform the region's leaders, Foreign Secretary George Brown traveled to Washington to break the news. The Americans reacted "with horror and consternation."[8]

Confusion reigned in Bahrain over how the announcement affected Bahrain's long-standing relationship with Great Britain and Britain's defense commitments. It was suggested that the Bahrainis join a federation with Qatar and the Trucial shaikhdoms. On 27 February 1968, Bahrain did sign an agreement to establish a Federation of Arab Emirates, however, Iran quickly reminded the parties of its long-standing claim on Bahrain. Facing this complication, and with concerns that Bahrain would dominate any federation because of the size and sophistication of its population and economy, Qatar and the Trucial shaihkdoms did not push to implement the 27 February 1968 agreement.[9]

Over the next two years, the future of the Gulf continued to be murky as politicians in London debated whether to reverse the January 1968 decision because of concerns about Bahrain's security. Then the shah of Iran acted. Although the prospects of regaining Bahrain after nearly two hundred years of Arab rule had been a long-desired fantasy, such an outcome could not be certain. It was certain that Britain had committed herself to leaving the Gulf, and the prospect of the Gulf waters being dominated by the Imperial Iranian navy seemed within reach. Deciding that the timely departure of the Royal Navy was far more desirable, the shah sought to eliminate any excuse the British might use to stay. Thus in 1969, he approached the UN secretary general to work with the British to determine Bahrain's status. In early 1970, the secretary general appointed an Italian diplomat to visit Bahrain to evaluate the attitude of the Bahraini people toward the shah's claim.

THE BRITISH WITHDRAWAL   49

He reported back that the Bahrainis desired to become a "fully independent and sovereign state." The shah accepted this conclusion and dropped
his claim to Bahrain. The British were free to go.[10]

Back in the United States, Chief of Naval Personnel Vice Adm. B. J.
Semmes met with Rear Adm. Marmaduke Gresham Bayne to discuss Bayne's
next assignment: "Duke, this is a job I want you to take. I had it, and it's the
best job I ever had in my life!" Bayne accepted, and in the spring of 1970, he
and his wife, Sibyl, were en route to Bahrain.[11]

The Baynes arrived at Bahrain at an interesting time. With the British
withdrawal imminent, there was intense debate within the American government over its policy in this region. The Americans faced three options:
they could follow the British and leave the region, they could continue on
as before, or they could expand the American presence to fill the vacuum
left by the British.

Given the growing Soviet presence and the oil deposits in the region,
the first option was not seriously considered. Rear Adm. Walter Small,
COMIDEASTFOR at the time of the British withdrawal announcement,
clearly favored the third option. A few days after the announcement, Small
sent a message up his chain of command proposing the establishment of a
naval support activity in the region. On 8 May 1968, he formalized his proposal in a letter. Finally, on 8 June 1968, three days before he was relieved,
Small sent a message expressing his concern about the operational readiness of the ships being sent to his command. He noted that with the closure of the Suez Canal, it could take augmentation forces up to forty days
to reach the Middle East. It was crucial that the ships assigned to him be
in optimum condition. Small cited major deficiencies with three ships that
were currently deployed with him and recommended that the option of
establishing support facilities ashore "be actively pursued."[12]

However, with the Gulf rid of the British, the shah of Iran expected that
there would be American interest in establishing a ground presence. On
27 January 1968, his prime minister, Amin Abbas Hoveida, declared: "The
Imperial Government can protect, with utmost power, its interests and rights
in the Persian Gulf and will not permit any country outside of the region to
interfere. . . . Britain's exit from one door must not result in American entrance
from the other door—or in the British re-entry in another form."[13]

In Washington, the CNO's staff, the Joint Chiefs of Staff, the Assistant
Secretary of Defense for International Security Affairs, and the State
Department all studied the situation in the Middle East to determine what
course to take. Newly elected President Richard Nixon and his advisor,
Henry Kissinger, wanted to improve U.S. relations with Iran. Having an

American military facility on an island long claimed by Iran could be counter-productive to this objective. In an April 1969 letter to the Atlantic Fleet commander, CNO Adm. Thomas H. Moorer wrote that Small's letter of the previous May "appears somewhat ambitious." He added:

> The political instability of the area precludes substantial investment and current thinking here favors some suitable leasing arrangement. It is important that no increased U.S. presence be reflected either by having Bahrain appear to be "headquarters" for the Middle East Force, with "Flag" facilities duplicated ashore, or by giving the impression that we are developing a permanent forward base. Our facilities must be kept as austere as possible, without placing undue hardship on personnel assigned to the flagship and staff. The establishment of a Naval Support Activity connotes, in certain quarters, an increased naval presence and, therefore, future planning should instead provide for the expansion of the mission and organization of the Naval Control of Shipping Office to handle additional support functions.[14]

At this time the Joint Chiefs and the major area CINCs involved with the Gulf concurred with the CNO's position. A year later, on 5 June 1970, the National Security Council recommended that the then-current level be maintained. President Nixon approved of this position in December 1970.[15]

Although not mentioned in Moorer's letter, budgetary concerns may have been another factor. The U.S. Navy was downsizing in 1970. World War II vintage ships faced block obsolescence. With defense expenditures going toward supporting the effort in Vietnam and building a strategic deterrence, the ships due to be retired had few replacements.

Admiral Moorer's position conformed to what would later be known as the "Nixon Doctrine," a policy that postulated that allied nations were expected to defend themselves against Communist threats. While the United States would still assist those nations in need, it would no longer assume most of the combat burden. In the Gulf, the Nixon Doctrine would become known as the "Twin Pillars" policy. As allies close to the United States, Iran and Saudi Arabia would be supplied weapons, and together they would serve U.S. interests by providing stability in the region. To maintain continuity, Middle East Force would simply retain its composition of a flagship and pairs of destroyers rotated in.[16]

Reflecting over a quarter-century later, retired Admiral Bayne argued that in time, this "status quo" approach would be costly: "Until the day I die,

I will believe the Iran hostage crisis, the Afghanistan invasion by the Soviets, the increasing differences between India, Pakistan, and Bangladesh, would have been moderated, or simply not occurred, had we increased our presence when the British left and made it clear that the oil resources in the region were far too important to be left in some power vacuum."[17]

Soon after Bayne arrived, he discovered that maintaining the status quo would hardly be possible. One of those World War II vintage ships facing obsolescence was the *Valcour.* Bayne recalled: "She was held together with baling wire and glue. I am sure I have never seen a naval ship in worse condition."[18] While Bayne may have been exaggerating about the baling wire and glue, he wasn't exaggerating by much.

After nearly two years on station as the COMIDEASTFOR flagship, *Valcour* turned over the flag to the USS *Norfolk* (DL 1), and passing around South Africa, proceeded back to the east coast. After arriving in Norfolk on 1 June 1968, the former seaplane tender entered the Norfolk Naval Shipyard for a three-month overhaul. Repeated difficulties extended her stay for another three months. During the yard period, an Operations and Intelligence Center aft of the Combat Information Center featuring radar repeaters and additional communications equipment was added. Berthing spaces were rehabilitated, with more powerful air-conditioning units. Unfortunately, these improvements left *Valcour* terribly vulnerable to breakdowns, because her electrical generating capabilities were not increased.[19]

The command ship departed Norfolk on 17 April 1969 and rendezvoused with COMIDEASTFOR, embarked in USS *Dahlgren* (DLG 12), in Djibouti on 31May. *Dahlgren* had relieved USS *Luce* (DLG 7), which had relieved *Norfolk* as the flagship in *Valcour*'s absence. After transferring the flag, *Valcour* arrived in Bahrain on 18 June. During the transit back to the Gulf, *Valcour*'s equipment had progressively failed and dropped out of commission. By the time the ship arrived in Bahrain, the No. 4 ship's service generator, the No. 2 boiler feed pump, the No. 2 fresh water pump, the No. 2 salt water circulating pump, the No. 1 boiler, the No. 1 fire and bilge pump, and the No. 2 diesel oil purifier were all inoperative. With no local shipyard or tender availability, much of the repair work had to be performed by the ship's own crew.[20]

Confronted with a flagship of questionable reliability and with the British leaving, Bayne started making noises about a more suitable flagship. Planners at CINCLANTFLT proposed to send a guided missile ship over, but Bayne resisted the notion and flew back to lobby for a less warlike ship: "What was needed was something that could be functional in the region, helping the small navies in the region, Iran, India, Pakistan, and offering counsel in other indigenous problems, tropical diseases, air conditioning maintenance, etc." Finally Bayne was told that *La Salle* (LPD 3) could be made available. He then went to Norfolk, where that amphibious ship was in overhaul. The possibilities with this ship overwhelmed him. Her modern equipment, huge sick bay and medical staff, helicopters, and well deck would greatly enhance his abilities as COMIDEASTFOR.[21]

With the arrival of a larger flagship, additional support personnel were needed ashore to take care of the needs of the ship's crew and their dependents. For twenty years, Navy Sailors and Hamza Kaedi had occupied office spaces at HMS Jufair through the permission of Her Majesty's government, after consultation with the local rulers. Now, with the landlords of HMS Jufair departing, Bahrain's rulers would soon have complete independence in internal and external affairs. Bayne sought to ensure the continued American presence ashore and to gain access to some of the facilities that the British were leaving behind. His predecessors had drafted proposals and sent them back to Washington, but no authorization had been granted to negotiate with either the British or the Bahrainis, because the status of the British presence was unclear, given the political debate in Parliament. Finally, on 24 December 1970, Bayne was given the authority to discuss with the British political resident and with Royal Navy personnel what facilities would be needed to sustain the American presence. He also received authorization to meet with the Bahrainis to discuss the nature of the desired facilities. Given the sensitivity of the situation, CNO Adm. Elmo R. Zumwalt Jr. asked Bayne to stay on for another year.[22]

Bayne visited with the amir, Shaikh Isa, to give an overview of a proposal for consolidating American activities into the central HMS Jufair compound. Bayne also explained to the Bahraini ruler that he sought to lease only ten of the one hundred acres of the soon-to-be-vacated facility, the receiving antenna field adjacent to the compound in the tidal flats, priority use of Berth No. 1 on Mina Sulman Jetty, and a small waterfront facility for work and recreation boats in the vicinity. Finally, on Muharraq Island, Bayne sought access to hangar and office space, a transmitter building, and the transmitting antenna field in the tidal flats adjacent to the transmitter building. "I did this, not expecting his highness to approve or disapprove what I presented to him, simply to give him the broad picture and try to detect any policy concerns the government might have." Knowing that other Gulf states such as Kuwait and Iran would oppose a continued U.S. presence, Bayne asked the amir if this could be a problem. "His Highness was very clear that Bahrain desired a continued U.S. presence."[23]

After Bayne's visit with Shaikh Isa, the actual negotiations commenced. Navy survey teams presented Bayne a wish list of facilities to seek. Bayne's guidance from the CNO was to keep the list down "in view of resource constraints."[24] He recalled:

> I went into the actual negotiations feeling that they would be pleasant with a partnership atmosphere rather than any conflict. Mr. Yousuf Shirawi, the Minister of Development and Engineering headed the Bahraini team, and with him were the Minister of Finance and three or four support people from the Mina Sulman dock and the Muharraq airfield. I had with me my Supply Officer and a contract official flown in for the occasion from Washington. I knew Yousuf well. We had eaten in each other's homes, our wives were good friends, we used first names when speaking to each other, but his greeting that Saturday morning gave me my first hint that this was not going to be a walk in the park. He said, "Good Morning Admiral, I think I should mention that we Arabs have been trading for thousands of years." Any thought I may have had that our calculations would be accepted as a basis for the agreement vanished. In reality, what could have been a quick agreement, took six months to complete.[25]

Educated at the American University in Beirut, Yousuf Ahmed Al Shirawi had held several posts in the Bahraini government and had the ear of the ruling family. With the withdrawal of the British, he handled the transition of the three British military facilities in Bahrain. In addition to HMS Jufair, there was a British army base, as well as the Royal Air Force facility at Muharraq. He dubbed himself "the Chairman of the Committee for the Liquidation of the British Empire."

Assigned to negotiate with Bayne, Al Shirawi was very aware that any agreement to extend the American presence in Bahrain would be scrutinized in the Arab world. Consequently, if an agreement to lease facilities were reached, Al Shirawi wanted to protect his government from further criticism for not receiving fair compensation. He recalled stating to Bayne: "Duke, let me push you as hard as I can and, when your back aches, start screaming."[26]

In the midst of the negotiations, on 14 August 1971, His Highness Shaikh Isa bin Salman Al Khalifa officially declared Bahrain an independent state. President Richard Nixon sent his best regards to Shaikh Isa and designated John Gatch as Chargé de Affaires to establish an American embassy in Manama. Five days later, upon returning from an Indian Ocean deployment, *Valcour* fired the first international twenty-one-gun salute to the new nation. On 16 December, the officially designated "National Day," Admiral Bayne presented Shaikh Isa with the shell casings from the first and twenty-first shells fired.[27]

At first the British had indicated that they might possibly maintain a limited communications facility in Bahrain. As the two negotiating teams discussed various options, the British indicated in August 1971 that their pullout would be total. This simplified the negotiations somewhat, because the Americans could simply take possession of the former British communications spaces. As Bayne and Al Shirawi negotiated, two important issues emerged. Al Shirawi wanted assurance that the Navy would provide proper support to the Department of Defense school for the dependent children. In addition to American dependents, many Bahrainis were enrolled. To Al Shirawi, this represented a personal as well as governmental interest. Five of his daughters would attend the school.

The annual lease fee was the other contentious issue. Because the Americans were going to occupy only a small portion of the British facilities, a fee comparable to the annual British fee of five hundred thousand pounds was considered excessive. In the end, the two sides agreed on a sum of about $800,000, to be paid in Bahraini dinar. On 23 December, the two sides signed the agreement to lease to the Americans a portion of the former HMS Jufair. In summation, Bayne thought that "the arrangement was fair and conducted in a friendly atmosphere." Al Shirawi agreed, citing friendship, honesty, and integrity as key.[28]

An immediate glitch occurred. The *New York Times* published an article claiming that Bahrain and the United States had signed a treaty without advising and obtaining the Senate's consent as called for in the Constitution. Kuwait immediately protested and offered to pay the Bahraini government double the fees agreed on to abrogate the "treaty." In Tehran, the shah also protested the "treaty," as did the governments of Iraq, Egypt, and Saudi Arabia. Finally, after wrangling with the State Department over language, the Defense Department prevailed on a senator to announce that no treaty had been signed, merely a contract to use Bahraini dock and airfield services. The matter soon blew over. Then on 5 January 1972, Admiral Zumwalt announced that the *La Salle* would relieve *Valcour* as the COMIDEASTFOR flagship.[29]

Protests notwithstanding, much work lay ahead to set up the facility and prepare for *La Salle*'s arrival. Hamza Kaedi recalled being called in by Admiral Bayne and being told that things were about to become really busy. Asked if he was up for the challenge, Kaedi responded, "No problem!"

He subsequently hired additional assistants and arranged for the U.S. Navy to hire the staff of the soon-to-be-vacated base pub and restaurant. In the meantime, *Valcour* pulled into port, and working parties were formed and sent ashore to help with the transition.[30]

During the week of 17–22 January, *Valcour* crewmembers worked with NCSO personnel to move their office from quarters they had occupied since 1950 into the recently vacated HMS Jufair headquarters building. Work also went forward to establish the exact boundaries of the new facility, to renovate the new NCSO headquarters building and the Public Works building, and to let contracts for fencing, lighting, and security. In the midst of the hustling Sailors, on 19 January, Secretary of the Navy John Chaffee visited the new facility and took the opportunity to tour *Valcour*.[31]

By the end of February, all departments except for supply, medical, and communications had moved into their new spaces. Public Works had completed the carpenter shop and the lumber storage area. Because the flagship and its medical staff were away most of the time, the Navy had sent Lt. Charles A. Veurink, a Medical Corps officer, to Bahrain in 1970 to provide care for the growing NCSO staff and their dependents. With office space limited at HMS Jufair, he established a temporary clinic at the American Mission Hospital. During March 1972, the clinic moved from the hospital to new spaces within the NCSO building. Also in 1970, a supply corps officer, Lt. (jg) James J. Mulva, had arrived in Bahrain to become NCSO's first disbursing officer. His experience in Bahrain must have served him well as Mulva would leave the Navy to eventually become chairman and CEO of ConocoPhillips. In April 1972, the Supply Department settled into new spaces and the Communications Department assumed occupancy of the former British communication building.[32]

During the summer of 1972, work on the compound continued at a hectic pace. Three unusable buildings were demolished, Hamza Kaedi's Personal Service Center was remodeled and improved, and the former British mess became an enlisted restaurant. Toward the end of the year, workers completed a theater adjacent to the Chief Petty Officers Mess and a communications office.

In addition, twenty-five *Valcour* volunteers helped move the Department of Defense Elementary School in Awali to new facilities adjacent to the new Naval Control of Shipping Office.[33] The elementary school or the "Bahrain School" as it became known, had been in existence since September 1968. Prior to 1968, with few dependents in Bahrain, children's education was not a major concern. In 1962, Admiral Semmes solved the problem for his family by sending one of his daughters to a boarding school in Switzerland

and his son to a boarding school in Rhode Island. His youngest daughter, eight-year-old Amy, attended Sacred Heart School, a Catholic school that had been in existence in Bahrain for about ten years. At Sacred Heart, Amy, a European girl, and their Bahraini classmates studied under the tutelage of Italian nuns. The nuns taught in Arabic as well as English. Consequently, Amy learned quite a bit of the native tongue. Admiral Semmes worried that Amy would fall behind her peers back in the United States, but when they returned, he found that she was months ahead.[34]

With the homeporting of *Valcour* in Bahrain and the gradual increase in the number of personnel assigned to NCSO, children's education became a concern. Junior officers and enlisted Sailors could hardly afford to send their kids off to Switzerland. However, the British were reluctant to allow Americans into their dependents' school and the Anglican school, St. Christopher's, informed the command that they would be unable to accept children after the 1967–68 season.

Consequently, Admiral Small prepared and sent a proposal to USCIN-CEUR to establish an American school at the Bapco compound at Awali. L. D. "Jo" Josephson, a Bapco official, offered the Navy a five-year lease for $6,000 per year for the use of his facilities. The director, U.S. Dependents' School European Area toured the site and pledged his support. The British and the Bahrainis also welcomed the proposal.[35]

The Bahrain American Elementary School received authorization from the Director of the U.S. Defense Education System European Area (USDESEA) to open on 4 June 1968. This authorization was, however, contingent on COMIDEASTFOR providing the facility, logistical support to the school officer, custodial personnel, and school supply personnel. USDESEA would provide the faculty.[36] Both sides held up their end of the bargain as the school opened in September 1968. The initial enrollment was forty; half were Navy dependents and the other half was a mix of children from the American and European business community as well as Bahrainis. They included some children from the ruling family. The staff consisted of a principal and three teachers.

In 1969, the return of the *Valcour* along with its dependents, and applications from more Bahraini families, doubled attendance at the school. By the time Admiral Bayne arrived in 1970, the student body had jumped to more than one hundred students, and the Awali facilities were becoming inadequate. He discussed the situation with Josephson, and they agreed to approach the Defense Education System to take on the administration of a larger school. The Bahrainis and the British agreed to the larger school, although the British attempted to modify the curriculum so that it conformed to European school systems—an understandable request given that many of the Bahraini and European students would continue their education in Europe. A compromise was reached when it was arranged for the school to offer curricula designed to prepare students either for American universities or for the British "O"- or "A"-level standards. Admiral Bayne credits Jo Josephson as being a "tower of strength." "It simply would not have happened without his support and resources."[37] By 1970, a school advisory council was formed to assist the principal, and two new rooms were constructed at the Awali site.

Unfortunately, there were also growing pains. The first principal, a Briton who insisted on being called "Headmaster," did not work out. Several other Defense Dependent School principals took turns running the school at Awali. By the end of 1971, the school hosted approximately two hundred elementary and correspondence high school students and strained the Awali facility.[38]

The former HMS *Jufair* had a track-and-field facility, a cricket field, and assorted structures that would not be needed by the Americans and that could be suitable for the school. But there were intense governmental discussions about the site because it was an ideal location for new port facility structures. The prime minister, Shaikh Khalifa bin Salman Al Khalifa, brokered a decision that preserved the site for the school. Thus the Department of Defense (DoD) school shifted from Awali to a new location adjacent to the old American NCSO building.[39]

The new school opened in August 1972 and was dedicated by the heir apparent, Shaikh Hamad bin Isa Al Khalifa, on 14 September 1972. By that time enrollment had grown to six hundred students in grades K through twelve, with twenty-three nationalities represented in the student body. Unfortunately and not too surprisingly, this large and diverse student body was difficult to manage. The Navy stepped in to help run the school and tightened discipline. Problem children were ejected, and Navy officers even took turns in front of the blackboard to teach various courses. Finally, Dr. Frithjof R. Wannebo, a secondary education coordinator in Athens, was flown in to meet with the school's principal and Admiral Bayne to address the challenges facing the school. Apparently Wannebo impressed Bayne. When he returned to Greece, his wife met him at the airport to tell him he had been promoted and reassigned to Bahrain to become the new principal.

Admiral Bayne later described Wannebo as "a marvel." "It was he who put the school on the map. To operate it, Dr. Wannebo had a staff of fifty-eight teachers, counselors, and administrators. Prior to Wannebo's arrival, "the Bahrain School Trust" was established to help maintain the school and provide funds for educational purposes in connection with the school. Over time, as its reputation grew, the school began to draw students from throughout the region.[40]

Reflecting back more than twenty-five years later, Admiral Bayne listed the effort he put into the school as one of his greater contributions. "I know the Distinguished Service Medal awarded me after that tour of duty was primarily for the school, not naval operations." Regarding the impact of the school on American objectives in the region, Bayne observed: " In my opinion, it was far more important to establish that school as an American-run school, exerting foundational American culture into the region through education, than running a few destroyers around the Gulf and Indian Ocean."[41]

His Highness Crown Prince Shaikh Salman bin Hamad Al Khalifa, who would graduate from the school in the late 1980s, expanded on the Admiral's observation: "The Bahrain School as being part of the Department of Defense System has given an opportunity, not only to Bahrainis, but to all from all over the Gulf to study at a premier facility. . . . It exposed us to not only American culture but culture from all over the world and in that respect it is very good."[42]

While Bayne worked on the education challenge, another problem loomed, literally, over the horizon, as Soviet warships entered the region. By 31 December 1971, the Soviet Indian Ocean Squadron had grown to include a Kynda and a Kresta I guided-missile cruiser, a Kotlin guided-missile destroyer, a Kashin guided-missile frigate, an Alligator LST, a mine-sweeper, seven submarines, and nine support ships. With the arrival of the Soviet navy, the loss of the British became even more regretted. Not only had British forces provided COMIDEASTFOR with a wealth of information about the region because of their centuries of corporate knowledge, but they had maritime surface and aviation assets that tracked Soviet shipping movements in the Gulf and the Indian Ocean.

To compensate somewhat for the loss of the British, Admiral Bayne approached Commandant De La Marine Djibouti and Commandant De La Marine Diego Suarez to exchange information about sightings of Soviet combatants and merchant ships. The French agreed, and a partnership was formed. As a result of this initiative, COMIDEASTFOR substantially enhanced its ability to track the Soviet navy in the region.[43]

In contrast to the growing Soviet presence, the U.S. Navy continued to maintain just a flagship and two to four destroyers in the region, only occasionally augmenting its forces to participate in the annual MIDLINK or other exercises. The changeover of flagships to the larger *La Salle* somewhat helped to correct the imbalance. During June 1972, as *Valcour* made her last deployment around the Indian Ocean, *La Salle* prepared to depart for her new duties overseas. Volunteers who had requested one-year unaccompanied tours or eighteen-month accompanied tours fleshed out the ship's roster. On 1 July, *La Salle* was redesignated AGF 3. Seven days later, loaded with forty-eight personal vehicles and tons of household goods, the ship departed Norfolk for the long trip around Africa. The *La Salle* reached Bahrain on August 23. The next day, Admiral Bayne transferred his flag to *La Salle* and the *Valcour* departed for Norfolk via the Pacific Ocean. In recognition of her long service as the COMIDEASTFOR flagship, the CNO authorized the removal of *Valcour*'s bell for placement in the Bahrain Jufair chapel.

Shortly after *Valcour*'s departure, *La Salle* got under way for port calls in the Gulf and Indian Ocean. Besides showing off the new flagship to foreign dignitaries, the *La Salle*'s crew hosted parties for school children and provided "Project Handclasp" materials to the International Red Cross, the Catholic Relief Agency, and the Port Louis Public Library in Mauritius. After a quick stop in Bahrain, the new flagship departed to participate in another MIDLINK exercise with the British and Iranian navies.[44]

In addition to fostering good relations throughout the region, COMIDEASTFOR assets continued to be ready to react to emergencies. For example, on 19 November 1972, a tank at Bapco's Bahrain refinery containing nineteen thousand barrels of naphtha base stock for jet fuel ruptured, spilled-two thirds of its contents, and exploded into an enormous fireball. The fire destroyed four other tanks, damaged three others, and took six days to put out. Hamza Kaedi recalled that Sailors from NCSO joined up with oil company workers and Bahraini firefighters to control the huge blaze.[45]

Americans responded to another oil disaster a few weeks later, this time in the Gulf of Oman. In the early morning darkness on 19 December 1972, USS *Charles C. Ware* (DD 865) approached a bright light on the horizon and discovered that two supertankers had collided and were ablaze. For the next half day, *Charles C. Ware* picked up survivors from both ships, provided preliminary medical treatment, and sent fire-fighting parties on to one of the ships to battle the inferno. When additional ships arrived on the scene, the destroyer rushed the survivors needing further medical attention to Bahrain.[46]

In the wake of these two oil disasters, Bayne's relief, Rear Adm. Robert J. Hanks, wrote to Walter O. Stolz, Bapco's president, to arrange for *La Salle* Sailors to use its fire-fighting training facility. He said: "It would be mutually advantageous for the U.S. Navy to use your facilities. *La Salle*'s crew would be available to supplement your standing force in case of an emergency, such as the unfortunate fire last year at your installation." Stolz agreed and the fire-fighting sessions commenced.[47]

Throughout 1973, the Naval Control of Shipping Office settled into its new facilities. A sum of $42,000 in repair and maintenance funds was used to improve the facilities within the NCSO compound and at the Bahrain School. New vehicles arrived, including a fire truck. Sailors assigned to *La Salle*'s engineering spaces (dubbed "Snipes") greatly appreciated the arrival of a mobile steam boiler that allowed the flagship to go "cold-iron" when in port. Service contracts in the amount of $305,000 were let to provide additional recreational and welfare services. On 10 September 1973, the new Bahrain School facility opened with 510 students representing twenty-two nationalities. The faculty increased to sixty-one.[48]

In addition, this period marked a change of operational command. In July 1969, President Nixon and Defense Secretary Melvin R. Laird appointed a Blue Ribbon Defense Panel to review the Defense Department's organization and management. Although the panel's recommendations for reorganizing the unified command structure went unheeded, the review did stimulate additional studies within the Department of Defense. Once again, the CNO's and the Marine Corps Commandant's proposals were countered by proposals from the Chiefs of Staff of the Army and the Air Force. Deputy Secretary of Defense David Packard, working with the Joint Chiefs, reconciled the proposals. Changes to the Unified Command Plan forwarded to President Nixon on 5 March 1971 included extending USEUCOM to cover "the Mediterranean littoral, the Red Sea, Persian Gulf, and Iran," and adjusting the PACOM area to adjoin the EUCOM area east of Iran. USSTRICOM was stripped of its overseas planning responsibilities but retained its domestic mission of preparing combat forces for deployment overseas. For the mission, the command was redesignated as United States Readiness Command (USREDCOM), with its headquarters remaining at McDill Air Force Base (AFB) in Florida.[49]

On 1 January 1972, with the abolition of USSTRICOM/USCINCMEAFSA, operational control in the Gulf and the Red Sea again reverted to U.S. Commander in Chief, European Command (USCINCEUR) and his CINCUSNAVEUR component commander. CINCUSNAVEUR continued as the administrative boss for COMIDEASTFOR as well.[50] But Commander in Chief, Atlantic Command (CINCLANT), who retained planning and operational control in the western Indian Ocean up to the Gulf of Oman, found the new command structure unworkable. For example, in a message to the Joint Chiefs, CINCLANT discussed the COMIDEASTFOR agreement with the French to share intelligence on the Soviets. "CINCLANT would like to pursue this excellent undertaking, but objects to its being negotiated by a naval component commander of another unified commander for actions which are clearly a CINCLANT (unified) responsibility." After citing several other cases to illustrate a broken chain of command, CINCLANT recommended that the JCS assign COMIDEASTFOR additional duty to CINCLANT to perform those functions assigned to CINCLANT in the unified command plan. Eventually, on 30 October 1972, CINCLANT and USCINCEUR agreed to an arrangement whereby COMIDEASTFOR would have duties to CINCLANTFLT on a not-to-interfere basis with its duties to USCINCEUR.[51]

COMIDEASTFOR was not the only Navy activity on Bahrain to undergo a change in command structure. Established during World War II, the Inspector of Naval Material Petroleum Products, Middle East Area had the distinction of being the Navy's first activity in Bahrain. However, on 1 January 1973, the office became part of the Defense Fuel Supply Center, a Defense Department Agency. Eventually it evolved into Defense Energy Region Middle East, a component of the Defense Energy Support Center at Fort Belvoir, Virginia.[52]

In contrast to the first two decades of American presence in Bahrain, the years spanning 1968 through 1973 represented a dramatic transition. The 1967 Arab-Israeli War and continuing tensions, the British withdrawal from east of Suez, the ambitions of regional rulers such as the shah of Iran, Arab nationalism, and the introduction of the Soviet navy into the region all created a complicated situation for American political and military leaders to sift through. Although Admiral Bayne argues that the United States decided to chart a status quo path, in reality there were significant changes in the U.S. presence over the period. In 1968, NCSO operated as a guest of Her Majesty's government at HMS Jufair with the consent of the Bahraini government. By 1973 the NCSO was occupying facilities on a small section of the former British post that had been directly negotiated for with the newly independent nation of Bahrain.

Despite manpower shortages in 1973 resulting from the drawdown of U.S. forces following the end of the Vietnam conflict, the number of officers, Sailors, civilian workers, and dependents ashore at NCSO had increased, especially in the wake of the *La Salle*'s arrival. To accommodate military dependents and other children within the region, a partnership among government, business, and Navy officials led to the creation of a new school adjacent to the NCSO compound. And, of course *La Salle*'s arrival represented a tremendous increase in capability as well.

Admiral Hanks also continued to build on the strong relationships established with the Bahrainis by his predecessors. Despite protests from other regional leaders, a direct, warm relationship between the U.S. Navy and the government of Bahrain had been forged. Over the next few years, world events would transpire to challenge that friendship.

PHOTO 1.

(PHOTOS 1–2) When oil flowed on 1 June 1932 from Jabal Ad Dukhan No. 1, it represented the first strike of oil in the southern Gulf. The well was drilled by Bahrain Petroleum Company Limited, a Canadian chartered company that was then, in reality, a subsidiary of The Standard Oil of California. *Photos courtesy John Bouvia*

PHOTO 2.

PHOTO 3.

(PHOTOS 3–6) USS *Rendova*'s visit to Bahrain in May 1948. Shaikh Salman bin Hamad Al Khalifa and royal family toured the escort carrier and hosted the wardroom to a sit-down feast. *Photos courtesy Naval Historical Center*

PHOTO 4.

PHOTO 5.

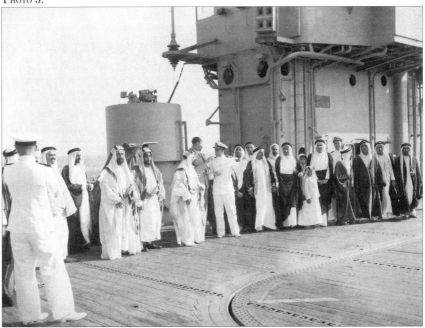

PHOTO 6.

PHOTO 7.

(PHOTOS 7–8) Liberty in Manama, Bahrain, in the 1950s. *Photo 7 from* Greenwich Bay *cruisebook; photo 8 from 1952* Valcour *cruisebook*

PHOTO 8.

PHOTO 9.

"Mr. Hamza," Hamza Kaedi, was hired as an office boy in 1948 to work at the Naval Control of Shipping Office and would remain on the American payroll for the next half century. *Photo courtesy Capt. James Wombwell*

PHOTO 10.

Passing "the sack," which contained turnover items for the Middle East Force flagship, became a tradition between the *Greenwich Bay, Duxbury Bay,* and *Valcour. 1966* Duxbury Bay *cruisebook*

PHOTO 11.

(PHOTOS 11–13) Middle East Force flagships *Greenwich Bay*, *Duxbury Bay*, and *Valcour*: *Photo 11 from 1951 Greenwich Bay cruisebook. Photos 12 and 13 courtesy Naval Historical Center*

PHOTO 12.

PHOTO 13.

PHOTO 14.

Rear Adm. John H. Maurer as Commander Middle East Force meets with Shaikh Isa
bin Salman Al Khalifa, circa 1966. *Photo 1965–66* Duxbury Bay *cruisebook*

PHOTO 15.

Rear Adm. Marmaduke G. "Duke" Bayne negotiated with the Bahrainis to maintain an American presence after the British departure from the Gulf. *Photo courtesy Naval Historical Center*

Photo 16.

(Photos 16–17) In 1972 *La Salle* replaced *Valcour* as the Middle East Force flagship and would perform that mission for more than two decades. *Photos 16 and 17 from 1987–88 La Salle cruisebook*

PHOTO 17.

PHOTO 18.

The Desert Dome served as an enlisted club and hosted VIPs and top-quality enter-tainers. *Photo courtesy John Bouvia*

PHOTO 19.

Bab Al Bahrain—The old customs house served as an entryway to Manama's shopping district, popular with Sailors on liberty. *Photo courtesy John Bouvia*

Photo 20.

Mannai Plaza Hotel, established as a quarters for American Sailors and Marines, became a security liability after the Khobar Towers bombing. *Photo courtesy John Bouvia*

Photo 21.

"Desert Sailors." *Photo courtesy NSA Bahrain*

PHOTO 22.

His Majesty King Hamad bin Essa Al Khalifa presents Vice Adm. Charles W. Moore
with the Bahrain First Class Medal upon his departure as Commander, U.S. Naval
Forces Central Command and Commander, U.S. Fifth Fleet, circa February 2002.
Official U.S. Navy photo

PHOTO 23.

Vice Admiral Moore hosts His Majesty the crown prince and commander-in-chief of the
Bahrain Defense Force, Shaikh Salman bin Hamad Al Khalifa, circa 1999. *Official U.S.
Navy photo*

CHAPTER FIVE

Eviction?

The years 1973–78 represent a period of significant disquietude and turmoil with regard to the American naval presence in Bahrain and the Gulf. At the beginning of the 1970s, as American forces were leaving Vietnam, President Richard M. Nixon enunciated what became known as the "Nixon Doctrine." During his State of the Union Address on 22 January 1970, Nixon proclaimed, "We shall be faithful to our treaty commitments, but we shall reduce our involvement and our presence in other nations' affairs."[1] While the United States was willing to provide military and economic assistance to friendly anticommunist nations in places such as the Middle East, Nixon insisted that America's regional allies had to take the lead in their own defense. This policy was well received by some nations of the Gulf—such as Iran and Kuwait—while others were less sanguine about it.

The Nixon-Kissinger foreign policy team foresaw that Iran and Saudi Arabia would provide for the defense of the Gulf. With its important strategic stake in both countries, the United States was willing to furnish each with arms and other military-related assistance. There were, however, numerous problems with trying to forge a closer military relationship between Iran and Saudi Arabia, dubbed the "Odd Couple" by State Department analysts. The prospect of promoting cooperation between the two nations was daunting. Friction existed over territorial claims, religion (Sunni Saudi Arabia versus Shi'ite Iran), and economic development (the Iranians viewed the Saudi approach as overly conservative, while the Saudis worried that the fast pace of Iranian economic development would foster internal instability).[2]

The shah of Iran eagerly embraced the American policy, because he envisioned Iran as the dominant military power in the region. America's reluctance to fill the vacuum left by the British withdrawal from the region and its willingness to provide him with military assistance made that goal appear attainable. As oil prices increased rapidly in the post-1973 period,[3] Iranian arms purchases increased exponentially—from a total of $1.6 billion during the period 1950–72 to $11.6 billion between 1973 and 1976.[4]

Saudi Arabia, the other pillar of U.S. foreign policy in the Gulf, took a more measured approach to its military buildup. Because the Saudis, in contrast to the shah, exhibited no interest in dominating the Gulf either militarily or politically, their focus was on defensive measures. Much of their military budget was spent on improving roads, ports, training facilities, and air bases. But their military forces were not ignored as all branches of the Saudi military achieved quantitative and qualitative improvements.[5]

As the Arab nations of the Gulf matured politically and prospered economically, American foreign policy options became more complex and difficult, especially after the October 1973 Yom Kippur or Ramadan War broke out. The United States, confident of Israel's military prowess, initially attempted to act in a neutral fashion to avoid Arab resentment. However, within three days the Israeli military situation became desperate and the United States committed itself to a massive resupply effort.

Led by Saudi Arabia, Arab oil-exporting nations established an oil embargo against the United States. As the war continued, Henry Kissinger added to his reputation as a masterful diplomat by arranging for a cease-fire that finally held at the end of October. Still, within the Arab world, the American actions on behalf of Israel were unforgivable, and the embargo would remain until March 1974. The oil-import–dependent United States managed to sidestep the embargo by increasing domestic production and by increasing imports from non-Arab sources such as Venezuela and Iran. Still, the rise in the price of crude oil produced a worldwide recession that strongly affected the American economy: gross domestic production declined 6 percent during the period 1973–75; unemployment doubled to more than 9 percent; and Americans confronted long lines at the gas pump and higher fuel costs.[6]

The Soviet Union saw the wedge driven between the United States and its traditional Arab friends as an opportunity for exploitation. The Soviet navy assumed a greater presence in the region and eventually established a foothold in Somalia. Between 1968 and 1973, the Soviet navy increased its presence in the Indian Ocean from 1,760 ship days to 8,543 ship days. In the aftermath of the war, the ship-day statistic, summarizing the total number of days a navy maintained ships in a region over an annual period, climbed to 10,500 in 1974 for the Soviets. Moreover, the Soviets were sending first-line combatants into the region, including *Moskva*-class helicopter carriers, Kresta II–class missile cruisers, *Krivak*-class destroyers, nuclear and conventional submarines, and Tu-95 Bear D aircraft. In contrast, the U.S. Navy's presence in 1973 in the region was limited to 2,154 ship days and increased only slightly in 1974 to approximately 2,400 ship days. The greater Soviet naval presence was somewhat offset by the French navy, with which COMIDEASTFOR fostered a strong working relationship.[7]

Besides the disruption of relations with its Arab friends and the growth of Soviet sea power, the United States also saw the demise of one of its staunchest allies with the death of Emperor Haile Selassie. As Ethiopia was torn by internal turmoil and rebellion by independence-seeking Eritreans, India and Pakistan remained at odds. In Iran, opponents to the shah's regime gathered strength.

The 1973 Arab-Israeli War, the Arab oil embargo, the military build-up in the region, and the growth of Soviet sea power changed both Arab and American perspectives about what military role America should play in the Gulf.

Twenty minutes after the Syrian and Egyptian forces had struck on 6 October 1973, Admiral Hanks received a flash message reporting fighting had erupted along the Suez Canal and on the Golan Heights. For Hanks, thinking about the possibility of having to evacuate American nationals from Arab countries, the timing could hardly have been worse. His flagship, USS *La Salle*, ideally suited to conduct evacuation operations, was moored at a Singapore shipyard receiving much-needed upkeep. The guided-missile destroyer USS *Charles F. Adams* (DDG 2), already en route to Bahrain, received orders to increase speed, and the destroyer escort USS *McCandless* (DE 1084) cut short a port visit to the Seychelles to head north to scout Soviet activity and patrol the Bab el Mandeb to observe maritime traffic in and out of the Red Sea.[8]

While Egyptian army units recaptured wide portions of the Sinai, back in Bahrain the Americans maintained a low profile. Hanks ordered all military personnel to don civilian clothes, and he alerted Sailors assigned to the NCSO to be ready to defend the Jufair installation against rioters. Late on the 8th, the *Charles F. Adams* quietly arrived at the Bapco fuel pier at Sitra to refuel and replenish food and supplies. The next day, the Director of Civil Aviation, Shaikh Isa bin Abdullah al Khalifa, called Hanks to inform him that the Council of Ministers had voted to join with other Arab nations to close airports to non-Arab military traffic. However, the shaikh then assured the admiral that the ban would not apply to the Middle East Force flag aircraft or to the weekly Military Airlift Command flight that arrived with supplies for NCSO and for MIDEASTFOR ships.

Having absorbed severe losses, Israel first mounted a counterattack against Syria. Reacting to the Israeli drubbing of the Syrian army and push toward Damascus, the Soviets began a massive air and sea lift effort to help their Arab client state. The Soviet effort led the Nixon administration to take similar actions on behalf of Israel.[9]

Unfortunately for Admiral Hanks, any American resupply effort would have grave consequences. On the evening of the 13th, Foreign Minister Shaikh Mohammed bin Mubarak called in acting U.S. Chargé de Affaires Sam Starrett to deliver a demarche warning that Bahrain was contemplating canceling the stationing agreement should the United States move forward with a resupply of Israel.[10]

However, as Starrett was briefing Hanks on the demarche, President Nixon was meeting with his top advisors to discuss this very subject. On the evening of the 10th, the White House received news that the Soviets had alerted three airborne divisions in eastern Europe. Clearly the introduction of Soviet troops into the region could threaten to turn the war into a superpower confrontation. Faced with this gloomy prospect, National Security Advisor Henry Kissinger recommended a massive airlift to enable Israel to conclude the war before the Soviets could intervene. But Defense Department officials, fearing hostile Arab reactions, resisted executing the massive resupply. Now meeting with his top advisors on the morning of 13 October, Nixon settled the issue. Before nightfall, a fleet of C-5s would be airborne en route to the Middle East.[11]

With ammunition and other essential stores arriving, Israel focused its attention on the Sinai, where its commandos crossed the Suez and began to destroy Egyptian surface-to-air missile sites. Egyptian counterattacks failed as Israeli aircraft and armored forces exploited the control of the sky to drive a wedge between the Egyptian 2nd and 3rd armies.[12]

Reacting to the changes in the ongoing conflict, the Arab Organization of Petroleum Exporting Countries (AOPEC) met in Kuwait and announced cuts in oil production to pressure America's Middle East oil-dependent allies to challenge Washington's support for Israel. Qatar added that it would immediately cease all oil exports to the United States.[13]

Back in Bahrain, the course of events hardly bode well for the U.S. Navy community. On the morning of the 16th, at the makeshift movie theater that had formally served as the British bowling alley, Admiral Hanks met with the wives of the officers and enlisted men who were deployed on *La Salle*. He told them to stay calm, stay out of the suq, and avoid unnecessary traffic about the island. Hanks expressed concern that anti-American demonstrations were possible, but the greatest danger lay in individuals venting anger due to loss of a relative on the battlefield. As a precaution should the need arise for an emergency evacuation, Hanks made sure that one of his two combatants remained within 48 hour steaming distance of Bahrain. Two days after *Charles F. Adams* departed Bahrain to patrol the Bab el Mandeb, the *McCandless* arrived at Mina Sulman pier to support any contingencies.[14]

On the 19th, the first demonstration occurred in the suq. From his Manama apartment, Lt. Cdr. Mike Gambacorta watched about five hundred protesters and observed a set of signs calling for the closure of the American base. Police dispersed the protesters. But the real threat to the American presence occurred behind closed doors as the Council of Ministers met to discuss the ongoing conflict. Walter Stolz, the president of Bapco, spent that evening as a guest of the amir and observed Shaikh Isa engaging in several phone conversations discussing the expulsion of the Middle East Force.

Stolz called Hanks at dawn to alert him of the discussions, and Hanks passed the information on to Sam Starrett and told him to expect to be called in to meet the Bahraini foreign minister. Indeed Shaikh Mohammed did call in the acting chargé de affaires, and in the early afternoon, Starrett visited with Hanks to announce that Bahrain had decided to invoke Article XIV of the Stationing Agreement—meaning that the United States had one year in which to withdraw its military presence from Bahrain.[15]

Early the next day, Starrett called Hanks to tell him that Shaikh Isa desired their presence at the Rifaa Palace that evening. The Bahraini ruler met the two Americans at the palace portico and escorted them into the majlis. Wearing a tropical white uniform, Hanks felt the chill of the palace air-conditioning system, which he noted seemed appropriate given the political situation. With the foreign minister at his side to translate, Shaikh Isa explained in Arabic that his government had made its decision to expel the Middle East Force with extreme reluctance. He greatly valued the friendship between the United States and Bahrain but Washington's favoritism toward Israel had interfered with the relationship. The amir noted that as they spoke, weapons provided to Israel by the United States were killing Arab brothers and that President Nixon had just sent a bill to Congress requesting two billion dollars of additional military aid to the Jewish state.

Sam Starret sat silently as Shaikh Isa spoke and chain-smoked as his foreign minister translated. He concluded by again expressing his deep regret for having to take the action he did. Responding on behalf of the Middle East Force, Hanks expressed his regrets and sadness over the action of the Bahraini government and that he understood the diplomatic pressures that must have been exerted by other Arab states. The admiral also expressed his appreciation for the friendship that Bahrainis had always shown to his Sailors and their families. The amir then turned toward Hanks and began to speak in English, expressing concern that if the fighting did not stop the only winners would be the Soviets, whose influence would spread throughout the region. As the audience concluded, Hanks noted the amir's coffee table still contained the plaque commemorating the first gun-salute rendered to Bahrain upon independence. Could this be a hint that the Bahrainis were amenable to reverse the decision?[16]

Admiral Hanks met with Walter Stolz the next day, and the Bapco executive informed the admiral that if the war could come to a quick settlement—one acceptable to the Arabs—he sensed that it could be possible to reverse the decision.

In Washington, the Bahraini move did not surprise Chairman of the Joint Chiefs of Staff Adm. Thomas H. Moorer. He later noted that the decision to terminate the lease was "directly related to the assistance that was given to Israel during the October War. There was a general reaction to that and they [the Arabs of the region] were looking around for some kind of retaliatory action."[17]

The fighting between the Egyptians and the Israelis stopped with a tenuous ceasefire that was broken and then reinstated. Meanwhile, the oil embargo remained as a pressure tactic to secure American leverage against Israel. For the Middle East Force, the impact was immediate as Saudi Arabia and other Arab states cut off their oil to American merchantmen and warships. Bahrain quietly provided fuel to the Middle East Force. On 31 October, La Salle, having returned from Singapore, pulled alongside the Sitrah refueling pier and began to receive 450,000 gallons of fuel oil. On the other side of the Indian Ocean, a task force centered on the carrier USS Hancock (CVA 19) entered the Straits of Malacca.[18]

With the ceasefire holding, Henry Kissinger began what became known as his shuttle diplomacy. In Bahrain, the amir again summoned Admiral Hanks for a private chat. This time Hanks arrived at Rifaa Palace in civilian attire where Shaikh Isa awaited on the portico with an honor guard standing rigid behind him. The Shaikh escorted the admiral into the private majlis room to the right.

Hanks later wrote: "Between routine arrivals of the incomparable Arab coffee, the famous Palace orange juice, and heavenly sweetened tea, we had a warm and friendly chat." Shaikh Isa asked Hanks if he had started to take action to remove the Middle East Force. The American responded that he had not, because he hoped that events would permit U.S.-Bahraini relations to return to normal. The amir expressed concern that the 20 October eviction notice had created consternation among the Navy dependents living on the island. He was relieved, however, when told that the families had been informed that they didn't need to pack their bags immediately.

The conversation turned to the tragedy of the war and the increasing peril of Soviet incursions. Being an idealist, the amir observed how much better the world would be if its treasures could be used to improve the human condition. Hanks agreed with the amir's sentiment, but he had a more realistic outlook, one based on historical examples. The admiral shared his concern that Bahrain was surrounded by more powerful neighbors and therefore had reasons to worry. He added that "so long as the United States Middle East Force remained in his country, he and his people would have little to fear from adventuristic states in the region."[19]

In an 11 November message sent to his boss Adm. Worth Bagley, the Middle East Force Commander stated, "We are in something of a state of limbo here with our future entirely dependent on outside events whose progress is unpredictable. I have just ordered a review of the preliminary planning for a phased and orderly withdrawal. I chose 30 June as the target completion date."[20] For the present, Hanks recommended, "We make no overt move. I would continue to let dependents come. When we finally decide that we must begin to move, we can call a halt."[21]

Admiral Hanks embarked on *La Salle* and departed Bahrain on 21 November with *Charles F. Adams* and rendezvoused with *McCandless* to participate in the annual ten-day MIDLINK exercise. On the diplomatic front, there was little progress and the AOPEC continued to pressure Washington with the oil embargo. So long as the two sides remained at odds, Bahrain's decree to evict the Americans would stand.

On the morning of 3 January 1974, Admiral Hanks arrived at Rifaa Palace to call on the amir during his public appearance to celebrate the Moslem holiday *Id al-Hajj* (The feast of the pilgrimage). Rather than arrive with the diplomatic community, Hanks appeared at the time when foreign businessmen and Bahrainis were to greet the ruler. Almost immediately after Hanks took his place in the greeting line, one of Shaikh Isa's aides pulled him out and escorted him directly to the amir. Hanks bid him *Id-kum mubarak* (Happy Id). Rather than having the admiral to greet his son the crown prince, the amir kept Hanks at his side as well-wishers flowed past. Shaikh Isa told Hanks he was glad to have the admiral at the majlis so his people could see him. Later Hanks discovered that Mrs. Hanks was accorded similar treatment when she called on the amir's wife.[22]

During this period, Petty Officer Daniel Wyckoff and his family also were made to feel welcome by most Bahrainis. Assigned to the *La Salle* as an electronic technician, Wyckoff enjoyed duty aboard "the Great White Ghost of the Arabian Coast" because of the quality of its communications equipment: *La Salle* was only the second ship in the fleet to receive SAT-COM capability, as satellite communications was in its infancy. On a negative note Wyckoff did lament that *La Salle*'s air-conditioning system had difficulty keeping up with the Middle Eastern heat, forcing crewmembers to

sleep on the deck near the air ducts, and that drugs were a problem, especially when the ship visited Karachi.

Ashore in Manama, Mrs. Wyckoff and her three-year-old daughter
enjoyed living in a nice apartment. (During his two-year tour she gave birth
to a son at the American Mission Hospital.) With the exception of some items
such as diapers that could be purchased at *La Salle*'s ship store, Mrs. Wyckoff had to purchase all of her goods from the local markets, and prices were
high. As for dining out, beyond the traditional restaurants, the Wyckoffs
had a choice of Kentucky Fried Chicken and Wimpy Burger. They felt safe
on an island that experienced virtually no crime and whose people seemed
very relaxed and friendly.[23]

Unfortunately, the hospitality that Hanks and the Wyckoffs found in
Bahrain was lacking elsewhere. Because of a concern about generating an
Arab backlash, African and Asian countries were reluctant to refuel transiting American warships. In the Middle East, eleven countries closed twenty-
eight ports to the United States in retaliation for American support of Israel
in the recent war. In the region, besides Bahrain, the only ports open to U.S.
ships were Port Louis, Mauritius; Karachi, Pakistan; Colombo, Sri Lanka;
and the Iranian ports of Bandar Abbas and Bandar Shahpur. Making matters worse were the inbound relief ships for the *Charles F. Adams* and the
McCandless. Equipped with pressure-fired boilers, the USS *Brumby* (DE
1044) and USS *Koelsch* (DE 1049) could burn only aviation-type fuel—a
difficult commodity to obtain. Foreseeing great challenges, Hanks zeroed
in on a solution and requested an oiler to be assigned to Middle East Force.
He received word that he could have one as early as June.[24]

In the meantime, Hanks had to consider planning for a Middle East
Force departure from Bahrain. A well-organized withdrawal would need six
months to execute, so Hanks hoped that there would be a Bahraini change
of heart before 1 April. There were positive signs. On 10 March, Andrew
Kilgore presented himself at Rifaa Palace as the new American chargé de
affaires. The amir immediately brought up the issue of the American presence, and he said that he expected that AOPEC ministers would vote to
lift the oil embargo against the United States in recognition of the American effort to bring about a peace settlement. He shared that King Faisal of
Saudi Arabia, who led the embargo, did not care to see the U.S. naval presence in the Gulf fade away.[25]

Unfortunately, a vote to lift the embargo taken on 18 March was tem-
pered by a caveat that it wouldn't be lifted until 1 June, assuming the United
States maintained pressure on Israel for a settlement. The half-measure left
the amir noncommittal when Admiral Hanks called on him on 24 March.

The next night Chargé de Affaires Kilgore and his wife hosted Hanks and his wife along with Yousuf Shirawi at a buffet dinner. Shirawi, besides serving as Bahrain's minister of development and engineering services, was Bahrain's representative to AOPEC. He shared Arab thinking about taking a wait-and-see approach on the peace talks and thus expected that no decisions could be made regarding the Middle East Force until June at the earliest.

The news distressed Hanks, who had given himself a 1 April drop-dead date. A few days later, Dr. Wannebo, the principal at the Bahrain School, briefed Hanks about a recent Bahrain School Trust meeting. Dr. Ali Fahkro, the minister of health, wanted to continue to operate the school but lacked the means to do so if the Americans departed. On 27 March, the topic of the school came up in a conversation when the admiral called on the director of civil aviation, Shaikh Isa bin Abdullah al Khalifa, to renew his customs and immigration pass. The shaikh's daughter was enrolled in the school, and he inquired if the school would remain open. Hanks turned the question around by stating that it depended on whether the Middle East Force had to leave. Offering a thin smile, the shaikh responded, "I really don't know."[26]

The Middle East Force commander decided to take a risk by hoping for a reversal and not packing. He reflected: "Given the stakes involved, it seemed essential that the United States retain this quarter-century old military foothold in the Middle East rather than abjectly surrendering it."[27]

During April Admiral Moorer visited Bahrain and called on the amir and several ministers. He recalled, "They didn't want to give some kind of indication to their countrymen, particularly the opposing groups, that they are not just U.S. puppets."[28]

While awaiting the Bahraini decision, the Middle East Force staff continually worked to keep the fuel bunkers of the three Middle East Force ships filled. This logistical nightmare eased on 6 June 1974 when USNS *Marias* (TAO 57) reported to COMIDEASTFOR for duty. Over the next six months, the venerable old oiler would pump in excess of 4.5 million gallons of fuel into Middle East Force ships.[29]

By the end of June, there was no word. Hanks had to force a decision. On 30 June two of his junior officers arrived at Government House, one with a check for 285,000 dinars ($750,000) for presentation to Finance Minister Sayyid Mahmoud Ahmed al Alawi to cover the lease payment for 1975, and the other with a letter to be passed to Yousuf Shirawi discussing the U.S. intention to lease Bahraini facilities in 1976.

The next day, former Chargé d'Affaires John Gatch, in Bahrain for a brief visit, called on the amir, who was joined by the prime minister, the foreign minister, and the crown prince. Shaikh Isa expressed pleasure in welcoming Bahrain's "Good Friend" again and then immediately turned to seeking Gatch's advice about the U.S. Navy presence. Although both the amir and the prime minister favored a continued American presence, the prime minister interjected that there were difficulties with the current agreement regarding criminal jurisdiction and *La Salle*'s berthing priority at Mina Sulman Pier.

Gatch stated that those issues were negotiable, after which Foreign Minister Shaikh Mohammed asked what to do about the check presented the day before, given that it extended payment beyond the eviction date. "Cash it" responded the prime minister, "We'll adjust later if necessary."[30]

At this important juncture, the United States upgraded its diplomatic representation to Bahrain as Joseph Twinam arrived as the first U.S. ambassador. On 23 July, he received formal notification that the U.S. Navy was welcome to stay.[31] Reflecting nearly a quarter century later, Tariq Almoayed, the former minister of information, noted that the easy course of action would have been for the government of Bahrain to evict the United States and that the amir took a "brave position" by quietly letting the termination notice lapse in October 1974.[32]

Negotiations progressed slowly. One sticking point was the provision in the 1971 Stationing Agreement granting the United States "exclusive criminal jurisdiction over members of the U.S. Forces, including dependents and non-indigenous DoD civilian personnel." The government of Bahrain began to question the propriety of the provision when, in the spring of 1973, a young Saudi national was killed in an auto accident involving a Navy petty officer. Although the case was settled in a civil court, the government did not drop its request for retrocession of criminal jurisdiction in this case.[33]

In early November, the new CNO, Adm. James L. Holloway III, arrived in Bahrain, called on Shaikh Isa, and shared a pleasant exchange. With Admiral Holloway's departure, the Middle East Force staff resumed preparations for the 1974 MIDLINK exercise, which included a task group built around USS *Constellation* (CVA 64). Unfortunately, from Hanks' perspective, the Ford administration had decided that if the *Connie* entered the Gulf, it could intimidate the Arabs into softening their negotiating stance with Israel. Hanks feared an opposite reaction; furthermore, the deployment could disrupt the ongoing negotiations with Bahrain. Despite his recommendations to the contrary, the *Connie* was detailed to the Gulf. To make matters worse for Hanks, the execute order came at a key juncture in the MIDLINK exercise with the British, French, Iranian, and Pakistani navies.

Hanks' diary entry for 21 November 1974 reflected his anger: "*Connie* going to Gulf. State notified all CENTO posts. Arabs will be told *only* when

Connie, Berkeley, and *Cochrane* enter Gulf! Damage now triple compounded: Carrier to the Gulf on short fuse; surprise Arabs; gut MIDLINK. We are truly our own worst enemy."[34]

Returning to Bahrain, Admiral Hanks and Ambassador Twinam met with Foreign Minister Shaikh Mohammed and Yousuf Shirawi to discuss the terms for agreeing to maintain the U.S. Navy in Bahrain. Shirawi drove a hard bargain, asking to increase the annual payment to four million dollars. Hanks, understanding the internal and external pressures the Bahrainis faced, sent a message to Washington recommending payment. After a month of deliberations, the Pentagon agreed to pay the higher figure. However, other factors presented themselves to put a final settlement on hold. Admiral Hanks would not be there to sign an accord. On 21 February 1975, a Singapore Airlines Boeing 747 took off from Bahrain with Hanks and his wife aboard. Rear Adm. Thomas J. Bigley now commanded Middle East Force.[35]

Admiral Bigley was not initially enthusiastic about commanding the Middle East Force. At about the time he was being considered for a new assignment, he ran into the chief of naval personnel, Vice Adm. David Bagley, in a Pentagon corridor. Bagley asked him if he would like to command the Middle East Force. Bigley declined, stating he would prefer to command a cruiser-destroyer group instead. After further discussion, Bagley said with a laugh, "Give me your answer on Monday or give me your retirement papers." Not quite yet ready for retirement, Bigley found himself on an airplane heading to the other side of the world. Before he left, he sat down with Deputy Secretary of Defense William Clements. Bigley recalled that Clements, a Texas oil man who felt he knew a good deal about the Arab world, told him, "We got to turn this situation around or you're not going to be able to stay there. This is important for the United States."[36]

With a mandate to ink an agreement with the Bahrainis, Admiral Bigley arrived as the Soviet navy prepared for OKEAN 75, a worldwide naval exercise unparalleled in scope, involving 216 Soviet navy ships and hundreds of aircraft. With the twenty-three ships of the Soviet Indian Ocean Squadron participating in the exercise, Bigley positioned his flagship *La Salle* and the USS *Trippe* (FF 1075) near the Soviet operations area near Socotra Island to monitor Soviet tactical maneuvers and intercept Soviet radio transmissions.

One factor that became troubling for the Americans was the amount of logistical support that the Soviet navy was receiving through the Somali port of Berbera. On 13 June 1975, the American ambassador to Somalia protested the establishment of a Soviet base at Berbera. In response, the Somalis invited the U.S. Congress to send delegations to visit the port. Separate Senate and House of Representative delegations arrived in early July to find the port empty of Soviet warships. Stationed off the Somali coastline, the *La Salle* and the USS *New* (DD 818) watched the Soviets sortie just a few days before the American legislators arrived.

On the bright side, on 5 June 1975, the Suez Canal reopened and the transit of the *Trippe* and the USS *Joseph Hewes* (FF 1078) a week later marked the first complete transit by U.S. Navy ships through this waterway since 1967. With the canal open, the transit time for Middle East Force deployers homeported on the U.S. east coast was cut from forty to twenty days.[37]

The amir also faced distractions and difficult decisions during this period. Bahrain had adopted a constitution in 1973 calling for a National Assembly that became a reality with elections held in December 1973. However, the thirty representatives represented extreme factions, with eight supportive of the banned Pro-Marxist National Front for the Liberation of Bahrain while another six favored the imposition of strict Islamic customs and laws. With no solid bloc of moderate representatives, debates became virulent as the representatives challenged the amir on budgetary and internal security matters. Of concern to the NCSO was a resolution passed in the summer of 1974 calling on the U.S. Navy to leave its base. The amir was out of the country at the time, and when he returned he was horrified. According to Bigley's successor, Adm. William J. Crowe, Foreign Minister Shaikh Mohammed al Khalifa advised his cousin, the amir, that although he may not like the National Assembly's decision, a reversal by fiat would be a grievous error, alienating most of the governments in the Gulf that favored the National Assembly's action and causing resentment among his own people. Over the next year, the National Assembly continued to pass resolutions challenging the amir's authority. Convinced that this experience in democratic government had the potential to tear away at the fabric of the newly independent state, Shaikh Isa disbanded the National Assembly in August 1975.[38]

The timing of Bahrain's internal strife was inopportune with regard to the ongoing negotiations to settle on a lease. As the two sides approached a settlement, external and internal pressures mounted against an accord. Coinciding with the decision to disband the National Assembly, notice was given to Admiral Bigley that his command was once again facing eviction, with no specific departure date set.

With the oil embargo a fading memory and the twin pillars strategy apparently on track, the Bahraini announcement terminating the lease did not cause much concern in Washington. According to Admiral Bigley and his relief, then Admiral Crowe, there did not seem to be any definitive national policy on what the United States should do about the Bahraini termination notice. Crowe later wrote that there seemed to be "no clear understanding about why we were there in the first place. . . . In a sense, we were in the Gulf more as a matter of habit than policy." Crowe also noted that, from a "warfighting standpoint, it was hard for the Navy to justify the Middle East Force; it was essentially a 'showing the flag' squadron. But on general principles alone, the Navy did not want to leave a place where they were already established."[39]

To Bigley, the situation looked bleak. In September 1975, he reported to his boss that "retention of COMIDEASTFOR home based in Bahrain without a homeported flagship does not appear to be a feasible arrangement. . . . The GOB [government of Bahrain] has consistently referred to terminating the Navy presence in Bahrain, not just the flagship." In his message, Bigley proposed the following schedule for ending the American naval presence in Bahrain:

1. Immediate cancellation of dependent travel to Bahrain.
2. Termination of the Bahrain School at the end of the school year.
3. Withdrawal of *La Salle* on 30 June 1976.
4. Disestablishment of NCSO on 30 September 1976.
5. Disestablishment of CMEF on 1 December 1976.[40]

Although this self-imposed timetable for withdrawal eventually slipped into 1977, Bigley remained pessimistic. He reported,

> I do not believe that it is a choice between the status quo or nothing, but rather a question as to whether any presence, status quo or reduced, would be acceptable to the GOB. All indicators from here are that it would not be, as the political situation now stands. . . . It is my perception that to the GOB, it is the activity of the USN from Bahrain, which is objectionable. Personally, they display considerable hospitality and warmth to the Navy. . . . GOB's chief complaint is not who we are, nor how many of us are here—but rather what we do. . . . Unless we are prepared to go begging to the government of Bahrain, I see little chance of our presence here being extended under any circumstances.[41]

Admiral Bigley, however, had not given up seeking ways to reverse the Bahraini decision to terminate the Navy's presence. The amir, Shaikh

Isa, had asked Bigley to come see him every month to six weeks to keep him informed of Soviet activities in the Indian Ocean and the "Persians" (Iranians) in the Gulf. Bigley used these opportunities to talk about the Middle East Force activities and the cordial reception he received in ports throughout the region. Besides maintaining cordial ties with the amir, Bigley took the opportunity to play the "Bahrain School card" in conversations with government and private-sector Bahrainis, many having children attending the school, reminding them that DODDS administration would depart with the Navy.[42]

Admiral Bigley also felt the new U.S. Ambassador to Bahrain, Joseph Twinam, was not particularly keen on keeping the Navy in Bahrain. Bigley recalled that although Twinam was a "pleasant fellow with whom I got along well, . . . he also had his views about how the Navy should operate in the area. He was of the opinion that we really shouldn't have Navy or military facilities based ashore in the area. The Navy, he believed, should be over the horizon and we will call you if we need you."[43] As for the Bahrain School, Twinam envisioned the school becoming a State Department–supported private school.[44]

During Admiral Bigley's farewell call on the amir in late June 1976, no comments about the forthcoming Navy departure were made. However, when Bigley the next day made his farewell call on Prime Minister Shaikh Khalifa bin Salman Al Khalifa, he was surprised to find Foreign Minister Shaikh Mohammed bin Mubarak Al Khalifa and Crown Prince Shaikh Hamad also present. "The prime minister said he knew I had already seen the amir but the amir wanted me to know, because 'I was such a good friend' that the Navy would not have to leave Bahrain." Bigley thanked the prime minister and asked him to convey his appreciation to His Highness for informing him of the good news and said that he would inform his superiors in London and Washington, as well as Ambassador Twinan.[45]

In his report to his boss in London, Bigley stated that "the government did not want us [the U.S. Navy] to leave and that they wanted a close and continued relationship with the USG [U.S. government]. The Navy had always been welcome."[46]

The prime minister admitted that the decision again to evict the Americans was related to the June 1975 internal politics surrounding the National Assembly. Bigley zeroed in on what appeared to be the real motivation for the Bahraini change of heart, reporting that Shaikh Khalifa said, "What Bahrain desires is assistance from the United States to help them upgrade their defense forces. . . . Bahrain needs advisors and advice on their programs." To the prime minister, the rent money was not as important as the military assistance the Americans could provide, especially in view of recent arms acquisitions by Saudi Arabia, Iran, Kuwait, and the Yemen Arab Republic.[47]

Because Bigley was promoted to vice admiral and ordered to Hawaii to be the Deputy Commander in Chief of Pacific Fleet, Bagley, who was recently promoted to admiral and now assigned as Commander U.S. Naval Forces Europe, turned to Bigley's relief, Rear Admiral Crowe, who actually sought the Middle East Force job because of his background in politico-military affairs. As with Bigley, he too received marching orders to work with Ambassador Twinam to reverse the Bahraini decision. With the 30 June 1976 change of command being held ashore at NCSO because *La Salle*'s was being overhauled at Subic Bay, the new Commander Middle East Force faced a one-year deadline to accomplish his mission.[48]

Crowe echoed Bigley's assessment of Twinam, recollecting that "I did not believe that the ambassador's heart was in the project. He would not say that, of course, because the official policy was to try to stay. But many career diplomats in that part of the world felt that keeping American bases in Arab countries was a mistake, and that our presence at Jufair put the Bahraini government at a disadvantage and jeopardized our interests. I think that underneath, Twinam agreed with that, though on the surface he was trying to carry out government policy."[49]

Certainly evidence exists showing that resentment existed in American diplomatic circles over the decision of the Bahrainis to inform Bigley rather than Twinam of the decision to keep the Navy in Bahrain. Back in Washington, State Department officials wanted to slow the negotiating process on a future leasing agreement to enable the ambassador to regain a leading role.[50]

Fortunately for the new Middle East Force commander, Twinam was replaced by Wat Cluverius, whose grandfather and father had been naval officers. Once again, American and Bahraini officials sat down to negotiate a new lease. Despite being assured by Crown Prince Shaikh Hamad, who was also the defense minister, that "no one would sink the *La Salle* or try to force the Navy out"[51] if the Navy was still in Bahrain on 30 June 1977, the Americans continued to plan as if they would eventually have to depart. Admiral Crowe continued to proceed with the plan of action and milestones set up by his predecessor to cover the withdrawal contingency.[52]

The negotiations over the new lease dragged on. Crowe recalled: "After the first six months we felt as if we had been batting our heads against a brick wall."[53] Apparently, the Bahrainis were in no hurry to complete the negotiations, because they were under intense pressure from a variety of

sources not to sign an accord. The Kuwaitis chided them for having provided the United States with facilities at such a bargain. The Iranians and
the Saudis, on whom America depended to execute its twin pillars strategy,
expressed indifference toward the notion of the United States remaining
in the Gulf. Other Arab states disliked the implication of Western interference in the Gulf that the American presence implied, along with the
baggage associated with America because of its long-term commitment to
Israel. Counterbalancing this was an understanding by some Bahraini officials that the prosperity, security, and stability of the Gulf depended upon
a continued American presence in their country.[54]

Crowe agreed that the Navy needed to maintain a presence ashore, sending his boss a message explaining that "NSCO offers CMEF, the flagship,
and deployers a convenience in terms of logistics, flag aircraft, communications support, voyage repairs, and miscellaneous services which materially
enhance the force's operational efficiency, morale, and flexibility."[55]

Bagley strongly supported this position. The Commander in Chief,
Pacific Fleet, Adm. Thomas B. Hayward, agreed that retaining a shore presence was the best option. However, he opined that if Bahrain persisted in
"forcing termination of CMEF presence," the transformation of the command
into a smaller, exclusively sea-based command should not be ruled out. He
noted: "The Navy has enough commitments worldwide to meet with inadequate forces without persisting in fulfilling a commitment that is not perceived as essential by the countries being supported and where alternatives
add to the burdens shouldered by our Sailors and dependents."[56]

In the fall of 1976, Crowe received word that Deputy Secretary of Defense
Clements would be traveling in the region. To Crowe and Cluverius, the
implication was that they were failing in their mission and that he was heading to Bahrain to get the deal done. On 24 October 1976, Clements arrived
and headed straight to the prime minister's office from the airport. With the
amir and most of the leading Bahraini personages gathered, Clements proceeded to shun the traditional Arab customs for receiving visitors and told
them why they needed to maintain the U.S. Navy presence with a "shoot-
from-the-hip" directness.

The amir said, "Thank you" and deferred to Shaikh Mohammed, who
felt quite comfortable fending off pushy Westerners. The foreign minister
concluded by stating, "I'm afraid our decision still stands." Flabbergasted,
Clements beat a retreat back to the airport, telling the Bahrainis "that
with more reflection you'll change your mind." For Crowe and Cluverius,
"The two guys who had the problem previously still had it, except now it
was worse."[57]

The Americans used all of their cards in an attempt to bring the Bahrainis to an agreement. In November 1976, a Department of Defense Survey Team visited Bahrain to determine Bahrain's military needs. They examined Bahraini naval, air, and air defense forces. CINCUSNAVEUR recommended that the Pentagon use the survey team's report to advise the Bahrainis on how best to fill their needs and suggested that "consideration be given to implicitly linking it as a means of influencing the Royal family to be responsive to our needs regarding MEF tenure."[58]

Another factor coming into play was the Bahrain School. There is a strong element of "folklore" surrounding the importance of the school in keeping the U.S. Navy in Bahrain. Many people interviewed for this monograph commented on the role the school played in keeping the Navy in Bahrain. Both Admirals Moorer and Bigley noted in their oral interviews the importance of the school. Bigley recounted that the school was "important not only to the Americans but to the Bahrainis and other foreign nationals that lived in the Gulf area. I began to think no Navy in Bahrain, no school. I decided to play the school card, much to the consternation of the ambassador."[59] Dr. Wannebo, former principal of the school, said that he frequently used this argument about the importance of the school in maintaining the U.S. Navy presence in discussions with his superiors in the Department of Defense School System. He added that although he was never involved in any of the negotiations, he got the impression from Cluverius and Crowe that the school was an important factor.[60]

From the Bahraini perspective, the school may not have been as important as the Americans thought. Tariq Almoayed, one of the Bahraini officials involved in the lease negotiations, stated that it was not an important consideration per se. What the school did do, Almoayed said, was create a community of interest and friendship among influential Bahrainis and Americans. Dr. Wannebo added that "the school provided the Bahrain government with an educational institution it needed to encourage foreign businesses to establish offices in Bahrain." Thus, in a more indirect manner, the school helped keep the Navy in Bahrain.[61]

Despite the lack of progress, there was cause for optimism as Admiral Crowe was approached by many in the business community who saw the American presence as a moderating, stabilizing force. Finally, the Americans realized that it was semantics, not actions, that were important to the Bahraini government. Yousuf Ahmed Al Shirawi, who negotiated the 1971 agreement, confirmed this by stating that it was crucial for the government of Bahrain to be able to tell its critics that Bahrain was changing its relationship with the United States. In a message to Secretary of

State Cyrus Vance, Ambassador Cluverius explained it was the "image" of Bahrain hosting a foreign base that had to be removed. From the Bahraini perspective, this meant changing the homeport of both the flagship and the Commander Middle East Force. Foreign Minister Shaikh Mohammed told Cluverius that "Bahrain must be able to say in June that MIDEASTFOR has been withdrawn. . . . If Bahrain can say convincingly that there is no longer a U.S. base in Bahrain, then the number of days of ships' visits or amount of supplies they load here is Bahrain's business for which it need not apologize."[62]

Crowe saw the possibility for a breakthrough but had difficulty convincing Bagley that it was possible to reduce the American presence yet maintain operational capability. Bagley especially didn't care for the idea of changing *La Salle*'s homeport to Norfolk, but preferred keeping the ship in the Middle East with a crew assigned on one-year unaccompanied orders. However, Crowe felt these concepts needed airing in the Pentagon, and he arranged through his friend Rear Adm. James Stockdale to be recalled to Washington to brief officials on the status of negotiations.[63]

The message from the CNO recalling Crowe to Washington did not sit well with Bagley. When Crowe called him to suggest that he stop in London on the way back, Bagley growled, "You'd better." The discussion between the two men was strained, however. Bagley allowed Crowe to try to sell the concept to the CNO. When Crowe arrived in Washington on 10 January 1977, he was joined by Ambassador Cluverius, who had arranged to be recalled for "consultations."[64]

By April, Crowe was reporting that the government of Bahrain was committed to a continued American presence. A sticking point had been the working understanding on the legal status of Sailors ashore. Bahrain, while recognizing the need for some flexibility in handling individual cases, desired respect for its sovereignty. This matter too was settled to the satisfaction of both sides, leading Crowe to write that the government of Bahrain "is happy as the USN to resolve this thorny issue and once the dust settles, barring a major Middle East flare up, MEF tenure will not resurface as a significant issue for some time." He further speculated that if conditions improved in the Middle East, "The U.S. Navy could expand its privileges in Bahrain if it so desires."[65]

Among the issues implicitly understood but not directly addressed in the new lease agreement were the following: the Navy would limit the number of Sailors ashore to seventy-five at any given time; dependents of the staff and flagship's crew would not live in Bahrain; berthing in Bahrain would be limited to no more than 120 days per year; and the government of Bahrain would not take away any of the U.S. Navy's leased buildings or real estate, because these facilities at Jufair kept Sailors occupied and out of sight. In addition to these points, the amount of the lease was reduced from four million dollars to two million dollars, allowing Bahrain to make the case that the U.S. Navy presence had been substantially cut down.[66] On this last point, when the embassy cabled back to the State Department about the rent reduction proposal, the Middle East desk officer called Cluverius in incredulity, explaining: "In the last forty years of American diplomacy, no one has ever lowered the rent."[67]

The new lease agreement went into effect on 1 July 1977, although problems over congressional approval delayed the signing until 23 August. In conjunction with the new lease, both Commander Middle East Force and the *La Salle* were assigned on paper to Norfolk as a homeport, and a new shore entity was created: Administrative Support Unit (ASU) Bahrain. Four days later, on 4 July, Crowe was relieved by Rear Adm. Samuel H. Packer.

Crowe went back to Washington, eventually becoming Chairman of the Joint Chiefs of Staff. Yet reflecting back, he felt in terms of service to the country that the Bahrain agreement to keep an American facility ashore was probably his most important contribution. "Bahrain was to prove the cornerstone for all our subsequent naval operations in the Persian Gulf. Pound for pound, Bahrain has been about the best ally we have had in recent times."[68]

CHAPTER SIX

War in the Gulf

A s his predecessor had done, Rear Adm. Samuel Packer had expressed
an interest in the Commander Middle East Force job and had an
extensive political-military background that ideally suited him for
it. Although hampered by the "new format" that limited the number of days
that Middle East Force ships could be alongside the Mina Sulman pier and
forced a high personnel turnover resulting from the switch to one-year unaccompanied tours, the Middle East Force remained intact and Packer enthusiastically continued to show the flag, breaking down barriers that had been
thrown up throughout the region in the wake of the 1973 war.

With more regional ports available for visitation, Packer's staff managed to adhere to the Bahraini 120-day-per-annum restriction by arranging for *La Salle* and her accompanying combatant deployers to call at
ports in the United Arab Emirates, Saudi Arabia, Iran, Kenya, Djibouti,
Pakistan, Sudan, Jordan, Mauritius, Somalia, Kuwait, Oman, Yemen, and
the Seychelle Islands. The ships also spent more time under way, increasing the average number of steaming days per quarter from thirty-three to
forty-five.

Besides showing the flag, the Middle East Force continued to conduct
its other traditional missions. For example, two months before Admiral
Packer's arrival, a helicopter operating from *La Salle* evacuated an injured
crewman from an Indian merchant ship and transported him to Bahrain
for lifesaving medical treatment. Shortly afterward, the COMIDEASTFOR
C-131 flag aircraft coordinated a search and rescue effort to locate the crew
of a downed Kuwaiti Puma helicopter, and the *La Salle,* with a LAMPS helicopter from the USS *Trippe* (FF 1075) embarked, followed up the rescue
effort with an attempt to locate the sunken aircraft.[1]

Middle East Force ships continued to participate in the annual
MIDLINK exercise with ships from Iran, Pakistan, and Britain. Admiral
Packer continued to forge a close working relationship with the French
navy. The two maritime forces often operated and exercised together, keeping tabs on a Soviet navy that had been dealt a setback due to its eviction from the Somali port of Berbera after the Soviets failed to back the
Somalis' effort to bring the Ogaden region of Ethiopia under their flag.

Sharing intelligence, the French and American ships monitored this struggle on the Horn of Africa.

The Middle East Force composition of *La Salle* with two rotational destroyers or frigates continued with periodic augmentations to meet operational requirements or provide coverage when the "Great White Ghost" departed the region for maintenance. USS *Fox* (CG 33) served as Packer's flagship during one period, and USS *Davis* (DD 937) flew the admiral's flag during another. The latter 1950s-vintage destroyer impressed Packer as she made two deployments to the Middle East in two years and "did very well."[2]

Ashore in Bahrain, the new ASU performed the same functions as its NCSO predecessor. Unfortunately for this new entity, the desired perception that there was no longer a U.S. Navy facility in Bahrain extended back to the States, and it proved difficult to obtain support to improve the facilities. One exception proved to be the opening of Inshallah Pool, a long-anticipated event. Folklore has it that the pool received its name because *Inshallah* ("if God wills it") was the consistent response provided by contractors to the query, "Will the pool ever be completed?"

Despite a declining number of dependents, the Bahrain School survived as a DoD-administered school receiving support from the Bahrain School Trust, an organization with representation from the Bahraini government, from the U.S. Navy, and from the private sector. With the school structure deteriorating, the trust voted to contract with a firm to design and build a new complex at an estimated cost of $13 million. To fund the construction, government, civic, and business leaders disestablished the trust and founded a new organization, the Bahrain International School Association (BISA). Unlike the trust, the association could legally seek bank loans to underwrite construction. To recoup money needed to pay off the loans, parents of non-DoD children wrote a check to BISA for facility expenses and one to the U.S. Department of the Treasury to cover tuition. In addition to having to raise the money for the new school, BISA was seriously challenged when engineers condemned the schools' dormitories in 1978, forcing the departure of most of the boarding students.[3]

Arriving in 1977 to serve as Bapco's chairman, Donald Hepburn volunteered to preside over BISA. As president, Hepburn worked with the school's principal, Rod Wannebo, to steer through one of its most difficult periods. Part of the frustration came as a result of changing administrations in Washington putting new political appointees in charge of the Department of Defense School System. Many of these appointees were puzzled as to why a DoD school enrolled students of fifty different nationalities when DoD dependents were only a minority of the student population. While Wannebo worked through his administrative chain to answer questions posed by Washington, Hepburn occasionally traveled back to the United States to explain the history of the school and its value as a center of cross-cultural indoctrination. Not all were convinced that the Bahrain International School was a legitimate operation. Hepburn recalled that one appointee sent a ten-person audit team to Bahrain to "fix" matters, including having students recite the pledge of allegiance to the American flag. The school survived the audit.[4]

As for Admiral Packer's chain of command, it remained very simple, with operational and administrative control being exercised by the Commander in Chief, U.S. Naval Forces Europe, based in London. Although the Army and Air Force presence in the region in the form of military advisory groups was significant, the Navy continued to dominate the U.S. military presence in Southwest Asia as it had done for decades.

Packer could have hardly realized when he took the helm in July 1977 that the stable situation in the Gulf that he and his predecessors had enjoyed was about to unravel. With the abdication of the shah, the seizure of the American Embassy in Tehran, the Soviet invasion of Afghanistan, and the commencement of an eight-year war between Iran and Iraq, the region became the focus of world attention. Packer and his successors suddenly found themselves operating in one of the most volatile areas of the globe.

Over the next decade, the United States adopted a "neutral" position regarding the Iran-Iraq struggle, but clearly one that favored Iraq and the Gulf states that were supporting Iraq. The seizure of the American Embassy in Tehran, the ensuing hostage crisis and its aftermath, and, in particular, Iran's efforts to restrict the movement of shipping in the Gulf during its war with Iraq all served to reinforce the American bias against Iran. Keeping the sea lanes open would require that the United States put its Navy in harm's way.

Bahrain helped fund the Iraqi war effort. The fall of the shah proved ominous to the shaikhdom, as Iran's new ruler, the Ayatollah Ruhollah Khomeini, reinstated historical Persian claims on the island nation and Iranian-trained clerics and other agents attempted to undercut the amir's authority. But the American military presence on the island, though limited, did provide Bahrain some sense of security against the possibility of a direct Iranian attack.

Nor could one foresee the dramatic changes in the American command structure that would be unveiled. Within five years the Commander Middle East Force would be reporting to a unified commander in Florida rather than to one in Europe. To provide the context for the decisions and actions that would take place in the Gulf during the 1980s and beyond, the evolution of the American command structure needs to be explained.

With the effects of the 1973–74 oil embargo a recent memory, President Jimmy Carter issued Presidential Review Memo 10 in mid-1977 declaring "the Persian Gulf as a vulnerable and vital region, to which greater concern ought to be given."[5] Presidential Directive (PD) 18, signed by the president on 24 August 1977, called for the establishment of rapidly deployable light divisions, marking the origins of the Rapid Deployment Force.

In 1978, the Joint Chiefs of Staff reviewed the situation in the Middle East, identifying American interests and how best to protect them. Given the strain on American resources, the Joint Chiefs recommended that the United States encourage western European and Australian allies to deploy more naval forces to the region. The Joint Chiefs also contemplated the creation of a Fifth Fleet. When queried about this idea, Packer thought that establishing such a fleet to cover the Indian Ocean and up into the Gulf would provide resources needed to better support American interests, thus he welcomed the idea. However, the Army and Air Force Chiefs of Staff and Commander in Chief European Command (CINCEUR) opposed the idea, and elsewhere in the Navy there was little enthusiasm for it.[6]

Although PD 18 called for the creation of light divisions to form a Rapid Deployment Force, Congress did not provide funding, so the concept remained just that until the eventful year of 1979. Within the Pentagon, Joint Chiefs Chairman Gen. David Jones, along with the Army and Air Force Chiefs of Staff, favored the concept, while the CNO and the Marine Corps Commandant opposed it, along with CINCEUR who wanted the Gulf to stay in his area of responsibility. With Iran in turmoil, planning for a Rapid Deployment Force accelerated, and in November 1979, President Carter directed its formation.[7]

The formation of the Rapid Deployment Force coincided with the seizure of the American Embassy in Tehran by Islamic militants. With embassy staff being held as hostages, operational control of Middle East Force quietly shifted from European Command (EUCOM) to Pacific Command (PACOM) as PACOM anticipated the advent of increased reinforcements and operations in the northern Arabian Sea.[8]

During his 1980 State of the Union address made in the wake of the Soviet invasion of Afghanistan, President Carter committed American forces to fend off any external aggressors threatening the Gulf. With the mandate of the Carter Doctrine, on 1 March 1980 the Rapid Deployment Joint Task Force (RDJTF) was established as a command subordinate to U.S. Readiness

Command at MacDill AFB in Tampa. Commanded by Marine Corps Lt. Gen. Paul X. Keley, the command immediately initiated a series of command post exercises. Within a year, U.S. forces under Kelly were conducting exercises in Egypt and then in Oman.[9]

In the summer of 1981, Army Lt. Gen. Robert C. Kingston took command of the RDJTF, and by October, the command had assumed responsibilities for contingencies in the Middle East and Southwest Asia and had obtained independence from U.S. Readiness Command. As a joint task force, the RDJTF was chartered as a temporary organization designed to meet a specific military challenge. However, with Iran and Iraq embroiled in a death struggle and no sign of Soviet withdrawal from Afghanistan, the new Secretary of Defense Caspar Weinberger and National Security Advisor Frank Carlucci wanted a permanent unified command to cover the region. The Joint Chiefs, CINCEUR, and CINCPAC were not in favor of the concept. Vice Adm. Thomas Bigley recalled attending a meeting of the Joint Chiefs where multiple reasons against forming a permanent regional command were spelled out for the defense secretary. Weinberger simply repeated that the president desired to have a command structure similar to what existed in Europe and the Pacific put in place. Weinberger prevailed. On 1 January 1983, U.S. Central Command (CENTCOM) was established at McDill AFB, replacing the RDJTF. Kingston, the first commander, set out to establish his new unified command as a bona fide organization with actual forces assigned, similar in scope to the established European and Pacific commands. Operating in the CENTCOM area of responsibility, Commander Middle East Force and his ships now came under its operational control as did Air Force Airborne Warning and Control Systems (AWACS) and other aircraft based in Saudi Arabia. The Navy's leadership did not welcome this development.[10]

With the stand-up of the new unified command, the Navy had to provide a component commander. In the Pacific and European theaters, the officer assigned to command the Navy components was a four-star admiral. For Central Command, the Navy detailed a flag officer–selectee to be stationed at Pearl Harbor to coordinate administrative and logistic support for naval forces in the Gulf. In reality, the Middle East Force commander, having operational control of forces in the Gulf, served as the component commander. In the Gulf of Oman and the northern Arabian Sea, the 7th Fleet commander under PACOM operated fleet units.[11]

The Reagan administration's commitment to maintain freedom of navigation, protect U.S. shipping, and reflag and protect Kuwaiti tankers meant that the number of warships operating inside and just outside of the Gulf would climb. With the CENTCOM and PACOM line of demarcation at the

Strait of Hormuz, nearly everybody recognized that there was a command and control problem. To Navy leaders such as Pacific Fleet commander Adm. James "Ace" Lyons, the solution was to allow PACOM to extend operational control into the Gulf. Marine Gen. George B. Crist, who relieved Kingston in late 1985, countered that he needed operational control of the naval forces outside the Gulf. His arguments swayed Joint Chiefs chairman Admiral Crowe to establish on 20 September 1987 a Joint Task Force Middle East (JTFME) and appoint a Navy admiral who would have operational control of the military forces in the region.

Rear Adm. Dennis M. Brooks assumed duties as the first JTFME commander. Only a few months elapsed before it became apparent that the responsibilities of the two separate commanders, JTFME and COMIDEASTFOR, overlapped significantly. Commanders in Tampa and Washington quickly determined that a far more efficient arrangement and one that would conserve scarce staff billets would be to dual-hat a single commander. Rear Adm. Anthony A. Less relieved Admiral Brooks in December 1987 and additionally assumed the duties of COMIDEASTFOR when he relieved Rear Adm. Harold J. Bernsen in February 1988.[12]

Factors beyond events in the Middle East led to the evolution of the American command and control structure in the 1980s. The October 1983 Beirut bombing, killing 241 Marines, exposed weaknesses in the command chain that contributed to the passage of the Goldwater-Nichols Act of 1986. With his power enhanced by this law, Admiral Crowe did not need to obtain consensus from the Joint Chiefs to act when he saw fit.

However, starting with the abdication of the shah in January 1979, most of the command realignments in the Middle East did come as a reaction to the events in the region. Throughout 1978, Admiral Packer kept abreast of the growing protests in Tehran. The gravity of the situation struck home when at the conclusion of the fall MIDLINK exercise, the commanding officer of an Iranian warship expressed regret that he did not expect to see Packer in the future.[13]

With the seizure of power in Iran by the anti-American Khomeini in January 1979, a stunned Washington reacted by moving forces into the region. Saudi Arabia agreed to base twelve F-15s and AWACs aircraft, and the USS *Midway* (CV 41) steamed into the Indian Ocean from the western Pacific. The Pacific and Atlantic fleets augmented the Middle East Force with additional combatants to handle contingencies such as the anticipated evacuation of American and other foreign nationals from Iran. On 12 February 1979, the *La Salle* and the USS *Talbot* (FFG 4) arrived off Bandar Abbas, and Royal Navy ships and other craft shuttled evacuees from the shore.

Serving as the assistant intelligence officer on the Middle East Force staff at the time, then-Lt. Evan Robinson recalled that the evacuation operation was particularly challenging because of the need to transport evacuees from Tehran to the port city. A week later, the USS *Hoel* (DDG 13), USS *Decatur* (DDG 31), and USNS *Mispillion* (TAO 105) arrived to help with the evacuation. On 22 February, the HMS *Fawn* and the HMS *Hydra* transferred 266 evacuees to the *La Salle* to be taken to safety. For these individuals and others, safety meant Bahrain, where they received good treatment while they awaited air passage home.[14]

Coinciding with the arrival of the evacuees in Bahrain, Robert H. Pelletreau called on the foreign minister to present his credentials. Shortly afterward, this new American ambassador had an amiable session with the amir. The two men discussed the geopolitical situation in the Gulf. Given the instability in Iran, Shaikh Isa expressed his appreciation for the presence of the Middle East Force. He spoke fondly of his many close relationships with the various naval commanders who had served in Bahrain. He even humorously recalled the time when he was a teenager and he had gone forward to greet an admiral and had been mistaken for the hat boy.

The working cooperation between the Navy and the Bahrainis quickly became apparent to Ambassador Pelletreau when a few rowdy Sailors from a visiting U.S. warship caused damage to a local restaurant. Given the volatile situation in the region, Pelletreau feared that the incident could spark anti-American fervor. To head that off, the Navy took immediate action to punish the Sailors, the restaurant owner was quickly compensated, and nothing more came of it. Afterward, Pelletreau learned that Middle East Force commanders, in addition to developing close ties to government leaders, had cultivated the Bahraini business community by building personal relationships during receptions and ship tours. He also quickly discovered the unique role of the Bahrain International School in fostering close ties.[15]

The importance of the United States–Bahraini relationship soon impressed Pelletreau. With the fall of the shah, not only did the United States see one of its "twin pillars" crumble away, but it saw its once staunch ally become an avowed enemy, dedicated to ridding the country of Western influences and spreading Islamic fundamentalism to countries throughout the Gulf, including Bahrain. In the case of the island nation, the Ayatollah Khomeini rescinded the recognition given by the shah a decade earlier. Making matters worse, the region's geography challenged U.S. military planners. With Iran dominating the Gulf along its northern edge, allied warships operating in its narrow confines were within minutes of potential attack by Iranian aircraft and missiles. Iran also had the capability to mine the shallow Gulf waters and to militarily restrict the movement of ships through the entrance to the Gulf, the famous bottleneck known as the Strait of Hormuz. Restricting tanker movement through the strait would have disastrously affected the world's oil supply.

Armed with billions of dollars worth of sophisticated weaponry purchased from the United States and others, Iran posed an extremely credible threat. In addition, intelligence specialists feared that the new Tehran regime would provide sanctuary to terrorist groups. Responding to a report that the Popular Front for the Liberation of Palestine intended to launch terrorist strikes in the Strait of Hormuz on 9–10 June 1979, Packer dispatched the USS *Elmer Montgomery* (FF 1082) to patrol the vital waterway. Within a year, escort service provided there by U.S. and other nations' warships became a regular occurrence.[16]

On 4 November 1979, Iranian zealots burst into the U.S. Embassy in Tehran, seizing the staff. With the USS *Aylwin* (FF 1081) on station off the Iranian coast, Admiral Packer reacted by deploying the *La Salle* and then the USS *Claude V. Ricketts* (DDG 5) and the USS *Miller* (FF 1091). Meanwhile, the USS *Kitty Hawk* (CV 63) and her escorts got under way at Subic Bay to augment the *Midway* Battle Group on station in the northern Arabian Sea. On the island of Diego Garcia, Navy SeaBees worked with contractors to expand the facility there to host a squadron of prepositioned cargo ships loaded to support ground forces. Then in December 1979, the Soviets moved troops into Afghanistan, capping a most disastrous year for American foreign policy.[17]

Responding to the Soviet invasion, the Carter administration took several actions to rally international support in opposition to the Soviet aggression. In early 1980, the State Department directed Ambassador Pelletreau to approach the Bahrainis about boycotting the Moscow Olympics. After consideration, the Bahrainis agreed to support the American stand and withheld their athletes from that quadrennial event.[18]

The rest of the year brought little to cheer about as the hostage rescue attempt launched on 24 April 1980 from the USS *Nimitz* (CVN 68) failed to achieve its objective.

Rear Adm. Robert W. Chewning, who had relieved Admiral Packer in June 1979, had deliberately not been informed of the operation. *La Salle* was at Bahrain at the time of the rescue attempt and immediately joined ASU Bahrain in setting up security as a precaution against possible Iranian retaliation. None came.[19] Then on 22 September 1980, Iraq attacked Iran to secure control over the Shatt-al-Arab, the waterway dividing the two countries, and to acquire territory holding rich oil deposits in southwestern

Iran. After initial successes, including the capture of Khorramshar, the Iraqi offensive became bogged down into what would become an eight-year war. By October, the United States and its allies had placed sixty Navy ships in the region to monitor the belligerents and deter the conflict from spreading.[20]

The American public's disgust stirred up by the daily televised images of their countrymen being held captive haunted President Carter. In November 1980, Ronald Reagan was elected president. On the day of his inauguration, the 444-day hostage crisis came to a close as the Iranians set the embassy staff free.

The Iranian revolution had a significant impact not only on the United States but on a number of other countries, including Bahrain. Many natural ties existed between Bahrain's Shi'ite population and the Shi'ites of Iran. For instance, many Shi'ite clerics routinely underwent instruction in Iran's holy places. There was also a considerable minority of Bahrainis who had direct family ties with people in Iran. As a result, there was a large audience in Bahrain susceptible to the messages coming from Tehran urging the spread of the Islamic revolution. Riots broke out in Manama in August 1979 as Shi'ite demonstrators showed their support for the revolution. Additional demonstrations occurred in the wake of the U.S. Embassy seizure later that year. In every instance Bahrain's government took swift action. The rioters were quickly controlled and the ringleaders either jailed or deported.

It is understandable that Bahraini leaders were not unhappy to see Iraqi troops storm across the Shatt-al-Arab the following year. By this time Iran had begun to actively fund, train, and arm its supporters in Bahrain, and there is strong evidence that Iran's revolutionary leaders were intent on overthrowing the Al Khalifa. In late 1981 a purported plot to assassinate the royal family, aided and abetted by the Iranian chargé d'affaires, was uncovered. A number of arrests and deportations followed, ending any real threat to the Bahraini government. While no further serious internal unrest was noted in Bahrain during the years of the Iran-Iraq War, the government remained alert to the possibility that the Iranian revolutionary government would continue its attempts to undermine the legitimacy of the Al Khalifa.[21]

Along the Gulf's southern fringe, concern about the conflict to the north persuaded Bahrain, Kuwait, Oman, Qatar, the United Arab Emirates, and Saudi Arabia to form a political and military association. Created on 25 May 1981, the Gulf Cooperation Council (GCC) enabled the Gulf Arabs to pool financial assistance to Iraq more effectively and cooperate in thwarting Iranian-motivated revolutionaries.[22]

During 1981 the tide of the war changed, and by May 1982, Iran had recaptured Khorramshar and taken as prisoners thousands of Iraqi defenders. Iraq pulled its troops out of Iran and set up defensive positions along a seven hundred–mile front. Against these positions, the Iranians launched human-wave assaults. By the end of 1983, these tactics had cost the Iranians three hundred thousand killed and five to six hundred thousand wounded. In contrast, the Iraqis had suffered about sixty-five thousand killed and between one hundred and sixty-five and two hundred and ten thousand wounded.

Seeking a way to counter the pressure of Iranian ground assaults, the Iraqis began striking tankers traveling to and from Iran. For nearly two years, the Iranians debated on how to retaliate for these attacks because Iraqi ports were closed and there was no equivalent tanker traffic carrying Iraqi oil. Kuwait operated its ports as surrogate ports for Iraq, however, allowing the Iraqis to import tons of arms and export oil and other goods. The Iranians knew that attacking Kuwaiti shipping risked an escalation of the war and possible American involvement. American intentions were already becoming clear. On 22 February 1984, President Reagan committed the United States to keeping the Gulf's sea lanes open. Then, in early March, the USS *Lawrence* (DDG 5) locked on an approaching Iranian P-3. When the American-built patrol plane flew well within the five-mile "keep-out" buffer zone previously established by the U.S. Navy for its ships operating in the Gulf, the *Lawrence* fired machine guns and flares to ward off the intruder.[23]

As Iran pressed forward on the battlefield, Iraq began using poison gas, launching missiles against Iranian cities, and stepping up attacks on shipping in the Gulf. Beginning in March the Iraqis expanded the scope of their sea campaign, hitting tankers loading at the facility at Kharg Island in the northern Gulf. Despite their concerns over possible American intervention, the Iranians lashed out. On 13 May 1984, an Iranian F-4 attacked the Kuwaiti tanker *Umm Casbah*. This and following attacks alarmed the Gulf states, and on 21 May they asked the UN Security Council to address the issue. On 1 June the council passed Resolution 552 (1984) calling on all states to respect freedom of navigation. Tehran ignored the resolution. Over the next seven months, the Iranians attacked another fifteen neutral ships.[24]

Middle East Force commander Rear Adm. John F. Addams reacted by ordering his ships to begin escorting American oil tankers chartered by the Military Sealift Command. Throughout the remainder of 1984, Middle East Force ships monitored the ongoing struggle. In January 1985, the danger of operating in the northern Gulf just within an exclusion zone established by the Iraqis became apparent to the USS *John Hancock* (DD 981) when an Iraqi Exocet missile slammed into an innocent tugboat a mere five miles away. Addams immediately issued an order forbidding his ships to enter this dangerous area.[25]

For Bahrain and the countries of the GCC, the escalation of the tanker war had troubling implications. Besides bringing the issue before the UN Security Council, the Gulf states prepared to use military means if necessary. In June 1984, a Saudi F-15 shot down an Iranian F-4 over the Gulf. Five months later the GCC announced that it had approved the formation of a rapid deployment force of between ten and thirteen thousand personnel to be drawn from the six countries.[26]

As the GCC took steps to improve its defensive posture, Middle East Force strove to improve its own security ashore. In 1983, a bombing at the U.S. Embassy in Kuwait and then the Marine barracks bombing in Lebanon brought home the dangers of terrorism for those serving throughout the Middle East. At the Navy compound in Bahrain, additional barricades were set up and security was tightened to protect the eleven officers and eighty enlisted personnel assigned. Obtaining the resources for the security enhancements was a contentious issue for Admiral Addams. Although ASU Bahrain existed to support the Middle East Force, its commanding officer looked to Commander Naval Logistics Support Force Pacific for funding. Located thousands of miles away in Hawaii, this command had to be prodded to free up money for needed improvements. Later, Addams recalled the installation of bullet-proof glass and steel doors for his home and the posting of additional guards.[27]

Facing mutual threats, the Gulf states warmed to the U.S. military presence in the region. Kuwait hosted a visit by Commander Middle East Force for the first time in six years and other countries welcomed U.S. officials and warship port visits. While Bahraini Minister of Information Tariq Almoayed continued to deny the existence of an American base to inquiring reporters, the amir and other Bahrainis frequently asked the admiral why more of the Americans stationed at the ASU didn't have their families with them. Consequently, many went ahead and called for their dependents to join them. In keeping with the "low-key" image, Admiral Addams' predecessor as Commander Middle East Force, Rear Adm. Charles E. Gurney, always visited Bahraini officials wearing civilian attire. The new, more open, pro-American stance was apparent when Addams, meeting with the crown prince, was asked why he didn't wear his uniform. The civvies came off.[28]

Adding to the visibility of the Navy installation in Bahrain was the number of VIPs who began arriving on a regular basis to consult with Commander Middle East Force, the ambassador, and Bahraini officials. In 1985 visitors included Secretary of the Navy John Lehman, CNO Adm. James Watkins, CENTCOM commander General Kingston, and Assistant Secretary of Defense Richard L. Armitage.

Over the Gulf, Iraqi and Iranian aircraft continued to pummel shipping. In August 1985, Iraq stepped up its attacks against the Kharg Island oil terminal in an attempt to cripple Iran economically. The ground war continued to be a stalemate as the Iraqis reinforced their positions in anticipation of an Iranian "final offensive" in the spring of 1986.[29]

In June 1986, Rear Adm. Harold J. Bernsen relieved Admiral Addams. Bernsen had considerable experience in the Gulf. In 1980, as captain of the *La Salle*, he witnessed from offshore the initial Iraqi assaults on Iran. Just prior to his new assignment he had served as the Director of Plans and Policy at Central Command under Generals Kingston and Crist, making him the first COMIDEASTFOR to have any staff experience in the Tampa command. His close relationship with General Crist would be of great value as the tanker war became more intense, presenting increasingly difficult situations for the American Navy.[30]

For all factions in the Gulf, 1986 proved to be a pivotal year. Iraqi troops had driven off repeated Iranian attempts to seize Basra, and Iran amassed one hundred thousand men in February to attempt another frontal assault—so Iraq believed. Instead, the Iranians crossed the Shatt-al-Arab and seized the Al Faw peninsula, adjacent to Kuwait's northern boundary. As Iraqi attempts to drive off the Iranians failed, concerns grew in Kuwait City because now Kuwaiti harbors were within range of Iranian Silkworm missiles.[31]

Iraq continued to attack ships trading with Iran, using imported Super Frelon helicopters to great effect, and continued to use its jet aircraft to assault Iranian oil trans-shipment facilities at Kharg Island and elsewhere. Strikes on Sirri Island on 12 August and Larak Island on 25 November demonstrated that the Iraqis could hit any Iranian oil terminal within the Gulf.

With its American-built air force being worn away through attrition and lack of spare parts, Iran began to use surface-to-surface missiles against Iraqi oil facilities and employed surface naval forces against shipping in the Gulf. On 2 September, the Iranians stopped and seized the Soviet arms carrier *Petr Yemsov*. On 16 September, an Iranian speedboat made a night assault on the Kuwaiti tanker *Al Funtas*. A month later an Iranian frigate fired a Seakiller missile that struck the Panamanian tanker *Five Brothers*. As a consequence of the Iranian seizure of the *Petr Yemsov,* the Soviet navy began to escort its arms carriers bringing supplies to Kuwait for shipment to Iraq.[32]

While Iran's air force was slowly being forced from the skies, the fact that it was still flying missions with U.S.-built aircraft nearly seven years after relations had been broken off impressed many military observers. Then in December 1986, information leaked out about an "arms for hostages" deal between the United States and Iran. In an attempt to win the release of hostages held in Lebanon, members of President Reagan's National Security Council engineered the delivery of spare aircraft parts and ordnance to Tehran. Unaware of the operation, Secretary of Defense Weinberger called it "one of the most absurd proposals" undertaken by the Reagan administration. At a time when the United States was condemning Iranian attacks in the Gulf and publicly tilting toward the Iraqis, the arms deal, which became known as the "Iran-Contra" affair, undercut American credibility throughout the region. Fortunately, the military-to-military relationships among the United States and the Arab countries of the region established by CENTCOM and MIDEASTFOR had provided a foundation from which the United States could restore its good name.[33]

For the countries of the GCC, America's perceived duplicity was just one of several worries. Of major concern, the war had begun to wreak havoc on their oil-based economies. For Saudi Arabia, Kuwait, and the United Arab Emirates, oil revenues dropped from $186 billion in 1982 to $57 billion in 1985. The combination of a world economic recession, oil discoveries and production elsewhere, and Iran selling oil below the world market price to lure customers to its vulnerable ports created a glut of cheap oil. Furthermore, contributions to the Iraqi war effort drained billions more from GCC coffers.[34]

Bahrain was not far from the front lines of the Iran-Iraq War. As a student of the Bahrain International School, a young Shaikh Salman bin Hamad Al Khalifa, the present crown prince, saw the effects of the war in terms of increased insecurity. "We heard reports of the mines that were floating down the Gulf." He noted that patrons of Muharraq coffeehouses sat and sipped their brews while watching Bahraini naval vessels locate and destroy the "floaters" that had entered coastal waters. In one tragedy, two boys were killed on a beach playing with a mine.[35]

Unfortunately for Bahrain, on top of facing an economic crunch, floating mines, and a continuing threat from Iran, the long-standing dispute with Qatar over the Hawar Islands and the shoal of Fasht-e-Dibal heated up.

On 26 April 1986, Qatari helicopters fired on Bahraini construction crews building a station on the Fasht-e-Dibal reef and then landed troops to seize the workers and the station. Both nations then called military alerts and reinforced their positions. Diplomacy led to an easing of tensions and the release of the construction workers.[36]

In Washington, Vice President George Bush followed the situation closely. He had visited the region in February and appreciated Bahrain's efforts to support ASU and the ships of the Middle East Force and did not want to see the situation deteriorate. Rejecting a State Department recommendation to take a "hands-off position," Bush asked retired admiral James L. Holloway III to act as a personal emissary to work with the Saudis to resolve the Fasht-e-Dibal dispute between Qatar and Bahrain. The former CNO recalled, "George Bush believed that Bahrain deserved greater consideration from the U.S. in this quarrel because of our special relationship." Briefed on the intricacies of the dispute, Holloway flew to Saudi Arabia in May 1986 and then to Bahrain to meet with the amir. The Fasht-e-Dibal issue was deferred.[37] Qatari claims on the Hawars continued into the twenty-first century, with the issue to be resolved in the International Court of Justice.

Bahrain's revenues were helped somewhat by a renegotiating of the lease in 1986. The new payment reflected the increased use of Bahrain International Airport by American military aircraft and the increased number of days that Middle East Force ships were spending alongside the Mina Sulman pier. In 1987, the Americans paid an additional $700,000 a year to rent needed warehouse space.[38]

Resupplied with arms and spare parts provided by the United States, Iran saw an opportunity to exploit the GCC's economic plight and forged a strategy of applying pressure to force a reconsideration of support for Iraq. Because of its geography and size, Kuwait was especially vulnerable. In June 1986, saboteurs damaged two main Kuwaiti oil manifolds. This event was followed by uprisings among Kuwaiti Shi'ites and then by a concerted effort by the Iranian air force and navy to attack Kuwait-bound shipping.[39] Seeking a way to preserve its valuable tanker fleet, on 10 December Kuwait approached the U.S. Coast Guard to gather information on how to register a ship under the American flag. The Kuwaiti request caused considerable debate within Washington's power structure. The implications of reflagging were significant. Once the tankers were reflagged, the U.S. Navy would be obliged to protect them against potential Iranian attack. It was clear to all that by so doing the United States was likely to become far more involved in the complicated and dangerous game taking place in the Gulf. However, when it became known that the Kuwaitis had also asked the Soviet Union to help protect their ships from attack by the Iranians, the die was cast. The Soviets could not be allowed to increase their presence in the Gulf unchallenged. Both Secretary Weinberger and Admiral Crowe came down strongly on the side of reflagging. To Assistant Secretary of Defense Richard Armitage and Ambassador Robert Oakley on the NSC staff, the reflagging represented an opportunity to restore American credibility following the Iran-Contra debacle.[40]

After intense negotiations between American and Kuwaiti officials in which the Kuwaitis used Soviet offers of assistance as leverage, Admiral Crowe arrived in Bahrain on 10 March for consultations with the Bahraini leadership and Middle East Force's commander, Rear Adm. Harold Bernsen. At the time, the United States had committed itself to reflag eleven Kuwaiti tankers. Although it seemed that the Soviets were no longer in the picture, Crowe was dismayed to discover that the Kuwaitis had agreed to charter three Soviet tankers to move oil. Despite this apparent setback, the chairman felt the need to push forward.

Calling on Crown Prince Shaikh Hamad bin Isa Al Khalifa, Admiral Crowe sat down with his highness and family members, including son Salman, within a spacious office. After the traditional perfunctory hospitalities, the admiral suggested that the United States would be willing to reflag the Kuwaiti tankers. The young Shaikh Salman bin Hamad recalled watching his father turn and call the Kuwaiti crown prince and Prime Minister Shaikh Saad to say, "I have Admiral Crowe sitting next to me, the United States is willing to reflag your tankers and I urge you to accept." The Kuwaiti leader responded by extending an invitation to the admiral to come to Kuwait to finalize the arrangements.[41]

Two weeks later Admiral Crowe had his opportunity. Arrangements were made for him to stop in Kuwait on his way back to Washington from a trip to the Indian subcontinent. Accompanied by Admiral Bernsen, he had separate meetings with the Kuwaiti amir and the prime minister, the amir's brother. The meetings were extremely cordial, both Kuwaiti leaders welcoming the American offer of reflagging. While assuring the admirals that any Soviet involvement would be minimal, neither of them would disavow the Kuwaiti request to the great power to the north.[42]

In April, the CENTCOM staff in Tampa began planning the escort operation for the reflagged tankers. Fortunately for General Crist, he had two officers within his command with experience in the region. Having commanded *La Salle* at the beginning of the decade, Admiral Bernsen was familiar with the tricky waters of the Gulf. From the Middle East, Bernsen transmitted his thoughts on how to run the operation. In addition, Bernsen sent his operations officer, Capt. David Grieve, to work directly with the planners. Grieve also was familiar with the Gulf, having just finished a tour as commanding officer of the Middle East Force–assigned ship USS *Jack Williams* (FFG 24).

It should be noted that in many quarters Navy support for the escort operation was muted. Senior admirals expressed concern that getting directly involved in a shooting war in a confined body of water at the end of an extremely long logistics pipeline was not prudent. The realization that the CENTCOM planners were asking for a much larger number of ships for the escort operation than were currently deployed to the Gulf made the tasking even more onerous. When briefed at the JCS level, the CNO, Adm. Carlisle Trost, objected that the requirement for eight combatants to operate continuously in the Gulf would severely tax his resources.[43]

While planning for the escort operation, titled "Earnest Will," moved forward, Middle East Force ships continued to monitor the war. On 16 May, one of the Soviet tankers leased to the Kuwaitis, the *Marshall Chuykov,* hit a mine on approach to a Kuwaiti oil terminal.[44] The next evening, aboard *La Salle* in port at Manama, Admiral Bernsen was entertaining Samuel Zackem, the American ambassador to Bahrain, at a dinner honoring a departing staff member. At 2110, the watch officer called Bernsen to the bridge. The ambassador noted other officers leaving the wardroom so he also headed topside to find a shaken Bernsen, who turned to him and said, "Ambassador, the *Stark* has been hit."[45]

The USS *Stark* (FFG 31) left Bahrain at 0800 that morning to take station in the north central Gulf. Twelve hours later, an Airborne Warning and Control System (AWACS) aircraft detected an Iraqi F-1 heading south into the Gulf in the direction of the *Stark* and warned the missile frigate. In the ship's Combat Information Center (CIC), the incoming aircraft appeared on the radar scope, and shortly thereafter the plane's fire-control radar was detected locked onto the *Stark*. At 2107, the Iraqi French-built jet launched an Exocet missile at a range of 22.5 miles. A second launch followed. A lookout's report of the first incoming missile came too late as the Exocet slammed into the ship's port side in the vicinity of her crew's berthing, failing to explode but splattering fuel. The second missile did explode, igniting the fuel. The devastation immediately killed thirty-four Sailors and wounded many more. The blast knocked several men overboard.[46]

Upon hearing the tragic news, Bernsen ordered the USS *Conyngham* (DDG 17), USS *Waddell* (DDG 24), USS *Reid* (FFG 30), and his flagship to the scene to conduct search-and-rescue efforts and lend assistance to the crippled ship. To care for the injured, Ambassador Zackem called the amir and received permission to use Bahraini hospitals. ASU Bahrain mobilized to form a command center, coordinating the delivery of fire-fighting equipment, medical personnel and supplies, and explosive ordnance disposal experts to the burning ship. At 2300, a Navy H-3 helicopter lifted off from Muharraq with Lt. Cdr. T. A. Miller, the ASU Bahrain medical officer, on board. Arriving over the *Stark* at 0200, the helicopter dropped "Doc" Miller and supplies, and then conducted a limited, unsuccessful search for crewmembers who were thought to have been forced overboard.[47]

At about 0300, Crown Prince Shaikh Hamad bin Isa Al Khalifa received a phone call. At daybreak he had helicopters in the air heading unarmed into a war zone to assist with the search-and-rescue effort. One of the helicopters, with only twenty minutes of fuel to spare, spotted four Sailors clinging together in the water. Swooping down, the helicopter picked up William McLeod, Timothy Porter, Timothy Gable, and William Morandi. The three operation specialists and the fire controlman were puzzled about the nationality of their rescuers. The pilot pointed to his Bahraini Flag patch on his shoulder sleeve.[48] Saudi Arabia also dispatched helicopters to comb the waters around the *Stark* to locate missing crewmen. On the stricken frigate, heroic damage control efforts kept the ship afloat. Sadly, the attack would claim thirty-seven lives.

With the fires extinguished and a 16-degree list corrected, the frigate was taken under tow to Bahrain by the *Conyngham*. There she sat at the Sitrah anchorage, outboard of the *La Salle*, awaiting the arrival of the tender USS *Acadia* (AD 42). Meanwhile, Sailors injured with severe burns received superb care at the Salmoniya Medical Center. In 1988, Sailors at ASU Bahrain conducted a fund-raising event for the burn unit to show their appreciation for the care given.[49]

News of the attack attracted international notoriety and suddenly focused congressional attention on the proposed plan to escort reflagged Kuwaiti tankers. Many railed against the idea. Senator Edward Kennedy wondered whether, by showing such favoritism to Kuwait, the United States was not pushing Iran into an alliance with the Soviets. Senators John Glenn and John Warner traveled to Bahrain to conduct fact-finding visits. They were briefed extensively by Bernsen and his staff and came away supportive of the plan.

The administration would receive support on the Hill for the escort operation if it could demonstrate that the risks were minimal. Admiral Bernsen's original concept called for using the MEF ships he already had available to conduct the escorting. However, the *Stark* incident changed Washington's mindset. Secretary Weinberger told General Crist that if he didn't have the force needed to conduct the operation, "You should ask for it."[50]

In Baghdad, American and Iraqi officials set up "deconfliction" procedures to prevent a repeat incident. Meanwhile in Tampa and in the Middle East, staffs finalized plans for the escort operation. Of concern was the obvious threat of mines. As previously noted, the day before the *Stark* incident, the Kuwaiti-chartered Soviet tanker *Marshall Chuykov* struck a mine in the Mina Al Ahmadi channel just east of Kuwait. The Americans reacted by alerting Helicopter Mine Countermeasure Squadron 14 (HM-14) to be ready to deploy and sending a mine countermeasure assist team. The Explosive Ordnance Disposal (EOD) divers discovered Iranian-built mines based on a 1908 Russian design carefully sown across the Kuwaiti channel. Saudi minesweepers joined the effort to clear the Mina Al Ahmadi channel. With the channel cleared and protected, Admiral Crowe, General Crist, and Admiral Bernsen felt confident that the escort operation could move forward.[51]

In mid-July the Middle East Force conducted two dress rehearsals off the northern coast of Bahrain with the *La Salle* playing the role of a tanker. On 21 July, Ambassador to Kuwait Anthony Quainton raised the American flag over the *Al Rekkah*. The next day, the ship, now called the SS *Bridgeton,* joined up with the reflagged natural gas carrier *Gas Prince* and two U.S. Navy warships for a transit up the Gulf. On the 24th the convoy was passing approximately twenty miles west of the Iranian outpost on Farsi Island when the *Bridgeton*'s skipper, Capt. Frank Seitz, felt "a 500 ton hammer hit us up forward."[52] The mine opened up a ten-by-five meter hole in the four-hundred-thousand-ton tanker. Never in danger of sinking, Seitz's vessel plowed ahead at half speed, with the more vulnerable U.S. Navy escorts following in her wake. The image of the escorted ship acting as a minesweeper for the ships supposedly escorting her created great embarrassment to the U.S. government and its Navy. Admiral Crowe recalled: "The newspapers were raking us over the coals about the *Bridgeton*." Judging from the geographic location of the mine hit and other indicators, the Iranians apparently had sown mines using small craft operating from Farsi Island to interdict the *Bridgeton* and her escorts. This represented a major change in Iranian tactics; it appeared that the Iranian leadership had made the decision to risk attacking American military forces directly. The threat to U.S. warships and personnel throughout the Gulf had now become very real. In Washington, Crowe had to make a decision. Operation Earnest Will came to a temporary halt while planners sought minesweeping assets.[53]

In Norfolk, HM-14 stood ready to deploy. To operate in the Gulf, however, the minesweeping helicopters needed a platform from which to fly. Although the helicopter carrier USS *Guadalcanal* (LPH 7) was in the region, Bernsen initially rejected the idea of bringing her into the Gulf because of a concern over placing such an inviting target in harm's way. Instead, he called for minesweepers from Charleston to be sent over and in the interim proposed equipping civilian craft with minesweeping gear and running them up the shipping lanes. To find civilian minesweepers, the admiral arranged with the general manager of the Kuwaiti Oil Tanker Company to rig two of the company's ocean-going tugs, *Hunter* and *Striker,* with minesweeping gear. Many in Washington were skeptical about the plan. What was the U.S. Navy's liability if civilians were injured or killed? Admiral Crowe, anxious to resume the convoys and seeing few other solutions, gave Bernsen the go ahead. In early August, the two tugs arrived at the small Basrec shipyard in Bahrain for fitting out. Ready to go, one nervous tug captain asked Bernsen whether the scheme was safe. Bernsen responded, "I hope the Kuwaiti Oil Tanker Company is paying you double for this because I think you deserve it."[54]

Before the two tugs began their sweeping missions, Admiral Crowe ordered HM-14 to the *Guadalcanal*. After offloading Marines and taking on the helicopters at Diego Garcia, the LPH steamed into the Gulf. Eventually, a minesweeping scheme was developed whereby the helicopters swept ahead of the tugs, which swept ahead of the tankers, which were followed by escorting U.S. Navy warships. Over the next year, the two tugs safely led numerous convoys. Many in the mine warfare community questioned the effectiveness of the improvised sweepers, but it appeared that a problem was being addressed, and—more importantly—no ships were struck when *Hunter* and *Striker* were operating with a convoy. Eventually, Britain, France, the Netherlands, and Belgium sent sweepers to the Gulf to handle the mine threat "professionally." Six American Korean War–vintage sweepers arrived later in the fall.[55]

Army MH and AH-6 helicopters from the Army's 160th Special Operations Aviation Group arrived to supplement Navy helicopters to perform nighttime reconnaissance duties. The superior sensors of the Army Special Forces helicopters over Navy and Marine Corps helicopters dictated the extraordinary move to allow them to operate in a maritime environment. By mid-August two "Seabat" teams—each team consisting of an MH-6 and two AH-6 helicopters—were flying at night from two frigates stationed in the Gulf. Navy special boat units and SEALs also arrived. Several boats were shipped in USS *Raleigh* (LPD 1), USS *Mount Vernon* (LSD 39), and USS *Saint Louis* (LKA 116).[56] Aboard the tankers, small teams of Naval Reservists embarked to provide liaison with the civilian crews and the escorts. Cdr. Greg Hawkins, USNR, recalled leading a five-man detachment that would pick up inbound ships in the Gulf of Oman and outbound ones off Kuwait. When not riding through the Gulf, Hawkins and his team stayed in hotels in Manama and kept a low profile.[57]

With the initiation of Earnest Will operations, the number of ships and commands deploying to the Gulf grew exponentially. As Hawkins and his team had discovered, the space ashore for housing the many players was simply not available within the confines of the ASU at Jufair. The Naval Reservists were not the only ones living ashore in hotels and apartments outside the ASU compound. Hundreds of people, Sailors as well as technical representatives from many different agencies and companies, had been sent to Bahrain to help COMIDEASTFOR carry out the escort mission, and they needed a place to sleep. Thanks to the gracious understanding and accommodating policies of the Bahraini government and the hospitality of the Bahraini people, all were cared for. For example, limits on the number of "pier days" that American warships could be berthed were set aside or simply ignored. Storage buildings were made available to accommodate the ever-growing piles of supplies and equipment, and ramp space was allocated to facilitate the tripling and quadrupling of logistics flights into the international airport. Without the wholehearted support of the Bahrainis, the operation could not have gone forward as it did.[58]

With Earnest Will moving ahead, VIPs flew to Bahrain to get first-hand reports on the convoy operations. In September 1987 alone, the small U.S. facility hosted the secretary of defense, the secretary of the Navy, the chairman of the Joint Chiefs of Staff, and the commander in chief of Central Command. With the arrival of Army Special Forces and Air Force assets in the region, and given the concern about the division line between CENTCOM and PACOM at the Strait of Hormuz, Crist had sold Secretary Weinberger and eventually Admiral Crowe on the idea of having a Joint Force Commander senior to Bernsen to coordinate the forces inside and outside the Gulf. On 20 September, Joint Task Force Middle East, under the command of Admiral Brooks, stood up. Embarked in the Arabian Sea aboard the USS *Long Beach* (CGN 9), Brooks had an Air Force brigadier general serving as his deputy. Within a day, the new command could claim a major coup.[59]

On the evening of 21 September, the USS *Jarrett* (FFG 33) launched its MH-6 and two AH-6 helicopters to observe the *Iran Ajr,* an Iranian six-hundred-ton landing craft, of being a suspected minelayer. Flying close in, the MH-6 crew observed three Iranian crewmembers pushing cylindrical "mine-like" objects down a gangplank over the starboard side. Back on *La Salle,* Admiral Bernsen monitored the surveillance mission. When he heard the report, he recalled ordering, "Take them under fire." But his operations officer looked at him and cautioned, "Mine-like!" Bernsen responded, "Bullshit, they're mines." *Jarrett* relayed the order, "You are cleared to engage." As the MH-6 pulled away, the two heavily armed AH-6 birds reported "inbound hot" as they veered in. Machine-gun bullets and rockets ripped into the mine layer, and frightened Iranians jumped over the sides to dodge the destruction from above. Fireballs lit the sky as rockets set off secondary explosions. On *La Salle,* Admiral Bernsen recalled, "We all sat wondering what the hell we had done—sort of on tenterhooks." As one of the small Army attack helicopters prepared to make a third run, *Jarrett* ordered a ceasefire. The MH-6 swung in and observed that the ship had stopped with her stern ablaze. After five minutes another secondary explosion ripped through her bow. As one of the AH-6 helicopters rearmed and changed pilots on *Jarrett's* flightdeck, the two remaining helicopters noticed the stricken vessel begin to surge forward and crewmembers hurrying aft to resume the mining operation. After receiving permission to resume attacking, the remaining AH-6 helicopter expended the rest of its ammo, causing havoc. The rearmed AH-6 arrived and further pressed the attack. After *Jarrett* issued a second ceasefire, the helicopters observed little activity as many of the crew had jumped overboard. In the morning Navy SEALs boarded the vessel and found nine mines, three dead Iranians, and numerous documents unveiling Iran's hand in mining. The Americans captured twenty-six Iranian s ailors who were later repatriated. Secretary of Defense Weinberger ordered the *Iran Ajr* scuttled.[60]

By the end of September, twenty-four U.S. Navy ships, including the battleship *Missouri,* were operating within or just outside the Gulf. Getting supplies, mail, and people to these ships was the mission of Detachment 2 of Helicopter Combat Support Squadron TWO (HC-2) based in Norfolk, Virginia. HC-2 was stood up as a new squadron in April 1987 using components taken from three existing squadrons. Detachment 1 of the Jacksonville-based Helicopter Antisubmarine Squadron ONE (HS 1) became Detachment 2 of the new squadron. For years Detachment 1 and predecessor helicopter detachments had been called the "Desert Ducks." Public Affairs Officer Lt. Kevin Wensing recalled at the time of the Gulf War that the moniker dated back to shortly after *La Salle's* arrival in Bahrain in the early 1970s. Detachment 2 inherited an SH-3G Sea King helicopter. During the *Stark* incident, the helicopter flew close to twenty hours to provide assistance to the damaged frigate.

"Desert Duck Airlines" quickly established Navy-wide fame for its logistical support to Middle East Force ships. With the late summer buildup, the number of hours per month the detachment flew jumped from 68 to between 125 and 150. Keeping the aircraft up and flying given the increased flight hours in a harsh environment challenged the aircrews. Aviation Maintenance Administrationman Thomas "Leaky" Faucett noted, "When it's 115 degrees, and a guy is out on the tarmac working on an aircraft, your concern shifts from getting the aircraft fixed to keeping the guy who's fixing it alive." Commenting on the environment, Aviation Structural Mechanic Chief Timothy Walters noted that the dryness rots tires and rubber tubing, the heat bakes paint, and the salt and humidity cause corrosion. One of the pilots, Lt. Chuck Farrell, recalled, "The intense heat was my first shock when I got here. There were days when it was 123 degrees by 9 o'clock in the morning."[61]

Petty Officer Kevin Secord, a veteran of six tours with the Desert Ducks, recalled that during this period the detachment operated out of two Quonset huts tucked away at the airport. The very junior Secord had numerous responsibilities, including the care and feeding of Daisy and Vivian, two mallards that graced a pond adjacent to the huts. Other chores included selling ice cream, sodas, and t-shirts. The Desert Duck t-shirts were prized trophies for visiting VIPs. Secord remembered selling $800 worth to the Senate Armed Services Committee. For security, the aviators were initially provided with nightsticks. That would change.[62]

With the Americans taking a more active role in protecting the freedom of navigation, concern grew about the security of the small ASU compound against attack from Iranian commandos and terrorist threats. A Marine Fleet Anti-terrorist Security Team company based in Norfolk placed a platoon on twenty-four-hour standby, and the small command became a test bed for sophisticated sensors, anti-swimmer nets, underwater strobe lights, and, finally, the marine mammal program. The last program stirred public interest when reported on *NBC News* shortly after six dolphins arrived in October.

Intended to force enemy swimmers to the surface, the dolphins took turns patrolling the Sitrah anchorage and the Mina Sulman pier area for the next seven months. To house the dolphins, Bapco Chairman Don Hepburn underwrote the construction of pens near his Sitrah fueling pier. Besides having facilities built, the dolphin handlers were pleased with the tremendous support they received from the Bahrainis who worked at the facility. Unfortunately, one thing the Bahrainis could not offer was food. The feeding effort proved a logistical nightmare because the sea mammals consumed ten tons of Columbia River Mackerel, which had to be flown in from the States. Warming water impeded the effectiveness of the dolphins, and they returned home as summer approached the following year.[63]

Additional resources arrived in Bahrain to support the Middle East Force. The Maritime Liaison Office Bahrain traces its origins from this period. COMIDEASTFOR established this office to facilitate an exchange of unclassified information with companies and individuals throughout the Gulf involved in the maritime industry. By contacting port officials, shipping company officials, diving and salvage company personnel, and regional coast guard representatives, the office could keep Admiral Bernsen and his successors abreast of commercial activities in the Gulf. In exchange, the office gave the companies information about potential mine and other threats in the Gulf and stood ready to help coordinate search, rescue, and medical evacuation activities.[64]

Fortunately for these shipping companies, Middle East Force sea and air patrols eventually secured the southern Gulf from Iranian mine-laying activities. The success of U.S. operations in the southern Gulf served only to accentuate the difference between that relatively open and easily patrolled area and the northwestern Gulf, a region of shallow water, small islands, and many oil platforms. The latter had never been covered well by the U.S. Navy's surveillance assets. Despite the Navy's mine-sweeping efforts after the *Bridgeton* incident, Admiral Bernsen and his staff believed that mines still lurked beneath some of the area's waters. For this reason, they did not consider sending combatants into the area for routine patrols. Some other method was needed to maintain a good watch on Iranian activities and to prevent further mining attempts. Patrol by helicopters and small craft carrying SEALs and Marines seemed to be a viable solution. The question was how to support such forces.

Admiral Bernsen had begun looking for a helicopter support platform to support the escort operation in the northern Gulf as early as June. In July he traveled to Kuwait and talked to the same officials who had offered up the services of *Hunter* and *Striker,* inquiring whether the Kuwaitis could provide any assistance. They offered two Kuwaiti coast guard units equipped with helicopter platforms. The platforms were quite suitable, but the admiral declined the offer because of the lack of berthing space in the ships. Returning to Bahrain, Bernsen remembered having visited some very large oil drilling support platforms years earlier. A few phone calls later, and he had located two similar platforms owned by Brown and Root, the two "barges" that were to become part of the folklore of the "Tanker War," *Hercules* and *Wimbrown 7*. Because of the downturn in the oil business, they had been laid up, ironically alongside a pier at Bahrain. Assured of their seaworthiness and convinced by Bernsen of the need for their services, the Kuwaitis immediately agreed to pay for their refurbishment and operation, a tidy sum.[65]

Notwithstanding Kuwait's offer to pay the bill, the barge proposal stirred heated debate in Washington and in U.S. military headquarters from Norfolk to Honolulu. The CNO, CINCLANT, CINCPAC, and the Sixth and Seventh Fleet commanders all weighed in with objections. Navy Secretary James Webb, visiting the region, inspected the barges and saw the potential for a Beirut suicide bombing–type disaster. At a conference convened at Tampa to study the issue from 9–11 September 1987, General Crist argued that the plan was less risky than placing a high-value Navy ship in the area. Admiral Crowe, who had worked with similar barges during his riverine experience in Vietnam, signed off on the idea.[66]

Two officers recently sent to the Gulf to augment COMIDEASTFOR's small staff—Capt. Frank Lugo and Cdr. Dick Flanigan—were assigned to supervise the refurbishment of the barges and put the finishing touches on the surveillance force basing concept. Faced with an ever-increasing list of "must have" equipment, such as armor, 50-mm guns, and sophisticated communications equipment and radar, the two worked tirelessly to complete the assignment.[67]

By early October, workers had completed the necessary alterations to the *Hercules,* and tugs pushed the platform into the northern Gulf. Under the command of Lt. Paul Evancoe, the 400-by-140-foot barge accommodated more than 170 Sailors, soldiers, and Marines, as well as civilian deckhands to support a Seabat detachment of three Army helicopters, four Mk III craft, and two riverine patrol boats. On the evening of 8 October, a Navy LAMPS helicopter detected small craft near Farsi Island and directed the three *Hercules*–based Army helicopters to investigate. The MH-6 pilot recalled coming up on the craft and reporting "We have Boghammers." Upon further inspection the pilot noted there were three small craft and discerned that one was a Boghammer and the other two were armed Boston whalers. As the scout helicopter zipped by, the Iranians began firing machine guns. Seeing tracers leaping into sky, the two following AH-6s fired flechette rockets and miniguns firing at a rate of four thousand rounds a minute. The devastating fire broke one Boston whaler in half and set her sister boat ablaze. The Boghammer fired a missile; however, the warhead failed to arm because of the closeness of the helicopters. The helicopters reacted by attacking the enemy boat. Hit by a high-explosive rocket, the Boghammer sank in thirty seconds.[68]

A Navy Mk III patrol craft with SEALs embarked from the *Hercules* arrived to pick up survivors. One petty officer retrieved a Styrofoam case for a battery for the U.S.-made Stinger missile. The discovery proved quite disheartening. Apparently, the Iranians had obtained the deadly missile from the Afghanistani Mujahadeen.

Evancoe, however, had little time to dwell on this disturbing development as the LAMPS helicopter detected a massing of Iranian craft to the northeast. With his reinforced platoon of Marines and SEALs bracing for attack, Evancoe called for reinforcements. Three more Army helicopters and the USS *Thach* (FFG 43) sped toward his position. Suddenly, the charging Iranians turned away. The attack never materialized. The Iranian action marked the first and last attempt to challenge the presence of the American floating base. With the arrival of the *Wimbrown 7* in December, the Americans established a strong military foothold in the northern Gulf. When the Iran-Iraq War ended in late 1988, the two barges were returned to civilian use.[69]

Iranian Silkworm missiles and larger Iranian naval vessels still posed a threat. From captured territory on the Al Faw peninsula, the Iranians aimed the Silkworms at ships entering and leaving Kuwait. On 15 October, one of the missiles slammed into the tanker *Sungarai*, causing extensive damage. The next day, the reflagged tanker *Sea Isle City* took a hit, injuring fifteen crewmen. Four days later, a surface action group consisting of four U.S. Navy destroyers attacked and destroyed two Iranian oil platforms in the southern Gulf suspected to be command centers. The impact of 1,065 high-explosive rounds tumbled one of the platforms into the Gulf and the second one remained upright, ablaze, leaving it to the SEALs to finish the demolition job with C-4 explosives.[70]

In the aftermath of the oil platform attacks, naval representatives from the United States, Britain, Australia, Belgium, the Netherlands, Italy, and France met aboard *La Salle* to discuss information-sharing arrangements about known threats. While the 4 November meeting did not result in any formal alliance, it served to solidify the already excellent working relations that the allies had developed during months of escort and mine-sweeping operations in the Gulf. Through the efforts of COMIDEASTFOR and the other allied commanders, principally Al Indien (the French commander) and the senior British officer afloat in the Gulf, the allies continually shared intelligence and operational information and cooperated to render assistance in a number of instances. The combined forces' experience gained during this period was certainly a harbinger of the cooperation that would be achieved during Desert Shield–Desert Storm.[71]

Throughout the rest of the fall and winter, the U.S.-escorted convoys proceeded unimpeded. The success of the operations, however, covered up conflicts within the chain of command, especially between Admirals Brooks and Bernsen. Ironically Brooks, who General Crist had selected to be his joint task force commander, was more in agreement with the PACOM approach of acting conservatively in the Gulf. Bernsen, on the other hand, took bold innovative steps that mirrored the general's aggressive philosophy. The solution was simple. With Bernsen due to be relieved, Crist arranged for the two billets to be merged. Rear Adm. Anthony Less assumed command as commander of JTFME in December and in February became COMIDEASTFOR. Upon taking the two helms, Less streamlined the staffs and modeled his revamped organization on the Composite Warfare Command structure prevalent in the fleet.[72]

Shortly after Admiral Less arrived, the Iran-Iraq War intensified. On 1 March Iraq launched eighteen Scud missiles to commence a six-week "War of the Cities" during which both sides lobbed surface-to-surface missiles at opposing population centers. In mid-March, Iraqi Kurds allied with Iran conducted an offensive in northern Iraq to obtain autonomy. Iraq responded with the indiscriminate use of chemical weapons against Kurdish military and civilian settlements. Finally, both sides stepped up attacks against shipping, with seventeen vessels coming under fire during the last two weeks of the month.[73]

On 14 April 1988, lookouts aboard the frigate USS *Samuel B. Roberts* spotted three mines ahead in waters northeast of Qatar. Immediately the skipper, Cdr. Paul Rinn, sent the crew to general quarters. Unfortunately, in backing down, the frigate hit a fourth mine, blowing a twenty-one-foot hole in her port side, cracking the hull, and injuring ten Sailors. The damage control efforts of the crew have become legendary. They welded cables together to keep the ship from breaking in half. Within a few days, allied minesweepers combed the area and found more freshly laid mines. Judging from the markings, Iran was the clear culprit.[74]

In Manama, Tampa, and Washington, flag officers and staffs considered the proper action. At the highest level, President Reagan met with his national security team. Admiral Crowe wanted to go after Iranian warships. President Reagan instead favored the less confrontational approach of going after Iranian oil platforms that had been used for command-and-control purposes. However, Crowe did convince the president to allow for "a very good set of rules of engagement" that would permit the Middle East Force commander to engage Iranian warships should they challenge the American operation. Crowe hoped that the notorious Iranian patrol frigate *Sabalan,* a warship that had mercilessly attacked many merchant ships and had massacred numerous unarmed Sailors, would be drawn into the fray.[75]

Under the command of Admiral Less, three surface action groups of three ships each went into battle in what was dubbed "Operation Praying Mantis," with two going after the oil platforms and a third seeking out the

Sabalan. Overhead, aircraft from the USS *Enterprise* (CVN 65) provided cover. Iranians stationed on both platforms resisted but were overpowered by naval and helicopter gunfire. Marines and SEALs captured the two rigs, set demolition charges, and got off unscathed.

Meanwhile, the third surface action group, operating off Bandar Abbas, failed to flush out the *Sabalan*. Instead, the Iranian missile boat *Joshan* came out to challenge the Americans and fired a Harpoon missile at the USS *Wainwright* (CG 28). The cruiser maneuvered to reduce its profile against the cruise missile and fired chaff. The tactic worked as the missile locked onto the foil cloud one hundred feet off the starboard beam. The *Wainwright*'s skipper then called over to the Iranian missile boat on the bridge-to-bridge radio: "Abandon your vessel for I am about to sink you." The *Wainwright* immediately fired three Standard Extended Range (ER) missiles at the *Joshan,* disintegrating the vessel.[76]

Wainwright's surface warriors had no time to celebrate. With an Iranian F-4 quickly closing, the skipper ordered Standard missiles to the rail and away. Two birds streaked toward the jet, apparently causing damage as the plane rapidly lost altitude before returning to Bandar Abbas.

To avenge the morning actions against their two oil platforms, the Iranians sent *Sahand*, sister ship of *Sabalan*, across the Gulf to attack United Arab Emirates (UAE) oil platforms. The Iranian frigate never made it as A-6 E Intruder aircraft from *Enterprise* responded to surface-to-air missile launches by firing two Harpoons and four laser-guided bombs. USS *Joseph Strauss* (DDG 16) fired another Harpoon into what became a burning hulk.[77]

Finally at 1700, the scorned *Sabalan* cleared Bandar Abbas harbor and fired three missiles at passing A-6E aircraft. Avoiding the missiles, one of the American planes turned and dropped a single five-hundred-pound laser-guided bomb down the *Sabalan*'s stack, ripping apart the engineering spaces. Admiral Less requested permission to finish off the ship. In Washington, however, Admiral Crowe turned to Secretary of Defense Frank Carlucci and said, "We've shed enough blood today," and called off any further action.[78]

For Iran, 18 April turned out to be a very bad day. Besides losing a large portion of their navy, the Iranians suffered setbacks on land as an Iraqi assault reclaimed the Al Faw peninsula. For Tehran, the situation only worsened over the next few months. Eight years and hundreds of thousands of war dead had drained the revolutionary zeal of the Iranian people. Calls to raise a one-hundred-thousand-man "Mohammed Corps" went unheeded. Iranian leaders began to consider the desirability of ending the war with a non-military solution.[79]

On 29 April, President Reagan further tightened the screws on Iran by offering protection for all ships transiting the Gulf. On 2 July the frigate *Elmer Montgomery* responded to a distress call from the Danish ship *Karama Maersk* and broke up a machine-gun attack by Iranian small craft. The next day the frigate was joined by the USS *Vincennes* (CG 49) and came upon additional Iranian speedboats. When two boats broke to attack the Aegis cruiser, the *Vincennes* defended herself. Meanwhile, CIC reported an incoming aircraft to the commander officer. Thinking he was the target of a coordinated Iranian surface and air assault, Capt. William Rogers fired two Standard missiles—and tragically shot down Iran Air Flight 655, killing all 290 passengers and crew.

In the aftermath, Admiral Crowe tapped CENTCOM J-5, Rear Adm. William Fogarty, to investigate. After interviewing the men involved in the incident and carefully reviewing the records over a two-month period, Fogarty recommended that no punitive actions be taken because given the information Rogers had to work with, "He acted in a prudent manner."[80]

Iran confronted the United States in the UN Security Council but failed to obtain a condemnation. Vice President Bush contended that Iran had to accept some of the blame for the disaster because its refusal to end the war had maintained the hostile environment that had claimed those 290 lives. Iran found little sympathy elsewhere. Isolated, with Iraqi forces advancing into Iran, the Iranian leadership finally convinced Khomeini to accept UN Resolution 598. Reading a statement on Tehran radio on 20 July, the Ayatollah said that he felt the decision was "more deadly than taking poison."[81]

A month later a ceasefire went into effect. The end of the war meant a gradual withdrawal from the Gulf. By the end of the year, Middle East Force had been reduced to six ships. Still, dangers remained. A Christmas show by the Dallas Cowboys Cheerleaders on the barge *Hercules* was curtailed by general quarters when an unidentified vessel made an approach. In January 1989 a Bahraini dhow struck a mine, killing the captain. The minesweeping operations continued.[82]

Two months later, Admiral Less provided a progress report to the Manama Rotary Club. Regarding mines, Less stated that since 1987, U.S. naval forces and those of allied nations from within and outside of the Gulf had neutralized 182 mines, with 93 having been found floating on the surface, and the rest being located in seven "different and distinct minefields." Less also noted that after the *Bridgeton* mine incident, 184 Earnest Will escort missions had provided unhindered transit for 325 ship passages through the Gulf. Less concluded his talk by assuring the audience that the United States would maintain the force in "significant numbers to meet our commitment."[83]

The new CINCCENT, Gen. H. Norman Schwarzkopf, resisted further pullbacks in the Gulf including calls to disestablish the JTFME. He managed to maintain the joint command, but the Middle East Force lost one more ship in June 1990.[84] Because of Schwarzkopf's actions, Admiral Fogarty continued to wear two hats after he relieved Admiral Less. Fogarty got the first clue of his assignment at the November 1988 CENTCOM change of command when Admiral Crowe hinted to him that he could be heading to "warmer climes!" Five months later Fogarty found himself on the *La Salle,* turning to Admiral Less and saying, "I relieve you, sir!"[85]

Shortly after taking command, Admiral Fogarty and Ambassador Zackem called on Shaikh Isa. The visit was friendly, with the amir expressing his appreciation for all the United States had done during the Iran-Iraq War and pledging continuing support in the future.

With his forces being reduced, the new commander found it a challenge to maintain the high surveillance of regional activities. In the Gulf, mines still posed a threat, and the sweeping continued. Closer to home, he took steps to counter complacency over security.[86]

The U.S. Navy's performance in the Gulf during the 1980s would prove critical when the Iraqi army pushed across the Kuwaiti border on 2 August 1990. By allowing the United States to maintain a toehold ashore, Bahrain provided the United States the opportunity to demonstrate its value as an ally against bellicose neighbors to the north. In preventing Iran from exerting power across the Gulf, the fleet put to rest doubts about the reliability of America's security commitment. During the "Tanker War," naval units from a coalition of Western powers strove to keep the sea lanes clear to keep the oil moving afloat. To meet the challenges, the naval leadership in the region thought "out of the box" in coming up with a unique minesweeping scheme and the mobile sea base concept. The industrial infrastructure based in Bahrain allowed the Navy to implement these innovations. To support the more conventional ships conducting escort operations, Bahrain proved to be a vital through-point for thousands of Sailors, spare parts, and tons of mail for the ships of the Middle East Force. Furthermore, because the Mina Sulman pier was made available, many Navy Sailors had an opportunity to obtain some R&R during a very demanding deployment.

For Bahrain, the 1980s represented a challenging period. Future Crown Prince Shaikh Salman reflected, "Bahrain was always on the front line but because of our strong relationship with the United States we were able to meet those challenges."[87] With the strengthened Bahraini-American part-

WAR IN THE GULF   111

nership, the emergence of the GCC, and the efforts by the new U.S. Central Command to build links in the region, a new coalition formed the foundation of what proved to be a winning team in 1991.

CHAPTER SEVEN

Desert Shield–Desert Storm

At 0200 on 2 August 1990, Rear Adm. William Fogarty was asleep in his Manama residence when the phone rang. Picking up, the admiral heard the voice of Gen. H. Norman Schwarzkopf: "Bill, the Iraqis have crossed the border. Do all you can to thwart their advance, but I know you have only a few forces in the area—I'll keep in contact with you. Help is on the way but it may take awhile."[1]

Iraq had initiated its invasion of Kuwait. The Kuwaiti forces were overwhelmed, but some fought valiantly, allowing most of the Kuwaiti royal family to escape along with elements of the armed forces. Would the Iraqis stop at Kuwait? At the time, Iraq possessed the world's fourth largest army and could have easily seized Saudi oil fields.

To deter further Iraqi aggression, President Bush began building a coalition against Iraq through the United Nations. Key to any plan against Saddam was to obtain Saudi permission to deploy troops and aircraft to that Arab kingdom. Seeing that the Iraqis were continuing to pour forces into Kuwait, Saudi Arabia's King Faud informed Secretary of Defense Richard Cheney and General Schwarzkopf on 6 August that the United States could begin moving forces into his country. The president ordered the execution of OPLAN 1002-90. In a fortuitous coincidence of timing, General Schwarzkopf had led a Joint CENTCOM Command Post Exercise, "Internal Look," during the last two weeks of July at Fort Bragg and at Hurlburt and Duke Fields in Florida, which had validated the recently conceived operations plan for such a contingency. Using this plan, American forces immediately began deploying to the Middle East on 7 August. Two days later the plan had a name: Operation Desert Shield.[2]

During this critical period, sea power provided the majority of the coalition's fighting forces. When the Iraqis attacked, the guided missile cruiser USS *England* (CG 22), destroyers USS *David R. Ray* (DD 971) and HMS *York*, five American frigates, and USS *La Salle* were in the central Gulf. Operating near Diego Garcia in the Indian Ocean, the aircraft carrier USS *Independence* (CV 62) and her battle group immediately headed toward the Gulf of Oman, and coming from the eastern Mediterranean, the USS *Dwight D. Eisenhower* (CVN 69) and her escorts proceeded through the Suez

Canal on 7 August into the Red Sea. With an average load of seventy combat aircraft, the two carriers positioned themselves to protect airfields on
the ground, allowing the transport aircraft and ground-based combat aircraft to fly unhindered into the region. In addition, the embarked air wings
could help blunt any Iraqi thrust into Saudi Arabia.[3]

While Air Force transport aircraft ferried soldiers of the 82nd Airborne
Division to reinforce Saudi forces quickly, thousands of other soldiers and
Marines were being mobilized stateside and in Europe for overseas movement. By 14 August all three brigades of the 82nd Airborne—more than
twelve thousand soldiers—were on the ground in Saudi Arabia along with
more than two hundred Air Force combat aircraft. A day later, the first three
ships of Maritime Preposition Ship Squadron Two (MPSRON TWO) reached
al-Jubayl with their precious cargoes of tanks and light armored vehicles
for the arriving 7th Marine Expeditionary Brigade. MPSRON TWO, commanded by Capt. Dick Crooks, debarked his staff of some two dozen officers
and enlisted personnel at Bahrain, and established the lead element for what
would become Commander Military Sealift Command Southwest Asia, an
organization that would play a major role in the coordination of MSC and
chartered ships bringing vital equipment and supplies into the Gulf.[4]

General Schwarzkopf, as Commander U.S. Central Command, became
a worldwide celebrity overnight. What was less clear to the public was who
commanded the naval forces. At the start of the conflict, Schwarzkopf's naval
component commander was newly selected Rear Adm. Robert Sutton, based
in Hawaii. Clearly not having the experience or seniority to command the
growing naval forces in the region, Sutton yielded his title on 16 August to
Seventh Fleet Commander Vice Adm. Henry H. Mauz Jr. Upon assuming
the title of COMUSNAVCENT, Mauz appointed Sutton as Commander, U.S.
Naval Logistics Support Force (COMUSNAVLOGSUPFOR/CTG 150.3).

Admiral Sutton and thirty members of his staff had already relocated
from Pearl Harbor to Bahrain. "We were set up as a multi-faceted support command," recalled Sutton. Once settled in Bahrain, Sutton's team
had the mission of ensuring that every Navy unit had the proper supplies
including food, medicine, equipment, ammo, oil, and most importantly—
people. Mauz also appointed Sutton to be the harbor defense commander
for the region.[5]

Having arrived in Bahrain on the 15th, Admiral Mauz embarked on
the *La Salle* and proceeded to tour the GCC countries and ships in the Gulf
countries to develop critical relationships. He recalled first meeting Shaikh
Isa shortly after arriving on 20 August. Before the meeting Admiral Fogarty
told Mauz that the shaikh was very pro-American "but he (like most of the

key people in Bahrain) had to be careful not to be overly friendly in public for fear of inciting the significant fundamentalist movement in the country."

Mauz recalled that Shaikh Isa was very cordial and spoke of the many previous Middle East Force commanders he had known. "He was especially keen to hear of Rear Admiral and Mrs. Tony Less, for whom he had special regard." The shaikh spoke only in generalities about Iraq, "but he was clearly very supportive of the coalition effort and was going to do all he could to support our needs." Mauz concluded: "He struck me as being a warm and dignified man, quiet but well-spoken."

Mauz also met with the son several times, and the crown prince was always friendly and supportive of the coalition efforts. Mauz noted: "He was very much concerned about the long term—after the coalition wins and withdraws and Iraq was still there."[6]

Two days after the meeting between Admiral Mauz and Shaikh Isa, F/A-18s of the 3rd Marine Air Wing began to arrive at Shaikh Isa Airfield. On the 24th the Marine fighter-attack planes began flying combat air patrol stations along the northern Gulf to protect the flanks of debarking troops and equipment in Saudi Arabia. Until the start of the war, these Bahrain-based aircraft, later joined by Qatar-based Canadian F/A-18s, had maintained the vital mission of protecting the northern flank of the coalition ground forces from enemy air attack. In addition to hosting the Marine Air Wing, the Bahrainis would host a squadron of British Tornado attack aircraft. Furthermore, Bahrain provided fuel gratis to the coalition air and naval forces.[7]

On 1 September 1990, Admiral Mauz's flagship USS *Blue Ridge* (LCC 19) tied up to the Mina Sulman pier across from *La Salle* where the new NAVCENT commander was hosting a congressional delegation led by Congressman Dan Rostenkowski. On the next day, Mauz briefed another badly jet-lagged delegation aboard *Blue Ridge*. With the outside temperature at 107 degrees, the inside conference room was hot and overcrowded. Capt. J. Cutler Dawson, the NAVCENT plans officer, admired the vice admiral's grasp of the important details, which instilled confidence in the tired yet intensely interested delegation. During the upcoming months, Mauz would host numerous other VIPs who came into the region to observe the coalition buildup.[8]

With the arrival of General Schwarzkopf in the region in late August, Admiral Fogarty surrendered his title as Commander Joint Task Force Middle East but retained his hat as Commander Middle East Force and assumed responsibility for overseeing the maritime interception operations against Iraq. The impetus for these operations came on 6 August when UN

Security Council Resolution 661 (1990) imposed trade and financial sanctions on Iraq. Geography greatly benefited the coalition, because Iraq had
only limited access to the sea. The challenge for Fogarty and the coalition
was enforcing the resolution.[9]

The United States favored an aggressive approach. Gen. Colin Powell
issued the execute order for the Maritime Quarantine Force Operations
to begin on 16 August. He later issued an amending order holding off the
execution for twenty-four hours and renaming the operation a Maritime
Interception Force Operation. Immediately, the question arose: How much
force would be considered proper to enforce the sanctions? On the 17th,
USS *Reid* (FFG 30) and USS *Goldsborough* (DDG 20) intercepted the outbound Iraqi tanker *Khanaqin*. Refusing to heed to beckoning from *Reid* to
alter course, the *Khanaqin* received a warning in the form of shots across
the bow. Still the tanker plowed ahead. What now? Firing into an unarmed
tanker loaded with oil could have grave diplomatic and environmental consequences. In this case, President Bush elected to let the ship go.[10]

UN Security Council Resolution 665 (1990), which was passed on 25
August 1990, authorized coalition navies to use "minimum force" to enforce
the sanctions against the Iraqis. Adding to the tension were Saddam's
threats against the families of Iraqi shipmasters should they yield to the
coalition's warships. Still, on 4 September, a team from *Goldsborough*
led by a member of a Coast Guard Law Enforcement Detachment (USCG
LEDet) and the destroyer's executive officer boarded and seized the freighter
Zanoobia. Elsewhere in waters in and around the Arabian peninsula, coalition warships began to tighten the noose in a loosely coordinated effort.

To execute the sanctions resolution effectively, representatives from
twenty nations attended a two-day conference held at a hotel in Manama
on 9–10 September. The conference resolved many issues regarding patrol
areas, communications, procedures, diversion ports, intelligence sharing,
and logistics. Additional conferences held at various locations fine-tuned the
process. By the end of September, forty-two coalition ships from ten navies
were in the region working with sixty U.S. Navy ships to implement the UN
sanctions. Although sanctions failed to liberate Kuwait, the role of the coalition's maritime forces in denying the Iraqis strategic cargoes and opportunities to earn foreign exchange would later hinder the Iraqi war effort.[11]

In late September, General Schwarzkopf visited with Crown Prince
Shaikh Hamad bin Isa Al Khalifa. At the time the American strategy was
to find a diplomatic solution to the Iraqi invasion of Kuwait, but to Shaikh
Hamad such a development would have been a disaster. The crown prince
explained that because of Saddam's unprovoked attack on a fellow Arab state,

"Our war with Iraq has already begun." The general later wrote, "Not only did Sheikh Hamad want the United States to kick the living hell out of Iraq, but he promised that his own forces would fight by our side: 'America should lead,' he said, 'and we are ready to follow.' " Previously, Schwarzkopf had supported a peaceful resolution of the conflict so as to spare the lives of the servicemen under his command. However, if Saddam merely withdrew he would retain his arsenal for later use. "The Gulf Arabs realized something Washington hadn't yet: strategically speaking, anything short of an Iraqi defeat in Kuwait was a losing proposition."[12] A week later, on 2 October, *Independence* and her escorts entered the Gulf.

Before Iraqi tanks crossed over the Kuwaiti border on 2 August 1990, one senior petty officer labeled the eleven-acre American naval compound known as the Administrative Support Unit or ASU in Bahrain a "sleepy hollow." Indeed, following the Iraqi-Iranian ceasefire in August 1988, the pace of activity at the ASU had slackened. The invasion quickly changed the lives of the some twelve officers and 145 enlisted personnel assigned to the only American military facility in the region as they found themselves working nearly twenty hours a day to keep up with the expansion of operations.[13]

The Iraqi attack reaffirmed the strategic importance of the small naval facility within Bahrain: personnel stationed there had already developed good working relations with the local officials and contractors, had gained access to regional port facilities, had established aviation support capabilities, and possessed the capability to lease warehouse facilities.

These advantages came into play with the quick arrival of the prepositioned fleet, shortly followed by cargo ships bringing materials from the United States, Asia, and Europe. As the region's only American military facility, "ASU absorbed the initial force build-up and became a major support center for the transportation, berthing, billeting, construction, and supply functions required initially to deter Iraqi aggression and eventually liberate Kuwait."[14] Almost overnight ships and aircraft began arriving bringing components and detachments from various Navy commands as well as from other services. For example, advance elements of the 47th Army Field Hospital were among the early arrivals. In the ensuing weeks, the number of tenant commands rocketed from twelve to forty-six, creating overwhelming demands on an infrastructure consisting of fifty buildings mostly remaining from the old British base HMS Jufair.[15]

In August, Admiral Sutton as COMUSNAVLOGSUPFOR and his staff moved into spaces formerly hosting the recreation center. Later in the conflict Sutton noted, "What started out as a small corps made up of 30 people from my staff in Hawaii has grown to 250 headquarters staff and some 8,000 shore based personnel made up of one third reservists and two-thirds active duty Navy personnel."[16] Additional personnel from COMUSNAVCENT, the Army, the Air Force, and the Coast Guard beefed up the ASU Supply Department. Meanwhile the gym, day care center, and theater were converted to billet transient troops.

Not surprisingly, the new tenants needed to communicate with parent commands, and message traffic soared from an average of 350 messages a day to well over 1,200. The communications center struggled to keep up with the demand by installing new high-speed printers and upgrading transmitter-receiver capabilities. One of the first priorities to be filled after the war would be the installation of a communications hub unit to provide ASU Bahrain and the tenant commands the bandwidth and baud rate needed to maintain connectivity.[17]

With hundreds of additional reserve and active duty naval personnel arriving to augment the beleaguered desert Sailors, Sutton took steps as harbor defense commander to enhance security in view of the potential threat posed by Iraqi saboteurs. Ports at Al Jubayl and Ad Dammam in Saudi Arabia and at Manama were considered key to the success of the war effort. In September Sutton requested the activation of three Naval Reserve Mobile Inshore Underwater Warfare (MIUW) units and three Coast Guard Reserve Port Security Units (PSU) to augment active-duty Navy EOD diver units. Quickly mobilized, these units were overseen on a day-to-day basis by Capt. Dennis Vaughan, USNR, who filled the billet of deputy harbor defense commander. In addition, security lighting was installed around the Mina Sulman warehouse, and defensive positions around the compound were hardened in October. A Marine Fleet Anti-terrorism Security Team (FAST) company arrived to man the positions.[18]

Also in October 1990, an arrangement with the Bahraini government was concluded that allowed for the annexation of thirteen acres to the east of the compound on new landfill. A month later, with the arrival of tents, medical equipment, and personnel, the 47th Army Field Hospital spread out over the site. With the Army's occupation of the landfill site, Sutton found himself with a small problem when the Saudis at the eleventh hour declined to host a third Navy Fleet Hospital on their territory. Unfortunately, the Army had left little land on Bahrain for the construction of the Navy Fleet Hospital that was then stowed in 433 containers on a ship approaching the Strait of Hormuz. Phone calls were made. Bapco chairman Don Hepburn recalled that Ambassador Charles Hostler worked closely with the Bahrainis to find a suitable location for the facility. After an initial site search turned up empty, Hepburn offered some recently graded land adjacent to the refinery in Awali. When the containers were ashore, SeaBees, helped by Awali residents, set up Fleet Hospital 6 within five days. With the arrival of the USNS *Comfort* and the USNS *Mercy,* much of the coalition's medical resources lay in and around Bahrain. Once the American military medical infrastructure was in place, a regular professional exchange with the Bahraini medical community began.[19]

Besides providing land for the Navy Fleet Hospital, Bapco welcomed servicemen and -women to use the Bapco Club, a country-club style facility. In addition, every Wednesday, Don Hepburn and his wife invited eighty enlisted personnel to their home for a buffet dinner. Hepburn recalled how well-behaved and appreciative the Marines and Sailors were. Prior to the meal, the guests donned traditional Arab dress for a photo shoot. After dessert, the hosts provided copies of the photos for the departing visitors to send home. During December, a Christmas tree was added to the background.[20]

While there was a large influx of personnel into Bahrain, several Sailors with dependents assigned to ASU Bahrain opted to take advantage of a State Department program to fly out dependents. The Bahrain International School was temporarily closed, but teachers, parents, and students urged it be reopened. Armed escorts were assigned to the school buses. Master Chief Petty Officer Timothy Moes recalled how his daughters used to carry gas masks to school. With the dependent population thinned out, Moes boasted, "My kids received one-on-one instruction for the remainder of the war and then some. It was great for them."[21]

Out in the Gulf, the coalition naval force increased in size. To transfer mail, supplies, and people among these ships and Bahrain, HC-2 moved additional detachments to Bahrain to augment the overworked Desert Ducks. In July, the two helicopters of Det. 2 had transported 3,420 pounds of mail, 27 passengers, and 1,468 pounds of cargo. Two months later, in the wake of the invasion, the figures were 43,173 pounds of mail, 668 passengers, and 36,688 pounds of cargo. In one of the more unusual medical evacuations in military history, the mallard "Boots" was flown to the USNS *Mercy* to relieve the duck of a club foot problem.[22]

During this period, the USS *Iwo Jima* (LPH 2) sat outboard of the *Blue Ridge* at the Mina Sulman pier. Plagued with minor steam leaks, the old single-screw amphibious ship had been ordered to Bahrain by the amphibious force commander, Rear Adm. John B. LaPlante, to undergo repairs at the Arabian Ship Repair Yard. On 30 October, *Iwo Jima* got under way and was just a mile into the channel when a major steam leak instantly killed six of her crew; four more Sailors who were evacuated to the USNS *Comfort* anchored nearby later succumbed to their severe third-degree burns.

The subsequent investigation determined that brass nuts had been used in the repairs. With a black coating, they had been indistinguishable from the required steel nuts. Under intense heat, the brass nuts melted, causing a steam valve to burst. *Iwo Jima* was subsequently towed back in to receive proper repairs.[23]

In November 1990, President Bush decided to increase the size of the American forces stationed in the Gulf to allow for offensive actions to liberate Kuwait. The additional forces were soon en route to the Middle East. While most ships offloaded at Dhahran, several discharged their cargoes at the Mina Sulman pier. There, detachments from the Navy Cargo Handling and Port Group, the Naval Reserve, and Marines moved cargo off the ships and into the warehouses or sent it to the front. Quartermaster First Class Timothy Smith recalled seeing a long column of tanks on his way home after work one night heading toward the causeway connecting the island with Saudi Arabia.[24]

The ASU compound hosted a Thanksgiving dinner for four thousand troops. Some of those served were Soldiers and Airmen stationed in Saudi Arabia who occasionally were allowed to cross the causeway for rest and relaxation. To ease the burden posed by units being rotated in for R&R, a cruise ship was berthed at the Mina Sulman pier; aboard her, soldiers and airmen could kick back, enjoy nightclub acts, and sleep in comfortable cabins. In a "Host a Servicemember" program, Sailors stationed at the ASU invited Sailors or Marines assigned to visiting ships to stay at their rented apartments for a few nights for a change of pace. For other Sailors and Marines on ships making port calls, Morale Welfare and Recreation (MWR) set up tents offering beer, soft drinks, and other refreshments. Some of the visitors jokingly referred to the ASU as the "Alcohol Support Unit." The local community raised funds to support the establishment of a USO facility in Manama. Servicemen and -women from all branches enjoyed USO shows including visits from Jay Leno, the Pointer Sisters, Marie Osmond, Brooke Shields, Crystal Gayle, and Ann Jillian. In addition, thousands of care packages arriving from the States were distributed and greatly appreciated.[25]

MWR also offered a variety of concerts featuring military bands as well as local choral groups such as the Bahrain School Carolers and the Manama Singers. Sporting events included a Holiday Invitational Basketball Tournament in which an Air Force team beat one from the visiting battleship USS *Wisconsin* (BB 64) for the trophy. The Kuwaiti Embassy hosted a soccer tournament, and American servicemen teams played local squads at the national stadium. On 23 December, Admiral Sutton and ASU commanding officer Cdr. Gregory E. Bolan were on hand to cut the ribbon for the Desert Dome Sports Bar.

Not surprisingly, with war impending, worship attendance increased for both Protestant and Catholic services at the ASU. The Navy Catholic chaplain assigned to the ASU also looked after the spiritual needs of the doctors, nurses, medics, and other soldiers serving next door at the Army Field Hospital. In addition, the ASU chaplain's office distributed five thousand donated Bibles to servicemen assigned in the region. On the day after Christmas, Chief of Chaplains Rear Adm. Alvin B. Koeneman visited the compound, reassuring all he met of the strong support and feelings that existed back in the States.[26]

The space shortage at the ASU compound was eased somewhat in early December when the U.S. Embassy moved into a new facility that had been under construction for some time. Admiral Sutton quickly claimed the former embassy compound to accommodate the expanding staffs of COMUSNAVLOGSUPFOR and COMSCSWA. These two organizations were now overseeing several seaports and airheads, as well as harbor defense and deployed medical units.[27]

To detect any Iraqi preemptive actions against coalition forces in Bahrain, Saudi Arabia, and elsewhere, in the northern Gulf the USS *Worden* (CG 18), the USS *Bunker Hill* (CG 52), and a frigate established a positive radar advisory zone (PIRAZ). To provide additional radar coverage, in November an E-2C detachment from USS *Theodore Roosevelt* (CVN 71) was directed to start flying out of Bahrain. In addition, Bahraini-based EP-3 electronic warfare planes flew a racetrack pattern off the Kuwaiti coast to detect Iraqi electronic emissions.[28]

On 1 December 1990, Vice Adm. Stanley Arthur relieved Admiral Mauz as commander of the growing naval forces in the region. Arthur had been slated to relieve Mauz before the crisis and CNO Adm. Frank Kelso decided in November to allow the turnover to proceed, because there was no decision yet to commence hostilities.[29]

As the coalition armada built up inside the Gulf, Manama became an ideal location for supply, repair, hospital, combatant, and merchant ships to berth alongside or anchor. Immobile and lightly armed, these ships were highly vulnerable to sea and air attack. Recognizing the strategic importance of Bahrain and the ports of Al Jubayl and Ad Dammam, Admiral Arthur reinforced the already formidable defensive gauntlet to challenge any daring Iraqi warships or aircraft. Responsibility for Gulf anti-air defenses for most of Desert Storm fell on the *Bunker Hill*'s commanding officer, Capt. Thomas Marfiak, who oversaw the movements of tactical aircraft on the alert to shoot down any air intruders and to stalk and destroy any enemy surface combatants. To counter an Iraqi intruder, the airborne weapons were augmented by the surface-to-air missiles carried on Marfiak's Aegis-equipped cruiser and other combatants in Battle Force Zulu.[30]

Harbor defenses also were beefed up to defend against Iraqi small craft or terrorist attack. In response to Admiral Sutton's September request, three naval MIUW units and three Coast Guard Reserve small-boat units were mobilized and transported to the Middle East for deployment. The MIUW concept had its origins during the Vietnam War with the construction of portable land-based combat information center–type platforms that could be placed within a harbor to detect hostile activity. Called Radar Sonar Surveillance Center vans, these platforms freed afloat assets to pursue offensive operations. At Manama, the Brooklyn-based MIUW 202 arrived on Thanksgiving Day, and the unit members occupied an abandoned warehouse in a remote commercial area near the harbor. With its Coast Guard and Navy diver counterparts, MIUW 202 formed the backbone of Admiral Sutton's Port Security Harbor Defense Group 1. Initially, the MIUW commander was directed to place his radar van on a barge afloat in the center of the harbor. While this site provided good radar coverage, lights from the Manama skyline caused thermal and visual imaging systems to be ineffective. Consequently, the MIUW radar van was moved to the end of the Mina Sulman pier, an ideal location so long as the *La Salle* and the *Blue Ridge* were under way, and to the Santa Fe warehouse complex.[31]

At 0141 on 17 January 1991, the USS *Paul Foster* (DD 964) launched the first of a barrage of Tomahawk cruise missiles from American warships stationed in the Gulf. Aboard the Australian guided missile destroyer *Brisbane,* Commodore C. J. Oxenbould observed that it was "altogether a most incredible and unforgettable sight, which imposed stunned silence in the operations room as we listened to the calm, measured tones of the U.S. commanders unleashing their well planned strike on Iraq."[32] Back in the States, millions watched live network coverage from Baghdad as bursts of Iraqi anti-aircraft fire filled the sky with tracers in a futile attempt to knock down the Tomahawks. Among those in the States was Shaikh Salman bin Hamad Al Khalifa. A student at American University, the future crown prince candidly admitted that he was happy to see the commencement of Operation Desert Storm. Echoing what his father had told General Schwarzkopf in late September, Shaikh Salman reflected, "There was a fear that Saddam was going to just withdraw and his war machine would remain intact and could redeploy at any time."[33]

The massive air campaign by shore- and sea-based aircraft pummeled military targets in and around Baghdad and Iraqi troops and equipment in the field. Some 350 of the coalition aircraft operated from the two Bahraini airfields. Bahrain clearly did its share in the air effort. Besides Bahrain's hosting of and providing fuel to British and American squadrons flying from its airfields, Bahraini F-16s and F-5s flying from Shaikh Isa Airfield joined the fray and performed credibly. Having just received the F-16 into its inventory, Bahraini pilots flew 166 sorties with the top-line fighter and 122 sorties with the venerable F-5 to attack Iraqi radar installations, Silkworm sites, and artillery positions. Reports credited the Bahraini airmen with performing their missions with skill.[34]

Other coalition aircraft attacked a broad range of other targets. Priority targets for the American aircraft were the mobile Iraqi Scud missile sites. Although hardly more sophisticated than Hitler's V-2 rockets, they were terror weapons because of their potential for deploying chemical or biological warfare agents.

While the Bahraini government took care of the needs of its people through the distribution of gas masks, little was done in the way of instruction. American Sailors living in the community filled the void by hosting "gas mask" parties to teach neighbors how to don the equipment properly.[35]

Scud launches triggered air raid sirens, which kept many people awake at nights. At Shaikh Isa Air Base, the U.S. Army placed Patriot missile batteries in position to knock down the intruding projectiles. To pass the time, "Scud Parties" became a ritual in which folks of different nationalities got together on balconies and roofs to watch the skies over Dhahran. Bahrain was not immune from Scud attack. Saddam's forces targeted the island with nine of the missiles. Six fell into the water. Of the remaining three, Shaikh Salman stated, "Two I know exactly where they are—one might be a myth." Shot down by a Patriot missile, the warhead of one of the Scuds did fall close to Shaikh Isa Air Base. Fortunately, no casualties or damage were caused by the missiles.[36]

Prior to the outbreak of hostilities, MIUW 202 Sailors lived comfortably, being quartered and fed at some of Bahrain's finest hotels. However, once coalition aircraft began to bomb Iraqi positions, the threat of terrorist attacks on vulnerable hotel facilities forced the relocation of many Sailors to more secure locations. In the case of MIUW 202, the Sailors at the Santa Fe warehouse complex constructed berthing facilities from dunnage and built bunkers for perimeter defense.[37]

By mid-February 1991, with allied control of the skies over Iraq and Kuwait well established, the carriers of Battle Force Zulu closed in on Iraq,

moving into positions in the central Gulf a mere sixty-five to eighty nautical miles north-northeast of Bahrain.[38]

While aggressive coalition actions gradually eliminated the Iraqi air
and surface threat to Battle Force Zulu and Bahrain, warships and merchant vessels were exposed to the threat of Iraqi mines. Rear Adm. Raynor
A. K. Taylor, arriving on the scene to relieve Admiral Fogarty, reflected,
"Surprisingly, they [the Iraqis] did deploy their mines quite professionally."
He noted that—in contrast to intelligence reports stating that that mine bar-
rier extended thirty-five to forty miles out from the coast—the Iraqis had
actually designed and laid fields mixing acoustically triggered, magnetically
triggered, and contact mines some twenty miles farther out. Fortunately, the
Iraqis maldeployed many of the mines by failing to arm them properly.

Early on the morning of 18 February, luck ran out. The USS *Tripoli*
(LPH 10) had operated for eleven hours in an undetected minefield before
the ship bumped up against one of the explosive devices. The moored mine
punched a twenty-to-thirty-foot hole ten feet below the waterline forward
of the starboard beam. Fortunately, with only four Sailors injured, the
Tripoli's damage control teams quickly controlled the flooding and saved
the ship. Ten nautical miles away from *Tripoli* and a few hours later, two
underwater explosions rocked USS *Princeton* (CG 59). On the cruiser,
I-beams bent and snapped, a rudder and a propeller shaft were damaged,
the after fire main ruptured, and internal fuel tanks burst. Three Sailors
were seriously injured. With reduced mobility, *Princeton* continued to perform her anti-air mission for another thirty hours until relieved by USS
Valley Forge (CG 50).

With its modern shipyard facilities, Bahrain provided a haven for these
stricken ships. Towed to Manama by Toorani Company tugs, the *Princeton*
received immediate attention from yard workers who stabilized the damage in such a manner that a tow to Dubai could be completed within a few
days. *Princeton* underwent major permanent repairs in Dubai. Despite the
gaping hole in *Tripoli*'s hull, she remained on station for another ten days,
serving as a command ship and base of operations for mine-countermea-
sure operations. On 23 February 1991, Admiral Taylor relieved Admiral
Fogarty as commander Middle East Force and as commander Task Force
151/152. With the turnover complete, the *La Salle* steamed to the northern Gulf and relieved *Tripoli* of her mine coordination duties. Eventually
the extent of *Tripoli*'s damage was to be determined and repairs made in
a Bahraini drydock.[39]

A day after Admiral Taylor assumed command of the Middle East Force,
General Schwarzkopf ordered the commencement of the ground war. As U.S.

Army forces executed a "left hook" into Iraq to outflank the enemy, Gulf Coalition Council units serving in Joint Forces Command (East) slugged their way up the coastline to free Kuwait City. An elite two-hundred-man company of Bahraini soldiers fought as part of the GCC force and participated in Kuwait's liberation.[40]

The crucial role the ASU and Bahrain played in the coalition's success during the Gulf War cannot be overstated. The 1990 ASU command history narrative stated: "The self contributions of the officers, men, and women of ASU were instrumental in facilitating what must be seen as a historic achievement in terms of the speed and efficiency with which the build-up occurred and operational readiness was obtained. Operating in the shadow of advancing Iraqi troops and under the magnifying glass of the world, Administrative Support Unit, Bahrain, through sheer fortitude and determination, expanded its function by as much as 3,000% and delivered more people, parts, and mail to more units than has ever been done by a unit of similar size."[41]

Because Bahrain had permitted the U.S. Navy to maintain a presence for more than forty years, a cooperative infrastructure was in place that facilitated a rapid coalition buildup. A decade later, Admiral Arthur reflected, "The real key to everything that happened over there was the Navy relationship with Bahrain. Overall those decades of Bahrain allowing the COMIDEAST Force to be a piece of business that occurred in the Gulf was not lost on all the neighbors."[42] In addition to hosting coalition forces, Bahrain also made direct contributions to the air and ground campaigns. In sum, Bahrain made an invaluable contribution toward the coalition's success.

Operation Desert Shield–Desert Storm also proved pivotal in Bahraini–U.S. Navy relations. While the government of Bahrain had always been friendly to U.S. Navy officials, the relationship was deliberately kept quiet so as not to create external and internal pressures. Prior to 2 August 1990, the government restricted the number of days U.S. Navy ships could stay in port to twelve per month. During the crisis the restriction was rescinded. Before the war there were many Bahrainis who were unaware of the ASU compound. Bahrainis appreciated the American resolve to stand up to Saddam Hussein. Furthermore, they were impressed with the members of the American civilian community who remained in Bahrain when other expatriates left the country. As events played out, the Gulf War formed the foundation for closer future ties with the nations of the GCC. Crown Prince Shaikh Salman observed that while the Gulf War opened doors for the United States in the region, "We still think our relationship is a special one because we know each other."[43]

CHAPTER EIGHT

The 1990s

O n 3 March 1991, combat having ceased, inside a pitched tent at the Iraqi village of Safwan, Saudi general Khalid bin Sultan al-Saud, commander of the coalition's Islamic forces, and American general Schwarzkopf faced their Iraqi counterparts to sign an UN Security Council–imposed agreement that if the Iraqis complied with it would allow for a permanent ceasefire and a return to stability in the region.[1] Victory in Operation Desert Storm was a cause for celebration in Manama, Washington, and other capitals of the coalition forces. For Bahrain, whose civilian population was located within range of Iraqi Scud missiles, the joy of victory was mixed with enormous relief. At the Administrative Support Unit, the Morale Welfare and Recreation (MWR) branch sponsored several huge victory parties behind the Desert Dome.[2]

Coalition success in eliminating the Iraqi presence in Kuwait was complete, but the war had exposed weaknesses in U.S. Navy capabilities that needed to be corrected. The Navy had already learned of its vulnerability to mines from the SS *Bridgeton* and *Samuel B. Roberts* incidents in 1987 and 1988, only to be reminded when *Tripoli* and *Princeton* ran afoul of the devices during the Gulf War. In addition, during Desert Storm the Navy still resisted full operational integration into a joint command structure. It had been envisioned that, in the event of a conflict in the Gulf, Commander in Chief Pacific and Commander in Chief Atlantic, both Navy admirals, would "temporarily assign their naval forces to the Army or Marine general heading Central Command. In essence the fleet's warships, especially its carriers, would remain under Navy control."[3] Such expectations stemmed from a failure to understand or appreciate the tenets of the Goldwater-Nichols Act of 1986 or the needs of the responsible geographic unified commander. Having not "bought in" to the new command structure, Navy leaders found themselves on the periphery in key planning and execution decisions.[4]

The relationship with Bahrain would help over the ensuing years to allow the U.S. Navy to overcome some of these weaknesses. Bahraini cooperation in permitting the Navy to forward deploy modern *Avenger*-class minesweepers and letting the naval commander place his staff ashore would prove mutually beneficial because Iraq, although beaten, was not vanquished, and Iran remained as a threatening power to the north.

But before these corrections could be made, the immediate concern was getting the hundreds of thousands of Airmen, Soldiers, Sailors, and Marines who had served so well and their tons of equipment safely loaded and returned home. Among the first personnel to depart the region were former prisoners of war released by the Iraqis on 4 and 6 March. The repatriation of the POWs occurred with little notice. Admiral Sutton recalled joining with Ambassador Hostler before dawn at the Bahrain International Airport to greet the former Italian and American captives. Once in Bahrain, the ex-POWs were transported to the USNS *Mercy* moored in the harbor. After Admiral Arthur greeted them, they received physical exams and medical treatment as needed and the chance to take hot showers, eat hot food, and phone home. On 9 March, the American ex-prisoners were taken to Bahrain International Airport where a Boeing 707 designated Flight "Freedom Zero One" lifted off to carry them to a hero's welcome at Andrews AFB outside of Washington, D.C.

Other American and coalition forces also began leaving the region for warm welcomes back home. U.S. forces at the time of the ceasefire agreement included six aircraft carriers, two battleships, two command ships, twelve cruisers, eleven destroyers, ten frigates, four mine warfare ships, thirty-one amphibious ships, thirty-two auxiliaries, two hospital ships, three submarines, numerous military sealift ships, and numerous support forces ashore. With the majority of the 82,278 Navy men and women who were now war veterans embarked on ships afloat, departing the region simply meant weighing anchor and steaming home.[5]

Before many of them left, however, a liberty port call to Bahrain allowed many Sailors an opportunity to "hit the beach" before the long journey home. In contrast to three ships making three visits and dropping off 302 Sailors in February, sixty-one ships made sixty-five visits in March, flooding Manama with an estimated 31,567 bluejackets. To help provide the visiting Sailors good liberty, MWR sponsored large numbers of picnics, athletic competitions, and special events.[6]

Within a month, most of the support ships that played important roles in sustaining the combatants in the Gulf had flown from the Manama waterfront. Reservists ashore in Bahrain departed via Military Airlift Command (MAC) or chartered airline flights. The greater challenge proved to be backloading all of the military equipment and non-expended ordnance from the region. Military Sealift Command's (MSC's) Vice Adm. Francis R. Donovan had boasted that his command had delivered the equivalent of a city the size of Louisville into the region—now Louisville had to come back. During the first four months of the pull-out, U.S. forces often loaded more than twenty ships a week. More than a year later, the arrival of SS *Leslie Lykes* at Bayonne, New Jersey, represented the last of 456 shiploads of material sent out of the region.[7]

Meanwhile, thousands of land and sea mines remained in place in Kuwait on and off the shore. They had to be removed. As Commander Middle East Force, one of Admiral Taylor's first assignments was to reopen the Kuwaiti port of Ash Shuaybah. A multinational salvage team, led by Capt. John Shick, was formed to clear mines and other obstructions leading from the approaches to the port. On 12 March, *La Salle* and mine hunter HMS *Cattistock* led three supply-laden merchantmen into Ash Shuaybah, and work proceeded to clear Kuwait's four other commercial and naval instal-lations.[8]

When paths had been cleared through Iraqi minefields to allow shipping, work commenced to eliminate the long-term mine threat. A multinational force consisting of American, Belgian, British, Dutch, French, Japanese, Italian, German, and Saudi mine countermeasure ships combed the Gulf waters for the explosive devices. Australia, Bahrain, and Kuwait provided explosive ordnance disposal experts. Together, the forces of these twelve nations systematically destroyed 1,288 mines. The U.S. Navy and Japanese Maritime Self Defense Force ships completed their part of the campaign on 10 September 1991. USS *Guardian* (MCM 5) departed the Gulf on 15 January 1992.[9]

Traditionally, the flag officer holding the COMIDEASTFOR billet had been the senior U.S. military officer in the region. With the insertion of the Seventh Fleet Commander into the theater as COMUSNAVCENT, Admiral Taylor, continuing as Commander Middle East Force, found himself subor-dinate to Admiral Arthur. Appreciating the difficulties his staff faced using the command framework in place during the war, Arthur directed him to review alternative command structures.

Taylor recommended "in-theater, dual-hatting" the NAVCENT bil-let with his COMIDEASTFOR job, with the headquarters in Bahrain. Maintaining the Middle East Force post as "an independent entity," Taylor argued, allowed for a historical legacy that had "legitimacy in the eyes of our Gulf allies." Also, by placing the NAVCENT billet permanently in the region, Taylor saw the opportunity for the organization to mature into a true component command that could provide an operational planning capability for the unified commander. Arthur agreed, and on 9 March he recommended to General Schwarzkopf that a "seasoned two-star rear admiral who had prior battle group command experience" be dual-hatted as COMIDEASTFOR and COMUSNAVCENT. Taylor also proposed moving the COMUSNAVCENT billet that had been based in Hawaii to Norfolk and to rename it COMUSNAVCENT REAR. The one-star admiral assigned would have the benefit of being in the same time zone as the CENTCOM headquarters in Tampa.[10]

CNO Admiral Kelso agreed with Arthur's proposal as ideal in peacetime but stated that in wartime a three-star would have to be provided from either the Atlantic or the Pacific Fleet. Arthur felt otherwise. Given the volatile situation in the region, Arthur argued that the U.S. Central Command commander needed continuity with his naval component commander during transitional periods of peace and war. Kelso's view prevailed—in the short term. On 24 March 1991, Taylor relieved Arthur as COMUSNAVCENT, kept his COMIDEASTFOR hat, and remained embarked aboard *La Salle*. At the same time, Rear Adm. Robert Sutton became COMUSNAVCENT REAR. Additionally, Taylor's recommendation to move the Hawaii-based staff to Norfolk was revisited, and it was decided that this command should be upgraded to a two-star billet and co-located with CINCCENT in Florida. The relief of the one-star Sutton by the two-star David Rogers, coincident with the relocation from Hawaii to Tampa, demonstrated the Navy's commitment to supporting the unified commander since General Schwarzkopf's relief, Marine Gen. Joseph Hoar, benefited directly from the operational and logistical expertise provided by the two-star flag officer representing COMUSNAVCENT and co-located with his staff. In addition, the billet provided command continuity because Admiral Rogers could fly to the Gulf to command the naval forces in the region when COMUSNAVCENT was called back to the States.[11]

On 3 April, the UN Security Council passed Resolution 687 (1991) spelling out the terms for a formal end of the Gulf War. Included was a provision calling for Iraq to reveal the location of its nuclear, biological, and chemical weapons and ballistic missiles and assent to their destruction, removal, or neutralization under the strict supervision of an on-site UN Special Commission (UNSCOM). On 8 April, Iraq's National Assembly voted to accept Resolution 687 (1991), and a formal ceasefire was put in place.[12]

Given the situation in Iraq, with the armed forces decimated and Shi'ites in the south and Kurds in the north rebelling against the regime in Baghdad, it seemed that Saddam Hussein's days were numbered. However, enough of Saddam's army remained intact to put down the rebellions brutally. The Security Council reacted by passing Resolution 688 (1991), authorizing the use of force to provide assistance to Kurdish refugees in northern Iraq.

Under U.S. European Command direction, a multinational force of twenty thousand was inserted into northern Iraq to execute Operation Provide Comfort. To protect its forces, the coalition informed Iraq that a no-fly zone would be enforced in the airspace north of the 36th Parallel. The presence of the coalition troops enabled the Kurds to feel secure enough to return home from the refugee camps. By mid-July, the situation allowed for the withdrawal of the coalition forces, though the no-fly zone remained in place.[13]

Despite Iraq's defeat during Desert Storm, it soon became apparent that predictions of the Iraqi dictator's demise were premature. The Iraqi army still remained formidable with a force of 400,000 men and some 2,300 tanks, 5,500 armored vehicles, and 150 armed helicopters. Furthermore, although they had agreed to abide by Resolution 687, the Iraqis were holding back on sharing information with the UNSCOM. During September 1991, for example, the Iraqis blocked the UNSCOM inspection team from using helicopters and seizing documents discovered by inspectors relating to Iraq's nuclear weapons programs. In response, on 11 October, the UN Security Council passed Resolution 715 (1991) approving plans for ongoing monitoring and verification. Iraq countered that the resolution was unlawful and that Iraq was unwilling to comply.[14]

In addition to renewed Iraqi belligerence, although Iran remained neutral during the Gulf War, deep animosity remained between this Persian nation and the United States and its allies in the GCC. Consequently, Central Command implemented a postwar strategy of twin containment centered on power projection, forward presence, combined exercises, security assistance, and a readiness to fight.

One aspect of the forward presence component continued to be maritime interception operations. Until Iraq fully complied with Resolution 687, the embargo that had been established immediately after Iraq invaded Kuwait would continue. During 1992 alone, coalition ships intercepted 3,127 vessels, boarded 2,871, and diverted 157 from their intended courses to undergo closer examination. COMUSNAVCENT coordinated the operations, convening periodic meetings with coalition forces to plan the effort.[15]

With regard to security assistance, the United States helped bolster GCC naval forces in the region through military sales and agreements to conduct joint training exercises. For example, during Admiral Taylor's tenure as COMUSNAVCENT, there were 125 joint exercises with regional allies, whereas in the year prior to Desert Storm there had been but two.[16] Most of these exercises were small-scale in nature because most navies in the region were built around fast patrol vessels.

The commitment to conduct more Bahraini-American exercises was spelled out in a Defense Cooperation Agreement signed on 27 October 1991. Determined to maintain a presence in the region, the United States poured money into the facilities located ashore in Bahrain. In 1991, ASU Bahrain completed a forty-thousand-square-foot hangar and office complex at Bahrain International Airport.

One of the challenges Admiral Taylor immediately confronted was the excessive turnover aboard *La Salle* and ashore resulting from the agreement that had been worked out with the Bahrainis more than a decade earlier. Most of the people assigned to him were either there on 90- or 180-day temporary active duty (TAD) or one year unaccompanied orders. Taylor wanted continuity and the ability to attract top-quality Sailors to his command. However, local attitudes had changed and the Bahrainis were willing to allow the Americans greater flexibility in filling their manpower needs. A Bureau of Naval Personnel study recommended that all of the billets be changed to permanent change of station (PCS) billets of two to three years' duration.

The change attracted married Sailors because they could bring their families over to experience a unique culture in an interesting part of the world. The slow influx of families would cause a lot of changes at ASU. The MWR Department now had to plan activities for spouses and children. Whereas only thirty to forty dependent children attended the Bahrain International School in 1993, about 250 were registered there in 1995. The Supply Department had to expand the Ship's Store and expand the types of items that were carried. One former ASU commanding officer observed, "The Bahrainis liked the idea of families. It provided more stability and helped their economy. The impression I got was that while ships showed presence in the Gulf, families showed commitment to peace and stability in the region."[17]

Throughout 1992, Iraq and the United Nations continued their tug of war. In February, Iraq initially refused to comply with an UNSCOM requirement to destroy certain weapons-making facilities and items. A month later the Baghdad regime declared the previous existence of ballistic missiles but said that these weapons had been unilaterally destroyed the previous summer. In April, Iraq threatened to harm UNSCOM surveillance aircraft. However, in May and June, Iraq did provide disclosures of its biological, missile, and chemical warfare programs and allowed destruction of its chemical weapons and production facilities to commence in July. Yet also in July, Iraq refused an inspection team entry into the Ministry of Agriculture, only to back down after Security Council threats.[18]

While resisting UNSCOM inspection efforts, Saddam Hussein also took action against his own people. In May 1992, the Iraqi strongman launched five or six divisions to attack an estimated ten thousand Shi'ite rebels and two hundred thousand civilian refugees. By August, some sixty thousand troops backed by seventy combat aircraft were positioned to make a final move. To prevent a slaughter, on 26 August 1992, President Bush cited UN Security Council Resolution 688, which forbade Hussein to use military aircraft against his people, to justify establishing a no-fly zone south of the 32nd Parallel. British and French leaders backed Bush's decision with a commitment to provide aircraft to enforce the ban.

To set up the no-fly-zone effort, General Hoar turned to his Air Force component commander (CENTAF), Lt. Gen. Michael A. Nelson, to head a separate joint task force with Admiral Rogers serving as his deputy. To staff "Joint Task Force-Southwest Asia" (JTF-SWA), Nelson drew heavily from the CENTAF staff headquartered at Shaw Air Force Base in South Carolina and tapped the USNAVCENT REAR staff in Tampa.

The decision regarding where to base this operationally focused JTF was delicate. With Kuwait rebuilding its war-damaged infrastructure and Bahrain saturated with naval forces and distant from the no-fly zone, General Nelson saw Saudi Arabia as an ideal place to locate his command facility. The Saudis were initially cool to the idea of reintroducing American, French, and British forces into the kingdom. But after some diplomatic maneuvering, they quickly agreed to headquarter the new organization at the Royal Saudi Air Force Command Center in Riyadh. They also agreed to allow allied aircraft to fly out of bases near Riyadh and Dhahran.[19]

On 27 August, U.S. Air Force and Navy combat aircraft took to the skies over southern Iraq to begin Operation Southern Watch. On the ground, U.S. Air Force personnel made up a majority of the two-hundred-person JTF-SWA staff. Navy personnel, along with British and French personnel, assisted in planning, targeting, and communications. Learning from the lessons of the Gulf War, the Navy improved its communications capabilities aboard La Salle, and the on-station aircraft carrier could receive the air tasking order via electronic means.

The Iraqis refused to recognize what they perceived as a violation of their airspace. However, any menacing moves by them were thwarted on 9 September 1992 when coalition aircraft flooded the airspace over southern Iraq.[20]

With Iraq maintaining a threatening posture, Navy leaders took several steps throughout 1992 to upgrade the Navy's position in Bahrain. Accepting a recommendation from Admiral Taylor, Admiral Kelso authorized a name change, effective 25 June 1992, from Administrative Support Unit Bahrain to Administrative Support Unit Southwest Asia (ASU-SWA) with the mission: "To maintain and operate designated facilities throughout the United States Central Command (USCENTCOM) AOR which support operational forces and afloat units assigned or attached to United States Naval Forces Central Command (USNAVCENT), other joint and combined USCENTCOM Forces, and the DODDS School; to provide support to the American Embassy, Bahrain and with applicable Foreign Area Activities Support (FAAS) agreements and DOS/DOD regulations; to provide morale welfare and recreation facilities in Bahrain; and to foster policies and programs which build and maintain positive Arab-American relations."[21]

Given ASU-SWA's expanded regional mission, the ranks of the CO and XO billets were raised to captain and commander. Steps taken to support the new expanded mission included establishing a Naval Legal Service Branch Office, assigning a permanent Medical Department Head, and increasing MWR services for the returning and newly arriving dependent families. A year later, in September 1993, a Navy Family Service Center was established.

As was dramatically demonstrated during the Gulf War, logistics plays a particularly important role in sustaining operations. On 1 September 1992, Admiral Taylor activated Task Force 153 as a focal point for logistical support in the CENTCOM area of responsibility, which stretched from Egypt to Pakistan and Iraq to Kenya. At the activation Taylor stated: "We intend to streamline the logistics organization by enhancing communications, maintaining proper stewardship of critical logistics assets and scarce resources, and standardizing policies and procedures." To fill the billet of CTF 153, Taylor tapped his assistant chief for logistics and supply, Capt. John E. Tufts. Dual-hatted, Tufts saw his new assignment as "the first step in establishing a theater-wide infrastructure for naval logistics support within USNAVCENT."[22] One of the first missions of the new organization was to support the withdrawal of UN forces from Somalia.[23]

Symbolic of the growing logistical infrastructure in the region was the ribbon-cutting ceremony on 19 September for a new Navy Regional Contracting Center in Bahrain. Capt. Pat Cummings, Commanding Officer NRCC Naples, presided at the ceremony and remarked how the office had grown in a year from a two-man detachment into an organization of twenty-one civilians and three Sailors—larger than the forty-three-year-old London office.[24]

Of greater significance, Kelso determined that he wanted an officer of higher rank stationed in the region to support the unified commander.

On 19 October 1992, Vice Adm. Douglas J. Katz relieved Admiral Taylor aboard *La Salle* berthed at Bahrain.[25]

Katz, a surface warfare officer, felt he had been selected for the job because of his previous experience in the region. During the 1980s he had been the skipper of a COMIDEASTFOR-assigned destroyer, and he later had command of a carrier battle group at the conclusion of Desert Storm. Besides providing the Navy with more horsepower in the region, Katz's rank was duly noted among many of the local governments: major generals were promoted and given a third star. In Bahrain, Crown Prince Maj. Gen. Hamad bin Isa Al Khalifa became a lieutenant general.

One of the new commander's early priorities was to merge the staffs of USNAVCENT (in Bahrain) and USNAVCENT REAR (in Tampa) into a single organization. With both staffs possible separate administrative (N1), intelligence (N2), operations (N3), logistics (N4), plans (N5), and communications (N6) departments, Admiral Katz and Admiral Rogers crafted a merger with the aim of physically putting the functions where they made the most sense. Katz and Rogers agreed to place the time-critical departments (intelligence, operations, communications) in Bahrain and keep the other departments in Tampa to support the CINC. With the merger, the COMNAVCENT REAR billet went away and Admiral Rogers became Deputy COMUSNAVCENT.[26]

Although the United States had led the coalition that had liberated Kuwait the year before, Katz still found many regional leaders skeptical about America's staying power. How long could a nation located on the other side of the globe sustain an interest in the region? It would not be long until the forces under Katz's command, by being used in combat, would have the opportunity to demonstrate the American commitment. In January 1993, Saddam Hussein moved anti-aircraft missile batteries into the no-fly zones and directed Iraqi aircraft to penetrate those zones. In addition, Iraqi army units made incursions into the demilitarized zone established between Iraq and Kuwait and refused UNSCOM the use of its own aircraft for transport in and out of Iraq. On 13 January, after the Iraqis had failed to heed allied warnings, four air defense control centers and two concentrations of SA-3 missile batteries were struck by USS *Kitty Hawk* (CV 63) and French, British, and U.S. Air Force aircraft based in Saudi Arabia. Four days later, the USS *Cowpens* (CG 63) and the USS *Hewitt* (DD 966) responded to further provocative actions by launching forty-two Tomahawk missiles against a uranium enrichment plant on the outskirts of Baghdad. Not all of the missiles struck home. One missile struck a hotel that actually had a command center located under it. The media bombarded Admiral Katz with questions, and he attempted to anticipate them by keeping one eye tuned to CNN. After the strike Hussein asked for a ceasefire, offering compliance.[27]

After the military confrontation at the beginning of the year, tensions eased for a few months. At Bahrain, change was about to occur at the waterfront. After being continuously forward deployed for eleven years, *La Salle* departed Mina Sulman pier on 10 April for a badly needed overhaul at the Philadelphia Naval Shipyard. That later became awkward for the Americans, because the Bahrainis did not realize that the Great White Ghost was not coming back. Admiral Katz explained that several factors, besides the overhaul, outweighed any need for *La Salle* in the Gulf. First, in another Desert Storm scenario, it was envisioned that COMUSNAVCENT and many of his staff would join CINCCENT in Riyadh to provide direct support and that the deputy COMUSNAVCENT would come to Bahrain to assume operational control of the assigned naval forces. Hence *La Salle* was not slated to carry out the flagship duties she had been designed to perform. As for communications capabilities, a carrier in the Gulf would be able to handle the heavy communications requirement for afloat forces. Finally, the Sixth Fleet needed a command ship.[28]

Because Katz had built a close relationship with the Bahraini foreign minister, he was able to smooth over the fact that NAVCENT's presence ashore was to be permanent. Indeed, Katz was struck by the legacy of the Navy-Bahraini relationship with its forty-year positive track record. For instance, he would get calls from leaders who sought the advice "of a friend." While keeping the State Department and the intelligence agencies informed of his discussions, Katz said he always gave advice that he thought was in the region's best interest, even if it did not coincide with U.S. foreign policy.

Admiral Katz had great respect for the Bahraini culture, and he maintained a strict dress code. Any Sailors unwilling to conform "were out of there pronto!" His impression was that because of the contribution it made to the local economy, the Bahraini people did not mind the American presence. However, Katz hoped for America to make less of a contribution in the form of extravagant housing costs. Accordingly, a decision was made to lease the Mannai Plaza Hotel, and it saved the U.S. government millions of dollars in the short term.[29]

With the NAVCENT staff coming ashore, the ASU-SWA Public Works Department scurried to renovate "spacemakers" and "milvans" and complete sixteen projects necessary to support the move. Coinciding with the move, ASU-SWA established a Computer Support Staff Department on 20 April 1993 to handle data-processing needs within the region. The NAVCENT staff, settling into a headquarters complex consisting of several trailers bolted together, soon would have its first opportunity to command a combat operation from ashore. In June 1993, Iraq refused to allow UNSCOM to install monitoring cameras on missile test stands. Then Kuwaiti security personnel intercepted an Iraqi assassination team that targeted Bush when the ex-president visited Kuwait. Responding to the assassination attempt, President Clinton ordered American warships into action on 26 June 1993. The USS *Chancellorville* (CG 62) and USS *Peterson* (DD 969) fired twenty-three Tomahawks into the summer heat against an intelligence headquarters in Baghdad. Again, Iraq fell in line, agreeing to allow its test stands to be monitored and accepting Resolution 715 (1991).[30]

By June 1994, the UNSCOM team had completed the destruction of large quantities of chemical warfare agents and production equipment. Claiming that it had compiled with Resolution 687 (1991), Iraq set a deadline of 10 October for the United Nations to lift the embargo and threatened to cease cooperation with UNSCOM. Furthermore, Saddam built up the Iraqi army along the Kuwaiti border. The UN Security Council responded on 15 October by passing Resolution 949 (1994) calling for Iraq to "cooperate fully" with UNSCOM and to withdraw the forces facing Kuwait. The UN resolution was backed up by the American execution of Operation Vigilant Warrior to rush forces into the region. Having relieved Admiral Katz as COMUSNAVCENT a month before, Vice Adm. John Scott Redd oversaw the rapid deployment into the region of the *George Washington* carrier battle group and the *Tripoli* amphibious ready group and several other combatants. With naval forces in the region responding rapidly and ground and air forces mobilizing in other areas of the globe, Saddam once again backed down.[31]

In the wake of the crisis, NAVCENT received a Navy Unit Commendation from the secretary of the Navy. Covering the period from 1 August 1992 to 15 December 1994, the award recognized NAVCENT's role in the planning and execution of multiple missions including the ongoing multinational Maritime Interception Operations, the Somalia relief effort, the continuing Operation Southern Watch, and the recently completed Operation Vigilant Warrior.

At the time of the award, the tally of merchant vessels intercepted had reached more than twenty thousand. Some five hundred vessels were diverted for closer inspection to enforce the UN sanctions program. To ensure compliance, NAVCENT coordinated the movements of warships from fifteen navies in the Gulf and Red Sea regions, making the effort the largest of its type in history. The award also acknowledged that over the two-year time span, NAVCENT support forces had moved 82,343 tons of cargo, 17,020,150 pounds of mail, and 13,457 critical repair parts and had transported 40,873 passengers to and from units in the theater.[32]

By late 1994, the United States had withdrawn from the Horn of Africa in the aftermath of what many critics claimed was a failed nation-building effort. However, because of NAVCENT's coordination and direction of Operation Provide Relief in August 1992 and Operation Restore Hope in December of that year, tens of thousands of lives were saved from the scourge of starvation.

Operation Southern Watch would continue, and there was a glum realization that there would be future "Vigilant Warrior"–type operations. Understanding that Iraq and possibly Iran might be prone to saber rattle in the future, Admiral Redd and other naval leaders advocated establishing another fleet combat command, given that carrier battle and amphibious ready groups were routinely operating in the region. "If it looks like a fleet, acts like a fleet, and operates like a fleet, it's a fleet!" exclaimed Redd.[33]

Back in the States, serious discussions among the Navy staff, office of the Secretary of Defense, the Joint Staff, and the State Department focused on the merits of establishing another fleet. Proponents argued that the move would signal further commitment to the region, establish an appropriate geographic division among the U.S. joint commands, function as a needed echelon between the operating forces and USNAVCENT, and be able to be implemented with only a few staffing additions. Opponents questioned the need to create a new fleet at a time the Navy was retiring dozens of warships.[34]

After considering the arguments, on 10 March 1995 CNO Adm. Jeremy M. Boorda signed a memorandum asking Secretary of the Navy John H. Dalton to forward a proposal to Secretary of Defense William J. Perry for recommissioning the Fifth Fleet. On 4 May, Secretary Perry approved the creation of the first new fleet in fifty years. The original Fifth Fleet had existed from 1942 to 1947 as a force in the western Pacific that contributed mightily to bringing the Japanese empire to its knees. In prepared questions and answers for the media, COMFIFTHFLT was identified as a "numbered fleet command under COMUSNAVCENT, component command responsible to CINCCENT for contingency planning and operational matters and Fifth Fleet is responsible to COMUSNAVCENT for day-to-day operation of assigned forces." The guidance further explained that the creation of Fifth Fleet "brings the naval organization in Central Command in line with the Pacific Command which has the Third and Seventh Fleets; the Atlantic Command which has the Second Fleet; and the European Command, which has the Sixth Fleet."[35]

Throughout May and June, America's friends in the Gulf were consulted about the creation of the new fleet. Overall, a deliberate low-key approach was taken. In the ASU command center at 0100 Zulu 1 July, Operations Specialist Seaman Christine Foster announced over the radio nets the standup of COMFIFTHFLT and "the redesignation of the Execution and Battle Force Zulu nets to COMFIFTHFLT Execution and Battle Command." Later that day, at a ceremony at Admiral Redd's residence, the Navy formally stood up the fleet. With the creation of Fifth Fleet, Admiral Redd's title as COMIDEASTFOR seemed superfluous. However, because of the deep tradition involved, it was decided to pass that designation on to Commander Destroyer Squadron Fifty, Fifth Fleet's forward-based destroyer squadron.

In Bahrain the announcement of the creation of the Fifth Fleet was well received within the commercial establishment. Local businessmen anticipated a large influx, given the size of the Sixth and Seventh Fleet staffs. There would be some disappointment when it was explained that this would not be the case.[36]

Not all in the region were pleased. The Tehran government characterized the action as "symbolic of America's aggressive designs in the Gulf."[37]

Yet there were ten Iranians who might find it difficult to agree with their government's stand. On 24 May 1995, the USS *O'Brien* (DD 975) rendered assistance to an Iranian cargo dhow discovered adrift eighty-five miles northeast of Bahrain. Despite language and technical difficulties, Engineman First Class Anthony Padilla and Engineman Third Class Fred Coldsnow were able to repair the engine. Provisioned with food and water, the small vessel made her way to Abadan, Iran.[38]

As noted in earlier chapters, throughout the U.S. Navy's fifty-plus-year presence in the Gulf, it had been helping "those in peril on the sea." In March the USNS *Spica* rescued twelve crewmembers from an Indian vessel that had sunk.[39] In August, the USS *Stark* (FFG 31) and USS *Merrill* (DD 976) came to the aid of a Kuwaiti tanker that had suffered a boiler explosion while transiting the Gulf of Oman.[40] A rescue team from the *Stark* recovered and treated an injured Egyptian sailor.

The *Stark* and *Merrill* were part of the USS *Abraham Lincoln* Battle Group, which was involved in Operation Vigilant Sentinel. Once again, Iraq bucked up against UN oversight of its arms programs. After Iraq had provided a second "full, final, and complete disclosure" report claiming the cessation of its prohibited biological and chemical weapons programs, UNSCOM inspectors dug up irrefutable evidence forcing the Iraqis to admit the ongoing existence of an offensive biological warfare program. After a third full, final, and complete disclosure report on the prohibited chemical and biological weapons programs was submitted, Iraq's position against the United Nations was again severely undercut when Gen. Hussein Kamel, who had been responsible for those programs, fled to Jordan on 8 August. There he proceeded to reveal to UNSCOM inspectors the locations of many hidden biological and chemical weapons.

Saddam reacted initially by mobilizing forces. In response, the United States Central Command initiated Operation Vigilant Sentinel and placed twenty-eight thousand military personnel on alert to deploy to the Central Command theater. With the presence of the *Abraham Lincoln* Battle Group, Fifth Fleet's Gulf forces had swelled to more than forty ships—the largest buildup since Desert Storm. The GCC also mobilized its forces. In a show of solidarity, Bahrain deployed a squadron of F-16 aircraft to Kuwait.[41]

In an attempt to discredit Kamel, the Iraqi government blamed him for withholding key documents from UNSCOM, and then suddenly produced them. New disclosures revealed greater progress in long-range missile development and information on nerve agent and nuclear weapon production. Once again Iraq backed off on its threat to end cooperation.

Yet despite Iraq's apparent current openness, in November Jordanian officials seized a large number of missile components destined for Iraq. UNSCOM inspectors followed up to discover that some of the ordered components had already made it across the border into Iraq. The Iraqis remained relentless in their quest to seek weapons of mass destruction.[42]

Shortly after the stand-up of Fifth Fleet, Capt. Thomas Feeks relieved Capt. Marcus Williams as ASU's commander. Feeks was familiar with the region. He had been assigned to Dhahran, Saudi Arabia, in 1988 and had served as a placement officer for the region while assigned to the Bureau of Naval Personnel. However, nothing in his experience had prepared him for dealing with the Bahrainis. "Working with the Bahraini officials was an education and a lot of fun," he later recalled.

Feeks cited the example of a nuclear submarine port call to Bahrain in the fall of 1995. The visit had been approved at the highest diplomatic levels but needed a final okay from the port captain. Feeks had the benefit of having an XO, Cdr. George Zimmerman, who had been born in Saudi Arabia and was on his third tour in the area. First, they met with the deputy port captain and spent thirty minutes talking about fishing. They then met the port captain and "during the next two hours we sat, drank tea, talked about the weather, the first electricity in Bahrain, in-laws, more fishing. Time is running out. At 1400 the port captain stands, thanks me very much for coming, and he says he has to go visit his mother. As he goes out the door he turns and says, 'Oh Captain, about your submarine, it is no problem . . . welcome any time . . . have a good weekend!' "[43]

Internal security became one of Feeks' immediate concern. Beginning in late 1994 a series of events occurred to increase the problems faced by the United States in the Middle East. While global attention focused on the Iraq-UN confrontation, there was some unrest within Bahrain that the American guests could not help but notice. In November 1994, there was an annual charity marathon that drew many expatriates out to run on a hot day. Although the race had passed through Shi'ite villages during previous years, many younger male villagers took exception to the apparel worn by many of the female runners. Stones were thrown. Bahraini internal security quickly arrested a twenty-eight-year-old Shi'ite cleric and twelve followers for inciting the violence. The cleric, who had been trained in Iran, had previously been deported for subversive activities and had been readmitted to Bahrain only after pledging to halt his anti-government activities. The arrests led to a series of protests, car torchings, and widespread graffiti over the ensuing months. From the American perspective, this was strictly an internal matter of civil unrest. Fortunately for the Americans, those having grievances did not seem to regard the American presence in Bahrain as part of the problem. In one case a Sailor did lose a car to fire, but it was a case of being in the wrong place at the wrong time.[44]

What truly caused Feeks concern were some major incidents across the way in Saudi Arabia. In November 1995, terrorists successfully detonated a bomb near the Office of Program Management Saudi Arabia National Guard (OPMSANG). The dead included five Americans. Whereas previously only minimal force protection measures had been in place, the blast caused a reevaluation. Jersey barriers were put in place, and random spot checks were initiated at the gates. At the Mannai Plaza Hotel, a three-hundred-foot cordon surrounded by fifty-gallon concrete-filled oil drums laced together with steel wire was established. Additional security was sent to protect the Bahrain International School.[45]

A key player in obtaining Bahraini support to address American concerns was Ambassador David M. Ransom. After he presented his credentials in July 1994, one of his first challenges was to obtain Bahraini cooperation to permit the execution of Operation Vigilant Warrior. By allowing U.S. combat aircraft to be stationed at Shaikh Isa Air Base, the Bahrainis signaled they too had a low tolerance for Saddam's antics. Next Ransom worked with the Bahrainis to pave the way for the establishment of Fifth Fleet. In addition, he capably conveyed the requirements for force protection. The Bahraini response to the potential terrorist threat was considered extraordinarily positive.[46]

While Sailors ashore were alerted to heightened dangers, for those serving at sea danger had long been a constant. As noted earlier, during the winter months a dusty haze can quickly reduce visibility in one of the most traversed waterways on the planet. Under normal circumstances, ships would distance themselves from potentially dangerous radar contacts. But American combatants conducting maritime interception operations to query merchant ships and dhows about their cargoes had to approach closely. Twice in one week in early 1996, close approaches resulted in collisions. The bumping at night in heavy fog between a dhow and USS *Oldendorf* (DD 972) resulted in no damage or injuries on either ship. However, a collision on 5 February was more serious. The dhow *Ya Alimadad,* suspected of smuggling goods out of Iraq in violation of the UN sanctions, was being escorted by USS *Ford* (FFG 54) to a holding area when the dhow lost steering and collided with *Ford's* stern. Two of the dhow's crew and an American Sailor aboard the dhow were hurt, and another American Sailor who had boarded the small vessel to make repairs fell when the dhow made an unexpected roll. A dhow crewman and a Navy Sailor eventually were flown to Bahrain for proper treatment.[47]

Despite the hazards, U.S. and coalition navies continued to conduct the interceptions. By April 1996, the coalition had recorded its ten-thousandth boarding after flagging down some 22,000 vessels. The fifteen navies participating in the program had diverted 573 ships. After further inspection, 76 were declared to be sanctions violators.[48]

While the Fifth Fleet ships conducting maritime interception operations were being rotated through the Gulf as part of their six-month deployment cycles, two American ships arrived that would have a more long-term presence. As documented in *Shield and Sword: The United States Navy and the Persian Gulf War,* the official Naval Historical Center history of that conflict, the U.S. Navy fell short when it came to the timely arrival of capable mine-clearing assets in the region. With the situation in the Gulf remaining potentially volatile, it was decided to forward deploy two of the Navy's newest minesweepers—USS *Ardent* (MCM 12) and USS *Dextrous* (MCM 13)—to Bahrain to be on call to keep vital choke points in the region open. What made this forward deployment different was the decision to rotate crews from stateside-based minesweepers. Although unusual, the scheme had precedent in the Navy with the Blue-Gold crews of the ballistic missile force. The real problem would be to keep the two ships operational during an extended forward deployment in a challenging environment.[49]

Ardent and *Dextrous* arrived on 23 March 1996 in the midst of another growing crisis in Iraq. UNSCOM inspectors once again were blocked from entering five sites designated for inspection. Finally, the Iraqis admitted the inspectors after stonewalling for up to seventeen hours. In response, on 27 March the Security Council approved Resolution 1051 (1996) to establish an export/import monitoring mechanism and again demand Iraqi compliance with UNSCOM. In May and June, UNSCOM supervised the destruction of Iraq's main biological warfare facility at Al-Hakam.

In June 1996, the tug of war continued. Once again the Baghdad government restricted UNSCOM access to sites, and once again the Security Council passed a resolution condemning Iraq. Resolution 1060 (1996) further directed that the UNSCOM executive chairman visit Iraq to secure access to all sites for UNSCOM inspection. During the visit, Iraq produced its fourth full, final, and complete disclosure report concerning the prohibited biological weapons program. At this time Iraq also produced a third full, final, and complete disclosure of its prohibited chemical weapons program. A month later, the Baghdad government turned over a third full, final, and complete disclosure of its prohibited missile program.[50]

However, events in Iraq were temporarily overshadowed. On 25 June 1996, Khobar Towers, the U.S. Air Force barracks in Dhahran, was bombed. The explosion was so powerful that many in Bahrain felt the concussion. ASU-SWA medical personnel and chaplains crossed over into Saudi Arabia to aid their Air Force comrades. To prevent a recurrence in Bahrain, in excess of $6 million was immediately added to initiate additional force protection measures. "Best of all," recalled Captain Feeks, "the Marines." By 4 July, two USMC FAST platoons joined with existing Navy and Bahraini security forces.[51]

The Khobar Towers blast would prove to be a seminal event in the history of the Navy's presence in Bahrain. Commenting four years after it, Capt. John G. Steele observed, "The reverberations haven't stopped yet." From the rubble of the Khobar Towers, the term "Force Protection" became etched in the minds of civilian and military leaders. For the Navy in Bahrain, the arrival of the Marines represented the beginning of a process to make ASU-SWA one of the most secure military installations in the world.[52]

In the wake of the Khobar Towers blast, a new Fifth Fleet commander arrived. On 17 July 1996, Vice Adm. Thomas B. Fargo relieved Admiral Redd as the Central Command's Naval Component commander. A prospective fleet commander and as CENTCOM's only forward-deployed component commander, Fargo believed that his job would be operational in nature. In retrospect, he didn't realize he would spend about 40 percent of his time handling political-military issues. The security concerns of ASU-SWA and the apparent long-term need to maintain an American strategic presence in the region topped the list.

The security concerns were addressed by a commission appointed by the president to investigate the Khobar Towers tragedy and determine other vulnerabilities to American installations within the region. Led by retired Army general Wayne Downing, commission members toured the Navy compound in Bahrain in August. They quickly concluded that the cozy twenty-three-acre compound consisting of old British-era stucco buildings and temporary prefabricated metal structures was vulnerable to the type of explosive device that had killed U.S. airmen in Saudi Arabia. In addition, the five hundred Sailors stationed at the leased Mannai Plaza Hotel presented terrorists with another tempting target. To address these concerns, part of the solution became obvious.[53]

Discussions began to expand the American Navy compound beyond the ten acres that had been leased since the 1970s and thirteen acres added during the Gulf War. Admiral Fargo worked closely with Ambassador Ransom to obtain forty-five additional acres situated on landfill adjacent to the compound. Once the acreage was acquired, the Navy approached Congress to obtain military construction (MILCON) funds to build on the new property. In fiscal year (FY) 1997, Congress authorized funds for a new medical/dental facility and quality of life facility. A year later Congress funded infrastructure upgrades and the construction of the first of two transient barracks that would be built to allow Sailors to stay within the protective walls of ASU-SWA. The Bahrainis were very cooperative in renegotiating the lease and assisting with security concerns.[54]

As the Downing Commission investigation of the Khobar Towers bombing unfolded, Admiral Fargo realized that implementing effective counterterrorist measures meant more than erecting additional jersey barriers and posting more guards; it required a change in the cultural mindset. To change that mindset, Fargo directed his desert Sailors to switch out of their khakis and dungarees and wear desert BDUs or "chocolate chips" as the uniforms were affectionately called. By adapting the gear that the Soldiers and Marines wear in ground combat, Fargo sought to "operationalize Force Protection." Although at first many Sailors felt funny wearing the new threads, soon the uniforms were accepted because of their comfort in the harsh environment, and they gave the desert Sailors a bit of esprit de corps.

Another major contribution to changing the mindset was the establishment of the Force Protection Board, a committee made up of key personnel in country including representatives from the embassy, the Naval

Criminal Investigative Service, NAVCENT Intelligence, and Naval Security. The Fleet Marine Force Commander served as the executive secretary. At first, the board met twice daily to review physical security measures and ongoing training. Technical security devices were important but could help only so much. "You cannot underestimate the value of an effective guard force," stated Fargo. Initially, the Marine FAST platoons provided a "hard outer shell" meant to deter terrorists. By October, the FAST platoons had departed and the Marines had established a Marine Security Company. The Naval Security Force provided the interior defense.[55]

As Admiral Fargo stepped up his efforts to improve his forces on the ground, the Iraqi army moved against the town of Irbil in the Kurdish autonomous region of northern Iraq and launched surface-to-air missiles against coalition aircraft patrolling the no-fly zone. In response, CINCCENT, Gen. J. H. Binford Peay III, ordered the planning and execution of Operation Desert Strike. On 4 September 1996, USS *Laboon* (DDG 58) fired a salvo of twelve Tomahawk missiles in coordination with B-52 bombers carrying air-launched cruise missiles. The unmanned weapons ripped into Iraqi surface-to-air-batteries and command-and-control centers. While JTF-SWA had tactical control over the strikes, NAVCENT served as CENTCOM's executive agent for the employment of the Tomahawks. In conjunction with the missile strikes, the United States deployed more forces, including a second aircraft carrier, to the region. In addition, the southern no-fly zone was moved up from 32 degrees to 33 degrees north in an effort to further box in the Iraqi dictator's forces. The strikes and no-fly zone expansion forced the Iraqis to redeploy their fighter aircraft away from the southern no-fly zone, decreasing the threat against Kuwaiti and coalition air forces.[56]

During the renewed buildup, Bahrain made a strong commitment to become a regional naval power with the acquisition of an *Oliver Hazard Perry*–class frigate from the U.S. Navy. USS *Jack Williams* (FFG 24) was decommissioned 13 September at Naval Air Station Pensacola, Florida, and transferred to the Bahrain Amiri Naval Force, becoming the BANS *Sabha*. Admiral Katz, serving as Commander, Naval Surface Force, U.S. Atlantic Fleet, spoke at the decommissioning ceremony. With the American colors lowered, Katz turned the podium over to Shaikh Salman bin Hamad Al Khalifa, who presided as the guest speaker for the *Sabha*'s commissioning ceremony. With the Bahraini crew aboard, the Bahraini red-and-white flag was raised for the first time.[57]

Now the capital ship of the Amiri navy, BANS *Sabha* remained in Mayport to allow her crew to learn how to operate the ship for the trans-Atlantic journey. Back in the Middle East, Admiral Fargo continued to implement an American "dual containment" policy aimed at isolating both Iraq and Iran. On 13 October 1996, the Iranians signaled their displeasure with the U.S. Navy presence in the northern gulf when the patrol boat *Bayandor* bumped into the USS *Gettysburg,* causing slight damage to the Aegis cruiser's flight-deck safety nets.[58] Undeterred, the American ship continued to perform her duties.

Desert Strike exemplified the need for a long-term American commitment to the region. To support the American presence, the United Arab Emirates signed a defense cooperative agreement enabling American warships to make more port calls in the region. With sea duty in the Gulf being arduous at times, respites ashore were always welcomed by Sailors. Bahrain had long hosted visiting American warships. Soon, Jebal Ali in Dubai became the most visited U.S. Navy liberty port in the world, with more than five hundred thousand liberty days in 1998 (a liberty day = one Sailor on the beach for one night).

Local merchants especially embraced the port calls as Sailors spent tens and thousands of dinars on exquisite gold pieces, fine carpets, and other exotic items. MWR ran classes on bartering and on appreciating cultural differences to facilitate trouble-free visits. A week prior to the bumping incident, the *Enterprise* arrived in Bahrain for the first carrier port visit since 1948. Some five thousand Sailors descended on Manama's shopping districts to purchase gifts for friends and families. The carriers *Kitty Hawk*, *John F. Kennedy*, *Independence,* and *John C. Stennis* would follow in the wake of *Enterprise* over the next two years.[59]

With the real estate acquired and the rudimentary plans in place to expand the ASU-SWA compound, the arrival of Capt. Marcia L. Fulham would prove significant. With her background as the former assistant chief of naval personnel for personnel readiness and community support, Fulham injected lessons learned from other base MWR, family service, housing, and similar activities. Relieving Capt. Thomas Feeks on 23 July 1997, Fulham undertook initiatives to improve the quality of life. One initiative was to clear the old compound of vehicular traffic. Through the expansion of the parking areas onto the newly leased landfill, Captain Fulham converted the original twenty-three acres into a pedestrian-only zone in May 1998. Shortly afterward, a "Main Street" beautification project began, to provide shrubbery, flowers, and trees along the street leading from the Desert Dome to the Oasis Restaurant.[60]

As commanding officer, Captain Fulham worked with architects on the expansion project to ensure that the designs addressed cultural, environmental, and habitability concerns. To address cultural concerns, for example, architects designed perimeter guard towers to look like traditional Bahraini wind towers. Admiral Fargo also took a keen interest in the "look" of the new facilities. Initial plans called for a standard chain-link fence to surround the complex. Fargo insisted that a wall with windows be constructed to match local architecture. Designing the new structures to blend with local structures also made sense financially because local subcontractors could build using familiar construction methods.[61]

Being a woman in a male-dominated culture did not faze Fulham, who discovered that the Bahrainis respected her collar devices. However, after selecting a residence in Manama and heading back to the States to retrieve her family, she returned to find that the landlord had repainted the exterior of the house "pink." For the next two years she jokingly referred to her abode as "Barbie's house."

Like her predecessor, she found that force protection continued to be a primary concern. Yet despite the restrictions caused by the increased security and the challenges faced by her people, she detected high morale when she arrived. Reflecting late in her tour, she cited the high pay due to cost of living allowances and the sense of importance due to being at the tip of the spear as factors in creating high Sailor morale.[62]

Also arriving at the Mina Sulman pier was Bahrain's *Oliver Hazard Perry*–class frigate. The BANS *Sabha* made a flawless approach. Admiral Fargo commended the Bahraini minister of defense on the expert ship-handling skills displayed in full view of the amir and most of the rest of the Bahraini hierarchy.

As *Sabha* arrived, Iraq again threatened UNSCOM helicopter operations and blocked inspection teams from entering certain sites. The Security Council responded with Resolution 1115 (1997) demanding access and suspending periodic sanctions reviews.

In September, Iraq provided a fifth full, final, and complete disclosure report covering its prohibited biological weapons program. An international panel of experts at the United Nations in New York found Iraq's declaration to be incomplete, inadequate, and technically flawed. Back in Iraq, UNSCOM inspectors were harassed by government officials and denied access to some sites that were declared "presidential sites."

On 23 October 1997, the Security Council passed Resolution 1134 (1997), which included a demand for Iraq to cooperate fully with the UNSCOM inspectors. Four days later, the UNSCOM executive chairman, Richard Butler, wrote Deputy Prime Minister Tariq Aziz to suggest an agenda for forthcoming meetings in Baghdad. Aziz responded with a letter to the president of the Security Council, informing the council that Iraq had decided not to deal with personnel of U.S. nationality working for UNSCOM and demanded that all Americans working with UNSCOM leave Iraq.

The president of the Security Council immediately condemned Iraq's decision, and two weeks later, the Security Council passed Resolution 1137 (1997), which cited the continued violation by Iraq of its obligations, including its unacceptable decision to seek to impose conditions on cooperation with the UNSCOM inspectors. Reacting to Iraq's decision on 13 November 1997 to evict Americans working for UNSCOM, Butler withdrew most of the UNSCOM inspection team from Iraq, leaving a skeleton staff behind to maintain UNSCOM's premises and equipment. In addition, the Iraqis threatened to shoot down American U-2 surveillance planes that were conducting photo-reconnaissance on behalf of the United Nations.[63]

Saddam's actions were being closely monitored in Washington and in Manama, and the reaction was swift. USS *Nimitz* (CVN 68) sortied from Hong Kong and sped toward the Indian Ocean. Moving in from the Atlantic Fleet, the USS *George Washington* Battle Group made its way to the Suez Canal.

Russian negotiators stepped in, and following intensive diplomacy Iraq accepted the return of the UNSCOM inspectors. The inspectors, who had been temporarily withdrawn to Bahrain, returned to Iraq on 21 November and resumed their activities the following day.

For a few weeks during the Ramadan period, the tension in the region eased. However, on 17 December 1997, Butler reported that Iraq still would not permit his inspectors into the "presidential sites." In response, on behalf of the UN Security Council, the council president issued a statement calling on Iraq to cooperate fully, stressing that failure to provide immediate, unconditional, and unrestricted access to any site was unacceptable. Again, the United States reacted and more than ten thousand ground troops were deployed to Kuwait as additional air and naval forces sped toward the region in what became the largest military buildup since the Gulf War.

On 13 January 1998, Butler reported that Iraq had failed to cooperate with an inspection team on the pretext that it had too many American and British members. With the team still blocked the following day, the Security Council president demanded that Iraq cooperate fully and immediately without conditions. Still, the Iraqi deputy prime minister asserted that Iraq would not permit access to eight so-called presidential sites.[64]

At NAVCENT headquarters in Bahrain, the sea power available to the Fifth Fleet commander continued to grow to support what was being called "Operation Desert Thunder." In February the *Independence* Battle Group, with Rear Adm. Charles W. Moore in command, arrived in the Gulf.

In addition to some fifty American ships in the region, twenty-five warships from other nations' naval forces took station to show Saddam the seriousness of the coalition's resolve. Admiral Fargo described Bahrain's contribution to the coalition's efforts as "hugely supportive." In addition to providing a logistical base for the tens of thousands of Sailors on station in the Gulf, the Bahrainis made Shaikh Isa Air Base available to an Air Force air expeditionary wing.[65]

To address the stalemate, UN Secretary-General Kofi Annan dispatched a technical survey team to Iraq in mid-February to evaluate the eight presidential sites that were off-limits to UNSCOM's inspectors. Shortly afterward, the Secretary-General visited Iraq. With President Clinton announcing in a 17 February televised speech that the United States would act if Saddam didn't cooperate with the inspectors, Annan had some leverage with his Iraqi hosts. As a result of his meetings, on 23 February the United Nations and Iraq signed a memorandum of understanding reconfirming Iraqi acceptance of past UN Security Council resolutions and promising to cooperate fully with UNSCOM. Reflecting on the MOU two years later, Admiral Moore observed, "We avoided war in February 1998 when the Iraqis agreed with Kofi Annan when it was clear that the United States and Great Britain and possibly others were going to execute a military response."[66]

As tensions somewhat eased between Iraq and the United Nations, the Fifth Fleet continued building military-to-military relationships with friendly countries through numerous multi- and bilateral exercises. Unlike exercises conducted under traditional alliances such as NATO and centered on the coordination of large multinational ship movements, exercises in the region involved small units working together to perfect specialized tasks. To provide American participants for these exercises, Admiral Fargo had some unique assets at his disposal.

For example, Explosive Ordnance Disposal Mobile Unit 5, based on Guam, maintained a detachment in Bahrain to be on call to deactivate mines and bombs, and to conduct anti-limpet mine screenings. During the year, the detachment conducted training exercises with ordnance disposal experts from Saudi Arabia, Kuwait, Oman, and Bahrain. In the case of Bahrain, the detachment worked closely with both Amiri navy and air force personnel. In addition, the detachment sent members to Yemen to teach de-mining to Yemeni forces in the wake of a long civil war.[67]

Working closely with the EOD personnel were *Ardent* and *Dextrous*. During September 1998, the two forward-deployed minesweepers conducted "Red Rover," a multinational exercise with British, French, and Saudi minesweepers. Lt. Cdr. John Bowie, commanding officer of *Ardent,* learned much from the French and British, who had a long tradition of expertise in the field. He also was impressed by the professionalism of the Saudis in their minesweeping techniques.[68]

Meanwhile the ASU-SWA Medical Department solidified relations with Bahraini Defense Force personnel through a series of exercises. In a drill called "Neon Falcon," medical teams from the two nations reacted to a mass-casualty scenario involving a chemical, biological, and radiation attack. Neon Falcon involved two hundred personnel and took more than two months to plan.[69]

Reflecting on the joint exercises, Crown Prince Shaikh Salman said, "There is nothing like training with the people that you would be fighting side by side with to deter any further aggression and to maintain peace and stability. Not only are you fighting side by side but you are getting to understand the other's doctrine, you are getting to understand each other's methods and ways of communication, and you get to know the land—the environment."[70]

The spirit of cooperation was emphasized on 27 July 1998, at a ceremony at the Gulf Hotel in Manama. With Commander U.S. Central Command Marine Gen. Anthony C. Zinni presiding, Admiral Fargo turned to Vice Adm. Charles W. Moore and said, "I am ready to be relieved." In the aftermath of the ceremony, the new U.S. Naval Forces Central Command and Fifth Fleet commander met with officials of the six GCC states to pledge continued close cooperation. Escorted by Ambassador Johnny Young, Moore also paid the customary calls on Bahraini government officials. In meeting with Shaikh Hamad bin Isa Al Khalifa, Moore came away impressed by the crown prince's recognition of the role the United States had played in maintaining regional security and stability. Shaikh Hamad also expressed a desire for even closer military cooperation between the two countries. Later, the amir honored the outgoing and incoming naval commanders at a banquet at Gudaibiya Palace.[71]

Reflecting on his recently completed tour, Admiral Fargo stated: "In Bahrain we have good friends, valued allies, and vital national interests. That is why the U.S. Navy has been here for 50 years and why we will remain committed to the peace, stability, and economic prosperity of this tremendously important region of the world." Fargo lauded the amir for the bravery, foresight, and charismatic leadership "that has been the key to the peace and stability we have enjoyed."[72]

As the U.S. Central Command strove to build relations with Gulf partners, the regime in Iraq worked toward opposite ends. Between 10 and 15 July 1998, an UNSCOM team of international experts informed their Iraqi counterparts that their third declaration on biological weapons was not verifiable. On 3 August, Aziz suspended further talks with Butler, and then Iraq halted cooperation with UNSCOM pending Security Council agreement to lift the oil embargo, reorganize the commission, and move it either to Geneva or to Vienna.[73]

As Admiral Moore and his staff monitored the lack of progress of the UNSCOM team, on 7 August bombs ripped through the U.S. embassies in Kenya and Tanzania, killing more than two hundred people including twelve Americans. Although the bombings occurred in the heart of Africa, a Middle East connection with the terrorist network led by Osama bin Laden was quickly established. On 20 August, American warships in the Arabian Sea launched Tomahawk strikes against terrorist camps in Afghanistan and a pharmaceutical complex with suspected bin Laden ties in Sudan. General Zinni recalled that intelligence suggested that bin Laden may have been at one of the Afghan camps. He understood that the odds of hitting him were not good, "But I felt we had to take the shot."[74]

For many in the region, "Operation Infinite Reach," as the Tomahawk strikes were called, raised eyebrows. Because of operational security factors regarding the assigned targets, the United States broke with its long-established tradition of consulting with leaders in the region before taking military action. In this case, even the American ambassador to Bahrain and most of Moore's own staff were not told of the impending strikes. Moore recalled that there was a pall over a meeting he had with Bahraini officials shortly thereafter. Moore could sense them thinking, "Here is this Admiral Moore who fired all these missiles and he hadn't talked to us."[75]

The terrorist attacks in Africa served as a grim reminder to Admiral Moore and Captain Fulham of the threat that lay beyond the walls of the ASU-SWA compound. Fortunately, the initiatives taken in the wake of the Khobar Towers blast continued to deter potential aggressors. In his previous duty, Lt. Cdr. Gordon Sheek served as the CNO's advisor on Force Protection. A limited duty officer with prior enlisted service, Sheek was one of a small community of naval officers with a "security specialist" designator. After the Khobar Towers blast, Sheek led a CNO Vulnerability Assessment team to inspect twenty-seven Navy facilities in seventeen countries. When he visited Bahrain in January 1997, he stressed to Admiral Fargo the importance of having a good security officer to coordinate the various efforts. A year later, Sheek found himself posted in Bahrain to take on "the most challenging security job in the Navy."

Sheek found that to do the job he needed at least eighty more people. Unfortunately, he found that the Navy manpower system worked on a three-year cycle to create billets. He had some luck in that the closure of a ship's intermediate maintenance activity freed up some billets that he could acquire. It was also suggested that some of the positions could be contracted out. But to whom? Admiral Fargo noted that the U.S. Embassy in Bahrain had contracted the services of Gurkhas to augment its security needs.

ASU-SWA then contracted with U.S. Defense Services, a security firm that then sent a recruiter to Nepal to interview Gurkha candidates. For decades, Gurkhas have served as one of the elite ground units in the British forces. After undergoing a grueling one-year boot camp, each Gurkha serves out a fifteen-year military obligation. After retirement, each soldier earns a pension of approximately $30 a month. With a contract of $800,000 per annum, ASU-SWA acquired the services of twenty-six of these veterans. Lt. Cdr. Sheek noted that the cost of posting a Gurkha at ASU-SWA would be one-fifth that of using a Sailor.

To fill the newly created Navy billets, Sheek looked to the Navy's Basic Underwater Demolition School to acquire Navy SEAL wannabes who, for various reasons, could not make it through one of the most stressful and physically demanding courses in the military. Sheek understood that these young men already had a leg up because of their selection to the school and that they would still want to serve with an elite security force. To these eighteen- and nineteen-year-olds, duty in Bahrain offered an opportunity to gain maturity and learn additional discipline.[76]

With the potent combination of Marines, Sailors, and Gurkhas as well as the deployment of additional Bahraini security forces, the United States and Bahrain successfully deterred any terrorist actions. Unfortunately, diplomatic efforts to handle another threat yielded little. In late August Iraq suspended cooperation with the UNSCOM inspection teams. The Security Council passed Resolution 1194 (1998), condemning Iraq for its action, and demanded that Hussein rescind his decision. Iraq countered on 31 October 1998 that it would cease all forms of interaction with UNSCOM and halt all of UNSCOM's activities inside Iraq, including monitoring.

On 5 November, Security Council Resolution 1205 (1998) unanimously condemned Iraq's actions. In the Gulf, the crews of ships in the *Dwight D. Eisenhower* Battle Group readied for action. In Norfolk, the *Enterprise* made final preparations to get under way. At CENTCOM Headquarters at MacDill AFB, Florida, in JTF-SWA in Saudi Arabia, in NAVCENT in Bahrain, and in the Gulf, Iraqi targets were screened and selected for destruction under Operation Desert Viper.

Joint Chiefs of Staff Chairman general Hugh Shelton had directed Zinni to prepare a heavy attack plan and a light attack plan. When Zinni briefed the two options to the Joint Chiefs at the Pentagon on 7 November, he advocated the heavy attack option arguing, "If you're going to hit him, hit him." Much to his surprise, the Joint Chiefs opted for the light attack plan by a vote of four to two. Asked to provide an encore presentation to the president and key cabinet members the next day at Camp David, Zinni discussed the options. After debate, President Clinton approved a compromise recommended by National Security Advisor Sandy Berger directing Zinni to go with the light option but to retain the option for a more substantial aerial campaign.[77]

The approved plan would be called Desert Viper. Zinni had conceived Desert Viper as the best means of disabusing Saddam of his belief that he had leeway as to how far he could push the coalition before backing down. A pattern had been established in which the United States first sought regional approval to station forces, and then commenced a build-up of air, sea, and ground forces. But for Desert Viper, Zinni sought to use the forces already in place at sea and on land and to mask the strike by sending envoys to friendly Gulf states to request that they host additional forces. Meanwhile, the UNSCOM teams in Iraq remained in place as desperate negotiations were conducted to avert hostilities. The withdrawal of the UNSCOM teams on 11 November seemed to signal that the crisis had reached the point of no return.

With the execute order already in hand, on 14 November Admiral Moore received a message telling him to join with Ambassador Johnny Young to approach the Bahraini defense minister to request permission to bring in more units. Moore didn't lie to his host, but he didn't reveal that a strike was about to be launched. Meanwhile in New York, the Iraqi ambassador and the secretary general conducted a series of hurried meetings. Letters were exchanged signaling Iraq's intent to cooperate fully with the United Nations.

Returning to the Fifth Fleet command center, Moore got a call from Zinni saying that the president needed to know how much time it would take to call off the operation before the first missile was launched. Moore responded, "Ten minutes." Later Moore found out that President Clinton was told "forty minutes" because Zinni, the chairman of the Joint Chiefs, and the secretary of defense each added ten minutes to the tally. Upon learning of Iraq's decision to comply with UNSCOM's demands, the president pulled the execution order for Desert Viper. In Tampa at CENTCOM Headquarters, Zinni received a call from Joint Chiefs Vice Chairman Gen. Joseph W. Ralston, "It's a no-go: Don't shoot." General Zinni immediately called Admiral Moore. The strike was cancelled just thirty-one minutes before the first Tomahawk was scheduled to be launched.[78]

To General Zinni and Admiral Moore it appeared that Saddam had again successfully played the brinkmanship game. Did Saddam realize that his forces were about to get hammered? Intelligence showed that the Iraqis were moving sensitive equipment and files away from targeted sites believed to be associated with Saddam's chemical, biological, and nuclear weapons programs hours ahead of the planned attacks. The American surge of air power in the region in the days before Desert Viper led Joint Chiefs chairman, General Shelton, to believe that Saddam was tipped off, and Shelton called the CENTCOM commander to express his concern. Shelton posed the question about the possibility of striking Saddam with just the assets already in the region. He observed, "We need to do something that outfoxes him. . . . We ought to call the next strike 'Desert Fox.' "[79]

After some detailed staff work, Zinni concluded that the air forces stationed in the region could deliver a more crippling blow if they struck before Saddam had a chance to hide his high-value assets. Because anybody with a pair of binoculars could observe bomb-laden land-based aircraft preparing to launch, Zinni decided to conduct only sea-based cruise missile launches on the first night. With the urging of Admiral Moore in Bahrain and Rear Adm. Mark Fitzgerald in Tampa, Zinni added Navy tactical air into the initial attack.[80]

Meanwhile through reports on CNN, Bahraini leaders learned just how close the United States had come to launching strikes. Twice the new Fifth Fleet commander had failed to consult with them. As the holiday season commenced with almost nightly receptions at embassies and prominent Bahraini homes, Moore found himself the target of barbs suggesting that his presence assured that there would be no surprise American attacks that evening. Then on 15 December, the Special Commission reported to the security general on the subject of Iraq's cooperation with the commission. Butler concluded that he had not been provided the full cooperation promised. Two days later the Special Commission withdrew its staff from Iraq and flew to Bahrain.

With the departure of the UNSCOM staff, President Clinton signed the execution order for Operation Desert Fox.

CHAPTER NINE

Kingdom of Bahrain

On 6 March 1999, His Highness Shaikh Essa* bin Salman Al Khalifa suffered a heart attack and passed away. In accordance with Islamic custom, he was buried within a few hours of his death. Thousands of men gathered at the cemetery to observe solemnly the burial of their beloved leader. Outside, women waited on the road leading to the cemetery trying to hold back the tears of grief. For many Bahrainis, Shaikh Essa had been the only leader they had known. His sudden loss was deeply felt within the population, and as the country declared an official three-month period of mourning. Bahrain's diplomatic community, dismayed with the sudden loss, expressed heartfelt sorrow on behalf of the governments they represented.[1]

Ruling for thirty-eight years, Shaikh Essa had led the transition of his country into a fully independent nation with a diverse economy. In his obituary in the *New York Times,* he was described as a diminutive man with twinkling eyes, "a man who enjoyed life and ruled with a mischievous touch." His leadership contributed stability to a part of the world that had experienced some of the most devastating wars of the late twentieth century. Part of his legacy was the strong relationship he had forged with the United States of America and its navy. By hosting a string of American naval commanders and their staffs during times when the American presence in the region was shunned by his peers, the amir fostered a greater understanding of the Arab world on the part of numerous Americans whose opinions later counted. Admiral Crowe clearly indicates in his autobiography that his approach to the Gulf during his tenure as chairman of the Joint Chiefs was heavily influenced by his tour as Commander Middle East Force.[2]

The amir's passing occurred shortly after Secretary of Defense William Cohen had visited him to conclude an arrangement to provide the Bahraini Defense Force fighter aircraft with updated air-to-air missiles. As the official American party departed, Admiral Moore stayed back and chatted with the amir for five minutes. He may have been the last to shake his hand.

---

* In 1998 the government of Bahrain designated "Essa" versus "Isa" as the correct English spelling.

Upon learning of the amir's death shortly after his departure from the meeting, the defense secretary consulted with Washington, and it was agreed that he would pay the official condolence call and then leave Bahrain. Admiral Moore remembers going to Shaikh Hamad bin Essa Al Khalifa's majlis and seeing the members of the grieving ruling family there with saddened faces. Secretary Cohen stated to the press: "Since he became a ruler in 1961, His Highness Shaikh Essa has been a force for peace and stability in the Middle East. He has also been a strong and loyal friend to the United States and particularly to the U.S. Navy."[3]

CNO Adm. Jay Johnson echoed the defense secretary's sentiments. Johnson had traveled to Bahrain the previous November to call on the amir to commemorate fifty years of U.S. Navy–Bahraini cooperation. For the occasion, Johnson had located from the operational archives of the Naval Historical Center a photograph of the amir as a teenager standing with family members on the flight deck of the USS *Rendova*. With the photograph, Johnson carried with him an inscribed small block of wood that had been carved out of a deck plank from the carrier. Upon hearing of the amir's passing, the CNO said: "He was a true friend of the United States Navy and a superb host to our Sailors and their families. We will miss the great vision, warm friendship, and staunch support of this brave and courageous leader."[4]

In Bahrain, Ambassador Johnny Young and Admiral Moore joined numerous dignitaries to call on the new amir, His Highness Shaikh Hamad bin Essa Al Khalifa, to express condolences. For Capt. Marcia Fulham, the death of Shaikh Essa represented the only time during her tenure in command at ASU-SWA that her gender became an issue. To pay her respects, she called on the wife of the deceased ruler.[5]

For Sailors stationed in Bahrain, Shaikh Essa was seen not just as the head of state. As documented earlier in this book, his paternal care for the Bahraini people extended to the bluejackets as well. For many years, the amir allowed personnel stationed in Bahrain to be guests at his beach estate on the western side of the island. Visiting this small paradise allowed Sailors an opportunity to gain some rest and relaxation from their challenging daily chores. When the amir was at the estate, he frequently would approach Sailors to ask about their backgrounds, interests, and thoughts about being stationed in Bahrain.

Not surprisingly, many Sailors felt obligated to sign and write personal thoughts in a eulogy book that Admiral Moore formally presented to Shaikh Hamad on 7 July 1999. The new amir expressed thanks for the sentiments, which represented a deep-rooted relationship between the two countries.

Recognizing the role of the Fifth Fleet, Shaikh Hamad commended the American effort to transform the region into an oasis of peace, security, and stability.[6]

Born on 28 January 1950, Shaikh Hamad came of age with Bahrain's independence and was directed by his father to form and head the Bahraini Defense Force. Although most of his training came "on the job," he did attend the Mons Officer Cadet School at Aldershot in Britain and the U.S. Army Command and General Staff College at Fort Leavenworth in Kansas. Serving for three decades as the military commander in chief, Shaikh Hamad had built Bahrain's armed forces from a constabulary organization into a potent service that incorporated the latest in sea, air, and ground weapon systems. As noted earlier, Bahrain's armed forces performed superbly during the 1991 Gulf War.

Shaikh Hamad had other interests besides the military. He prided himself on being a sportsman, participating in numerous individual and team sports. Admiral Moore would find him to be an exceptional golfer. In 1976, he demonstrated his interest in the environment and in preserving Bahraini culture by creating the Al Areen Wildlife Park and Historical Documents Center. His history of Bahrain, *First Light: Modern Bahrain and Its Heritage,* appeared in 1994.[7]

Even given his well-rounded background, few could have predicted the sweeping initiatives that the new amir intended to pursue.

In the realm of foreign policy, during his first year in office, Shaikh Hamad made several trips to improve ties within the Arab world and beyond. In addition, after appointing Shaikh Salman as the new crown prince, the amir soon dispatched his articulate elder son to represent Bahrain's interests abroad. For example, Shaikh Salman conducted a whirlwind tour of the United States in January 2000, meeting with President Clinton and other senior Defense and State Department officials to discuss regional security and economic issues.[8]

That Shaikh Hamad continued his father's diplomatic legacy by maintaining ties with traditional friends in the Arab world and with the United States was hardly surprising. However, his trip to Rome in November 1999 to visit Pope John Paul II was less expected. It sent a clear message to fundamentalists within both the Islamic and Christian religions that a spirit of tolerance and co-existence should be allowed and encouraged. Commenting on his talks with the pontiff, the amir said they "embodied a common desire to deepen the understanding between religions and civilizations of the world." As an exclamation point, Shaikh Hamad invited the pope to visit Bahrain, and the aging John Paul II expressed his interest in doing so.[9]

Shaikh Hamad scored an early foreign policy success with the final settlement of the long-standing Hawar Islands dispute with Qatar. Bahrain's eastern neighbor had hoped to win title to those islands at the International Court of Justice (ICJ) at the Hague. As crown prince in 1996, Shaikh Hamad had taken the lead in fending off Qatar's territorial claims. He had repeatedly urged Qatar to drop its ICJ claim, urging bilateral talks within the framework of the Gulf Cooperative Council (GCC) with Saudi Arabia serving as an arbiter to resolve the border dispute in a brotherly and amicable way. Clerics echoed Shaikh Hamad's call, claiming that foreign Western arbitration went against "Gulf religion, tradition, and customs and Arab and Islamic norms."[10]

There was some initial headway as the two sides allowed the GCC to set up a four-member ministerial committee to examine the issues. In March 1997, the two countries agreed to establish embassies in each other's capitals. Still, Qatar continued to pursue its claim at the ICJ, even after Bahrain demonstrated in 1998 that documents provided to the ICJ by Qatar had been forged. Additional written pleadings were subsequently submitted, and on 30 June 1999, the court ruled that the case was ready to be considered without additional pleadings.[11]

With the case before the ICJ for a final decision, Shaikh Hamad and his counterpart from Qatar, Shaikh Hamad bin Khalifa Al Thani, met in late 1999. Setting aside the Hawar Islands dispute, the two leaders established diplomatic relations at the ambassadorial level, established landing rights for Qatar's airline at Manama, and agreed to construct a causeway to link the two countries. The two Shaikh Hamads also decided to give diplomacy one last try, appointing their crown princes to lead a joint high committee to resolve the border dispute, with the understanding that an agreement would lead to the withdrawal of the case pending before the ICJ.[12]

The high committee led by the two crown princes made little headway, however, and on 29 May 2000, the ICJ opened oral arguments on competing territorial claims. During the month of June, the seventeen judges heard arguments presented by spokesmen backed by large teams of solicitors, councilors, cartographers, diplomats, and official observers representing the two Arab states. Despite all of the amiable talk prior to the hearing, both sides forcefully argued their cases before the bench.

With proximity as their strongest argument, the Qatari legal team spent a week introducing materials backing their claim for the Hawars and adjacent islands. On 8 June Bahraini representative Jawad Al Arrayed gave his opening remarks and turned the floor over to Sir Elihu Lauterpacht. The Cambridge professor demonstrated his belief that a good offense is often the best defense by claiming that the abandoned port of Zubarah on Qatar's northwest coast should come under Bahraini sovereignty, noting that in 1937 adherents to the Al Thani family had forcibly evicted from there Naim tribesmen who had been loyal to the Al Khalifa of Bahrain. In doing so, he illustrated that the Al Thani claim on the whole Qatar peninsular until recent times was tenuous, let alone the claim on the Hawars. With regard to proximity, Lauterpacht argued there was a closer natural unity between the Hawars and Manama as opposed to Doha because the islands were separated from Bahrain by easily navigable waters in contrast to the miles of harsh desert that impeded travel from Qatar's east coast capital.[13]

Back in Bahrain and Qatar, citizens gathered in front of television sets to watch the proceedings as they were transmitted back live. In his closing remarks, Jawad Al Arrayed stood before a hushed courtroom packed with many Bahrainis who had flown in for the final session and argued, "Qatar has become an immensely rich country and has developed an appetite for prestige. It is claiming Zubarah and Hawar as trophies!" Speaking with deep emotion, he continued, "Bahrain's claims have an entirely different foundation to Qatar's. It is the foundation of social roots and national identity. We are defending one third of our territory, but an even greater part of our national soul."[14]

Jawad Al Arrayed's pleadings aside, Bahrain's argument that the issue had been settled some sixty-one years previously through binding arbitration is what most impressed the judges. In 1939, the then two British protectorates had agreed to allow London to determine the issue of sovereignty over the Hawar Islands, and the British ruled in Bahrain's favor. When the ICJ issued its verdict on 16 March 2001, it cited the 1939 arbitration as binding, even after the independence of the two countries.

As the ICJ was explaining its decision, the streets and sidewalks of Manama were void of cars and pedestrians; the televised event had turned into the Bahraini equivalent of the Super Bowl. There was jubilation when the ICJ reaffirmed Bahrain's sovereignty over the Hawars. "Hawar Is Ours!" exclaimed the *Gulf Daily News,* and Prime Minister Shaikh Khalifa bin Salman Al Khalifa issued an edict declaring the day after the ruling a public holiday. However, Qatar did not come away empty-handed—the ICJ ruled that Qatar had jurisdiction over Zubarah, Janan Island, and the low-tide elevation of Fasht ad Dibal. Of mutual benefit was the judges' drawing of a maritime boundary.[15]

The United States was particularly pleased with the outcome. U.S. Navy leaders in Bahrain were concerned that to defend the Hawars, Bahrain was deploying some of its more capable forces, weakening the defense of the main island. Also, in the wake of the Gulf War, the Pentagon worked to build on military ties established with Qatar during that conflict by conducting military-to-military consultations and bilateral exercises. Relations with Qatar improved further when the United States became the first to recognize the newly formed government led by Shaikh Hamad bin Khalifa Al Thani, who had ousted his father during a bloodless coup on 27 June 1995. Within months, the Qataris agreed to allow the U.S. Army to pre-position equipment within the country and establish "ARCENT-Qatar" as an in-theater Army component command of U.S. Central Command. The ICJ settlement freed the Americans from being drawn into the long-standing border dispute, enabling them to pursue even closer ties with Qatar without slighting America's warm relationship with Bahrain. Subsequently, the two countries invested in expanding the Al Udeid Air Base, some thirty miles southwest of Doha. The base would serve as a key command center during Operation Enduring Freedom and Operation Iraqi Freedom.[16]

With the long-standing territorial dispute behind them, the two amirs immediately met to discuss future cooperation. For Bahrain, the settlement of the dispute meant that oil companies could resume exploration in the vicinity of the Hawars and that housing and other construction projects could commence. More important, the victory at the ICJ gave Bahrainis an additional feeling of national pride and identity; numerous rallies with large turnouts had been held during the ICJs deliberations. "It was a real coup for Shaikh Hamad," noted an observer who postulated that his handling of the situation in the victory legitimized his later moves in the eyes of many.[17]

While working to settle the territorial dispute with his eastern neighbor, Shaikh Hamad turned to the north. His initiative to continue improving relations with Iran had clear local aims. The Persian nation had long fomented unrest within Bahrain's Shi'ite population. However, with the Iranian election in 1997 of Dr. Sayyid Mohammed Khatami, the tone of Iran's rhetoric turned reconciliatory. Just over one month before Shaikh Essa's death, the two countries exchanged ambassadors. On 4 May 1999, the new amir dispatched Foreign Minister Shaikh Mohammed bin Mubarak Al Khalifa to Tehran where he met with his Iranian counterpart, Dr. Khalil Kharazi. The two men discussed improving bilateral relations and exchanged invitations for their respective leaders to make visits. Two weeks later in Qatar, Crown Prince Shaikh Salman met Iranian President Khatami for additional discussions during a state visit. As a follow-up, a few days later Shaikh Hamad and President Khatami exchanged additional views during a phone conversation.

As 1999 continued into 2000 and beyond, ministerial-level talks continued between the two countries. One agreement led to the establishment of a Bahrain-Iran Joint Economic Committee that held its first meeting in Manama in March 2000. Additional joint committees were formed to explore other areas of cooperation. Dialogue continued, and on 17–18 August 2002, Bahrain's leader visited Tehran to hold meetings with President Khatami and Ayatollah Ali Khamenei. Concerns about security in the Gulf, especially with respect to Iraq's resistance to complying with UN resolutions and American threats to take unilateral action, dominated the conversations. To continue the dialogue, Shaikh Hamad extended an invitation to Khatami to visit Bahrain. On the weekend of 17–18 May 2003, the two leaders held serious discussions at the Shaikh Hamad Palace at Gudaibiya on an assortment of economic, cultural, and regional security issues.

A centerpiece of the cross-Gulf summits was a security agreement, similar to the one Iran had signed with Yemen and Saudi Arabia. This accord promised cooperation on combating organized crime, drug trafficking, terrorism, sabotage, and cross-border infiltration. For the Bahrainis, the dialogue and agreement served a domestic agenda promoting economic growth and encouraging internal stability.[18]

No doubt the contacts with Iran facilitated the release of hundreds of prisoners and detainees, most of whom were of Persian descent and had been incarcerated in the mid-1990s during the crackdown on unrest. Three months after the passing of his father, Shaikh Hamad ordered the release of 41 prisoners and 320 detainees and pardoned 12 individuals living abroad. Over the next few weeks, additional releases occurred, and scenes of families being reunited made the evening news. Explaining his actions in July, the amir described "the pardoning of 'misled groups' as a clear step to foster national unity." He stated a commitment to treat all citizens equally "regardless of their creeds or origins."[19]

The initial and subsequent releases of prisoners and detainees served as part of a grandiose scheme by the new amir to make his government more democratic and inclusive. In 1992, in a controversial move, Shaikh Essa abolished the national constitution that had been suspended in 1975. In its place, he established the Shura Council as a thirty-member consultative body consisting of appointees from various elements of society. In 1996, after the conclusion of the council's first four-year term, the Bahraini leader expanded the number of members to forty.[20]

With the passing of his father, the new amir retained the council and then appointed eighteen "mayors" for Manama and the surrounding areas to establish open majlis in their homes where citizen complaints could be heard. Next he announced that Bahrainis would be allowed to elect their own town councils. When the time came to appoint a new Shura Council for the third session, the amir appointed four women as well as Ebrahim Dawood Noonoo, a Bahraini Jew, to signal his desire for greater inclusiveness. Finally, Shaikh Hamad appointed a Supreme National Committee and assigned it a mission of drafting a National Action Charter to establish a constitutional monarchy.[21]

Led by Shaikh Abdallah bin Khalid Al Khalifa, the forty-six-member committee, after several months of work, submitted the charter to the amir in late December. Among the more notable recommendations was the creation of an independent judiciary and a freely elected parliament responsible for passing legislation. The Shura Council would remain as a legislative body to create a bicameral system similar to that found within most Western democracies. Women would also have the right to vote and hold office in this new framework.

To encourage the large Shi'ite community to vote, a week before the polling, Shaikh Hamad declared a general amnesty for another 397 "prisoners and detainees held on security issues." The amnesty covered many who had already been freed and a number of those who had opposed the government and were living abroad. Included were 108 Bahrainis who were exiled abroad and given amnesty to return. Then, on the eve of the election, special amnesty was granted to an additional sixteen Shi'ite activists who had been behind bars. The gesture was reciprocated by an extraordinarily large turnout. On 13 and 14 February 2001, 196,262 Bahrainis stood on line at forty-seven polling places around the country to vote on acceptance of the National Action Charter. Pollsters noted that thirteen of the voters were older than 100 with the oldest being 108! To no one's surprise, the populace overwhelmingly supported the charter with a 98.4 percent majority. Having the popular mandate, the government proceeded on a path toward setting up further elections.[22]

On the first anniversary of the referendum, Shaikh Hamad took a major step toward building a constitutional monarchy through his proclamation that Bahrain was to become a kingdom. The amir would now be king! As part of his declaration, the king issued a new constitution drawn from the National Action Charter. Also significant was his announcement that municipal elections would be held on 9 May and that votes would be cast for parliamentary seats on 24 October.[23]

Although thousands of Bahrainis poured out onto the streets to celebrate the proclamation and Bahrain's self-elevation in status, not everyone in the new kingdom was celebrating. Many advocates had called for a restoration of the 1973 constitution with its unicameral legislature. These individuals saw the new bicameral system with an appointed upper body as impeding true democracy.

Still, many of these Bahrainis decided to remain engaged. When the government permitted the formation of political societies, eleven groups registered with the Ministry of Labor and Social Affairs. For the May elections to fill fifty seats on five municipal councils, the societies recruited many of the 304 candidates whose names would appear on the ballots.

In the weeks prior to the election, several of the societies and candidates employed Tammany Hall–type tactics, distributing free sacks of sugar, rice, and other food items and offering to pay off outstanding bills. Equating these campaign practices to bribery, clerics in their Friday sermons condemned these actions as contravening Islamic ethics. While some candidates attempted to buy votes, others reshaped their image by growing beards to look pious and taking position in the front rows when attending prayers at mosques.

While some clerics condemned and chided actions of some of the candidates, others actively endorsed candidates and invoked Islamic teachings. The combination of such activism by religious leaders and a gender-segregated society proved fatal for the female candidates. One-tenth of the candidates were women, and they struggled to overcome biases. To address religious concerns, Bahiya Al Ataawi sought and received a fatwa from influential Muslim scholar Shaikh Yusuf Al Qaradawi that cited passages in the Koran to justify women running for office, especially after childbearing years. However, one of her opponents obtained an opposing ruling from a Saudi cleric, citing the same text. When another woman candidate found that her open invitation for constituents to visit her home was being shunned, she erected a tent and moved it every few days as a mechanism to attract audiences.

When the elections were held on 9 May, none of the women were able to collect enough votes to win outright or force a run-off. Siba Al Asfoor, an engineer who ran for a seat in "Northern Governorate 5," competed against twelve male candidates and received only 115 of the 3,776 votes cast. While at many polling stations women constituted the majority of voters, prejudices held by people of both genders were a major factor in the outcome. Frustrated, Al Asfoor exclaimed, "Bahrain's people are not wise enough to accept women in the public arena. Even women lack faith in women's abilities to carry any kind of public responsibility."[24] Surveys of some of the women voters bore out her thesis. "Men just use their brains better, they know more about what is happening in the world," commented Safat Aysar, a forty-year-old hospital worker, after she had cast her ballot.[25]

Although not arguing against women voting, one of the newly elected candidates declared, "A woman's place is in the home and not in the chamber of the municipal council." Others argued to the contrary. Although women were not successful at the polls, the election process did stir a healthy debate about the role of women in society.[26]

Besides serving as a barometer on the role of women in society, the election showed the political potency of Islamic organizations. The fifty elected men all had backing from societies with religious connections, and twenty-two of these had ties to Islamic National Wefaq, a Shi'ite-oriented political society.[27]

After the 9 May election, debates raged within several political societies about how to handle their objections to the February constitution. Finally on 3 September, the leaders of four of those groups—the aforementioned Islamic National Wefaq Society, National Democratic Action, Democratic Nationalist Tajammu, and Islamic Action Society—declared that they would not run candidates in the 24 October election and would urge their followers to boycott it. Two weeks preceding the October contest, these groups appealed to the king to postpone the elections and launch a national dialogue on amending the constitution. Ignoring the plea, the government pressed ahead with election plans.[28]

With the boycott in place, only 174 individuals decided to run for office, only eight female. Tension existed in the days leading up to the balloting, because many feared that those boycotting the election might turn to violent acts. In turn, King Hamad urged calm and urged Bahrainis to vote. His wife, Shaikha Sabika, exhorted Bahraini women to participate in the polling. When the shaikha visited a Shi'ite community center, an elderly woman, expressing her appreciation for being enfranchised, exclaimed: "Thank you, for the first time our husbands are asking us what we think and are interested in what we have to say."[29] With the get-out-the-vote effort, the real drama came down to the turnout. Hoping to undermine the legitimacy of the new parliament, the opposition hoped for a low turnout of approximately 30 percent.

On election day, *New York Times* writer Thomas L. Friedman visited several polling places and was struck by the number of elderly women who lined up to vote. He observed: "Many of them illiterate, they would check the picture of the candidate they wanted to vote for and then stuff the ballot in the box." To prevent voters from being intimidated within their own precincts by the boycotting opposition, the government arranged for voting to take place at any polling station. This flexibility helped as the final tallies indicated a turnout of approximately 52 percent.[30]

When the tallies were counted, nineteen candidates had collected 51 percent of the votes and won their seats outright. Three additional seats already had been decided as a result of no-opposition. To fill the remaining eighteen seats, a run-off election was held with forty-two surviving candidates, including two women. Neither female candidate was elected.

Commenting on the election at an American Bahraini Friendship Society lecture in Washington, Dr. Jean-Francois Seznec of the Columbia Middle Eastern Institute observed that in the emerging democracy in the Middle East, religious political societies have an edge because they have been organizing for centuries. In Bahrain's case, half of the seats went to candidates backed by Sunni religious societies, and four additional seats went to candidates backed by Shi'ite organizations. Had there not been a boycott, that latter number would have been higher.[31]

In mid-November, the king appointed his cabinet and the new Shura Council. For this body, the king included six of Bahrain's most highly educated females, four of whom held doctorates. Of the thirty-four men installed by royal decree, one-quarter represented the business sector, five were from the military, three were from the media, three came from the royal family, and the rest were selected from diverse sectors of Bahraini society.[32]

On 14 December 2002, at a specially built open-air auditorium, King Hamad exclaimed that "Bahrain's destiny has been fulfilled" as he inaugurated the opening sessions of the Parliament and Shura Council, collectively labeled the "National Assembly."

Bahrain's transition to a constitutional monarchy did not occur in a vacuum. Major world events around the small Gulf island nation would have a domestic impact. Terrorist attacks, Iraqi belligerence, the ongoing Palestinian-Israeli conflict, a new administration in Washington, and war would adversely affect the relationship between the United States and the Arab world. Yet despite misperceptions that led some bigots in America to commit hate crimes against Arab-American citizens in the United States and caused virulent anti-American protests throughout the Middle East, the relationship between Bahrain and the U.S. Navy remained strong.

Illustrative of that relationship was the close cooperation that occurred in the wake of a tragedy that put Bahrain in the international spotlight. On 23 August 2000, Gulf Air Flight 072 flying in from Cairo made two aborted approaches to the runway at Bahrain International Airport. Ali Ahmed and Bassim Mohammed were sitting at a friend's seaside farm playing cards. Ali Ahmed observed that the plane had passed overhead twice, and on the third time, "We saw the same aircraft fly overhead, fully tilted on one side, with its nose pointing to the ground." Bassim Mohammed continued,

"We quickly scrambled to rush out of the main farm gate, just in time to see the plane crash into the sea. . . . The wing hit first and then there was a huge explosion over the water." Gulf Air Flight 072 plunged into shallow waters a mile and a half north of Muharraq Island with 143 passengers and crew embarked.[33]

Bahraini civil defense and fire rescue personnel immediately responded, as did dozens of fisherman and other villagers living on Muharraq Island. Recognizing the importance of getting as many resources as possible to the scene in the hope of recovering survivors, a call was made to the American naval facility. Within twenty minutes, a helicopter from the Desert Ducks was airborne and Sailors and Marines scurried to collect medical supplies and rush to the scene. Meanwhile, aboard USS *George Washington* (CVN 74) anchored off Sitrah, Cdr. Kurt Martin, standing battle watch duty, received the crash report and notified the command duty officer and the carrier's skipper, Capt. W. J. McCarthy. Within an hour *George Washington* launched two SH-60 helicopters loaded with search-and-rescue swimmers. They were joined over the scene by another Navy SH-60 from the USS *Oldendorf* (DD 972) and two Bahraini Defense Force helicopters. Meanwhile Captain McCarthy sent a rigid-hull inflatable boat, three fifty-foot utility boats, two liberty ferries, and his gig to join two U.S. Navy harbor patrol craft at the scene.[34]

Arriving at the north end of Muharraq Island, Crown Prince Shaikh Salman bin Hamad Al Khalifa took control of the recovery operation. To facilitate recovery coordination, the crown prince requested and received Assistant Operations Officer Cdr. Gordon Van Hook to perform liaison work for what sadly became a gruesome recovery operation. Into the early morning hours, Sailors and Marines worked closely with Bahraini rescue workers to bring human remains ashore. Two of the swimmers from *George Washington,* Boatswains Mates Alan Field and Bryan Hadley, recalled spending hours in the debris-filled waters hoping to find survivors. A volunteer Bahraini diver observed that the rescuers found themselves diving into an underwater world of horror. He exclaimed, "Bits of bodies, jewelry, clothing and other personal belongings were scattered on the sea bed. It was like a village down there, we didn't expect anything like this at all." Within five hours the joint effort of more than four hundred rescuers yielded all 143 victims—there were no survivors. For the rescue workers, the effort took a physical and mental toll. In the August midnight heat many battled dehydration. Bahraini Civil Defense and Fire Service chief Col. James Windsor told reporters, "A lot of us, including me, were suffering from tremendous headaches, which is the first sign of dehydration." One Navy petty officer in a rescue boat became unconscious and had to be taken ashore for treatment.[35]

With sunrise, divers from the USNS *Catawba* began to assist in the salvage operation to recover parts of the aircraft and the two flight data recorders. By mid-day the "black boxes" were in the hands of civil aviation authorities. Colonel Windsor reflected, "It was a tremendous effort by everybody. . . . All the practice we have done for years paid off today."[36]

Not surprisingly, the in-bound flight from Cairo was nearly half-filled with sixty-four Egyptians. In addition to the Egyptians, thirty-four Bahrainis, a dozen Saudis, and thirty-three individuals from other countries lost their lives. The lone American loss was a diplomatic courier making a delivery to the U.S. Embassy in Manama. Given the relative size of Bahrain, the impact of the tragedy was deeply felt. "Being a small community, it seems that almost every person had a friend or a friend of a friend on GF072," reported the *Gulf Daily News*. Shaikh Hamad led his nation in mourning.

That afternoon, Crown Prince Shaikh Salman met with many of the Sailors and Marines who had assisted in the rescue attempt to express his appreciation and shake their hands. Only twenty-four hours earlier, when asked about the future of the U.S. Navy in Bahrain, he had said, "We have continued to build on a relationship that has existed for fifty years. We don't see any change in our relationship." No doubt each handshake affirmed that conviction. More important, each handshake affirmed another observation he had made about the title of this book. His Highness had noted admirals as well as ambassadors leave lasting memories, "But it is the Sailors—without them nothing would really happen. It's the Sailors that leave the impression."[37]

They would continue to do so in the coming months.

CHAPTER TEN

USS *Cole*

Mid-morning on 12 October 2000, Master Chief Hospital Corpsman James Parlier stood on the hot, sun-drenched bridge wing of the USS *Cole* (DDG 67) as the warship slowly maneuvered toward a concrete platform fueling station in the northwestern reach of Aden harbor. As the command master chief aboard the new Aegis-guided missile destroyer, Parlier served as the senior advisor on all enlisted Sailor matters to Cdr. Kirk S. Lippold, the ship's commanding officer, who was also on the bridge along with a Yemeni harbor pilot and other Sailors serving on the "special sea and anchor detail."

Parlier peered out at jagged mountains beyond the coastline that enveloped the *Cole* on three sides. Below the ridges, activity bustled as vehicles traversed city streets and ships loaded and discharged cargoes in a port that had served as a major base for the Royal Navy for decades. In the years after the British withdrawal of its forces from east of Suez, the strategic port at the tip of the Arabian peninsula suffered as competing groups fought for control of the country. Ahead in the distance, the rusting hulk of a Soviet ship marked a time when a leftist regime had invited the Red navy to use the port to support Soviet Indian Ocean operations. Following the fall of the Soviet Union and the end of a Yemeni civil war, American relations with the new government remained distant for reasons that included Yemen's failure to support the UN coalition during the Gulf War.

That Parlier was now entering Yemen's main port on a United States man-of-war could be traced to Yemeni initiatives in 1996 and 1997 to improve relations with the world's remaining superpower. For the United States, the Yemeni overture seemed fortuitous, because ships transiting from the Suez Canal to the Strait of Hormuz had been calling at Djibouti, an African port that was crowded with small vessels, lacked security, and had an unstable government. CENTCOM planners also looked at Jiddah as a refueling stop, but the Khobar Towers bombing discouraged use of that Saudi Red Sea port. In that light, Aden began to hold promise in late 1997 as a potential refueling stop for Fifth Fleet ships. The CENTCOM commander, Gen. Anthony Zinni, USMC, visited Yemeni president Ali Abdullah Saleh twice in 1998 to discuss refueling visits and a wide range of cooperative measures in concert with the Clinton administration's engagement policies to strengthen Yemeni military, law-enforcement, and anti-terrorism capabilities. During his first visit, which began 22 May and lasted for several days, the Yemenis asked Zinni for help in training counter-terrorist forces and building a coast guard.

Touring Aden's harbor in a harbor craft, Zinni found the concrete platform fueling station located out in the harbor very appealing. Rather than coming alongside a pier, a U.S. warship could slip in and out with minimal exposure, almost like a car filling up at a gas station just off the interstate. Seeing a number of hulks sunken in the harbor, Zinni arranged to send divers to check the harbor and provide advice on steps needed to improve navigation.

When Zinni briefed Admiral Moore before the latter took command of the Fifth Fleet in July 1998, the Marine general told the Navy admiral that Yemen was one of the countries in the region that presented opportunities for closer engagement. Consequently, Moore traveled to Yemen in late September 1998 to meet with President Saleh and ministers within his government. Flying into Aden, Moore was hustled down to the harbor for his own boat tour. As with Zinni, Moore saw Aden's potential as a fueling stop and arranged for the Defense Energy Support Center to survey the port in November 1998. A month later a contract was let enabling American warships to conduct refueling stops.

In March 1999, the first U.S. Navy warship arrived at Aden to refuel under the provisions of that contract. *Cole*'s arrival marked the twenty-eigth such arrival.[1] As the destroyer's starboard side nudged up to the refueling platform, Parlier chatted with a junior shipmate about career opportunities. With the temperature approaching 100 degrees and the starboard side moored to the platform, both men lay below, seeking relief within the air-conditioned interior of the warship.

Parlier eventually headed to the weekly Morale, Recreation, and Welfare (MWR) meeting held in the second-deck training room aft. Sitting by the command master chief was Damage Controlman First Class Ernesto Garcia, along with representatives from other divisions. The XO, Lt. Cdr. Chris Peterschmidt, facilitated a discussion on acquiring new television sets for the crew's lounge. Meanwhile outside, two Arab men in a white boat that proved to be a floating bomb, approached the warship, waving at the sentries.

As the meeting ended, Parlier stood and left with the others, when "there was a huge boom, like an M-80 under a can, but only 100 times louder." Their knees buckled as the ship lifted up to starboard and rocked back to port.

The lights flicked off and on, and a television set crashed down on the deck. Peterschmidt grabbed an internal ship's telephone and found the line dead. He then yelled, "Go to GQ!"

Cole's crew didn't need to be told what to do. Months of repetitious training kicked in. Crewmembers instinctively ran to their battle stations amid shouts of "General Quarters, Pass the word" in the passageways. Hatches slammed shut and were dogged down as crewmembers set Condition Zebra throughout the ship to increase watertight integrity. With his extensive medical training, Parlier started heading back to the after battle dressing station. Immediately coming upon an injured Sailor, the master chief stopped to provide some first aid.

Garcia, meanwhile, rushed up a ladder to the main deck and ran into Hull Technician First Class Christopher Regal along the portside passageway. Donning emergency breathing devices, they rushed forward into smoke, with only beams from yellow battle lanterns marking their way. Upon opening the door leading to the mess deck, the two shipmates were startled to see no deck left on the port side. Other Sailors from a damage control team arrived, and Regal organized them to establish smoke and fire boundaries to isolate the crippled area. Garcia moved through the mess line, passing Sailors tending to injured shipmates. He helped extract a chief petty officer who had been knocked down a vestibule, and then comforted a female seaman, whose leg was pinned to the deck by a large piece of kitchen machinery, while other Sailors worked with metal cutters to free her.

Regal noticed that the ship began to list to port as water poured into the engineering spaces. Then from the Chiefs' Mess he heard, "There are chiefs in here—get us out!" The explosion had sheared the deck from the galley area, pushing it forward into the Chiefs' Mess and crushing the door to the space. The Repair 2 damage control team chopped a hole in a non-metal bulkhead to gain initial access to the space while another team worked to pry the door open, which they did some minutes later. With access gained, a team of Sailors pulled out the injured enlisted khaki.

Had it not been for the MWR meeting, Parlier may have been one of the trapped chiefs. Instead he was now working with Tayinikia "Baby Doc" Campbell, a recently minted third-class hospital corpsman treating patients back aft. Other crewmembers performed first aid, busted open locked medical supply cabinets, and ripped doors off hinges to serve as additional stretchers.

The blast knocked out the destroyer's communications suite. Fortunately, the assistant defense attaché who had greeted *Cole* from the pier when she arrived had come back to the ship aboard one of the initial Yemeni boats that had come to evacuate wounded, and he had brought his mobile phone. Commander Lippold borrowed it to make a call.[2]

Back in Bahrain, Capt. John "Greg" Steele was presiding over a farewell luncheon for his departing assistant security officer at the recently renovated "Oasis." A veteran helicopter pilot, Steele had relieved Marcia Fulham as commanding officer of Administrative Support Unit–Southwest Asia the previous year, just before the Navy renamed the installation Naval Support Activity (NSA) Bahrain. Steele's cell phone chimed. Flicking it open he heard the voice of Marine Col. Gary Supnick, the NAVCENT force protection chief: "Greg, we've had an event."

Excusing himself, Steele briskly walked from the dining facility over to the Fifth Fleet/NAVCENT Command Center. Entering the admiral's office, he saw the staff gathered around Admiral Moore, who had been apprised of the situation in Yemen and was calmly ticking off what needed to happen. "He knew what to do," recounted Steele, "using true classic leadership style, everyone there left knowing what they needed to accomplish. . . . It was a tragic trigger but the reaction was textbook." The destroyer *Donald Cook* (DDG 75), and the frigate *Hawes* (FFG 53), which had already cleared the Strait of Hormuz en route to the Suez Canal, were ordered to Aden at best speed. Both ships had been operating in the Gulf. *Hawes,* an *Oliver Hazard Perry*–class frigate, had been conducting communications, air defense, antisubmarine, and replenishment exercises with her sister ship, the BANS *Sabha.* Besides getting additional medical support and emergency repair equipment down to Aden, additional security forces were needed to protect the vulnerable ship and the many individuals who would be flown in to help the crew and begin to investigate the terrorist act.

Unfortunately, the Marine Fleet Anti-terrorism Security Team (FAST) platoon assigned to Moore, with its mission of responding to just such contingencies, was in Kuwait on a training exercise. Steele offered a platoon of Marines from his security force to fill the void. With the offer accepted, Steele left the Command Center and hit the speed-dial button on his cell phone for his senior Marine officer. "Meet me in my office in five."

Within hours, a dozen Marines had saddled up and crammed aboard a P-3 Orion maritime patrol aircraft at Bahrain International Airport, along with medical personnel and supplies, the DESRON 50 commander who would take charge as the initial on-scene commander, as well as an officer assigned to conduct the prescribed Judge Advocate General Manual (JAGMAN) investigation.[3]

As the plane flew south over the Arabian peninsula, the new CENTCOM commander, Army Gen. Tommy Franks, had formed a crisis action response team and was monitoring the situation from Tampa. Rear Adm. Mark Fitzgerald, as Moore's stateside deputy, spoke with his boss in Bahrain throughout the day and appraised and assisted Franks as the situation quickly grabbed national and international attention. One offer, quickly accepted, came from France. Within hours, a French medical evacuation aircraft was airborne, crossing the Red Sea from its base in Djibouti.[4]

The arrival of the French plane would prove fortunate. In the immediate aftermath of the explosion, Master Chief Parlier and "Baby Doc" Campbell triaged wounded Sailors on the fantail while Chief Hospital Corpsman Clifford Moser did the same work in the area amidships. Seeing the extent of the burns, broken bones, and internal injuries, the Cole's medical team knew that many would not survive in the 100-plus-degree heat and needed to be evacuated to emergency facilities ashore. Uninjured Cole Sailors lowered their injured shipmates down on to the concrete fueling platform, first using ropes and a ladder, and then down on the ship's steel accommodation ladder, which was put over the starboard side after a Herculean effort to move it from the port side.

The assistant defense attaché coordinated a flotilla of small boats that made themselves available for the evacuation effort. Starting with the more critically injured crewmembers, these boats carried the wounded to waiting ambulances ashore. About forty uninjured Sailors served as escorts to watch over their shipmates being treated at the local hospital. Eventually, some of the more severely injured Sailors were taken to a French aircraft that arrived that evening. They were flown to a military hospital in Djibouti where French doctors performed some timely surgery.

Within ninety minutes Parlier and Moser had gotten most of the critically injured off the ship. While they were concentrating on saving lives, others focused on saving the ship. Petty Officers Garcia, Regal, and other crewmembers climbed down into some of the auxiliary engineering spaces to find ruptured pipes and progressive flooding, with fuel and other flammable liquids presenting a potential hazard. The men applied some temporary patches, set up dewatering equipment, and set up flooding boundaries. Elsewhere, other crewmembers performing damage control work battled a noxious stench. The outside sun beat down on the ship's hull, and the air inside reeked of the smell of explosives and rotted food. Electricians worked to isolate damaged power lines and to string up cables to carry electricity that would be produced by an emergency generator.

As the sun set on that tragic day, Commander Lippold called the crew members to the fantail to praise them for their fine efforts to save the ship and their shipmates' lives. That night, the crew took turns sleeping on deck, watching the flooding barriers, and standing guard at posts to prevent a fol-low-on attack. Admiral Moore arrived the next morning with Ambassador Barbara K. Bodine, the U.S. ambassador to Yemen, to look over the scene. Escorted by Commander Lippold, the admiral could see recognizable human remains embedded in the overheads, pinned in place by a labyrinth of pipes and ripped metal.[5]

As Moore assessed the situation, *Donald Cook* and *Hawes* arrived. Once the two warships received diplomatic clearance, they entered the harbor and anchored near the stricken ship. Both ships immediately began send-ing rescue and assist teams and supplies to help keep *Cole* afloat. Besides assisting with security and damage control watches, the two ships provided a haven to *Cole* crewmembers in need of showers, meals, and sleep.[6]

Back in Tampa, Admiral Fitzgerald received a call from Moore, who saw the need for his deputy to come over to head up "Joint Task Force Determined Response" to look after the crews' well-being, facilitate the immediate inves-tigation, and oversee the eventual removal of the ship from Aden. Within two hours, Fitzgerald was on a plane heading to Bahrain. Arriving at Manama on Saturday evening, Fitzgerald spent an hour with Moore and other staff-ers getting briefed before catching a P-3 down to Aden.[7]

At Fifth Fleet Headquarters, Fitzgerald learned that several floors of Aden's largest hotel were being filled with Americans, including an inter-agency team that had arrived from Washington to investigate the terror-ist act and representatives from the U.S. Embassy in the capital city of Sanaa on hand to assist with logistics. Outside of the modern hotel, NSA Bahrain's Marines teamed with Yemeni forces to protect this potential ter-rorist target.

Security at the hotel was not the only area of concern. As Moore briefed Fitzgerald in Bahrain, Auxiliary Machinery Room Number Two inside *Cole* began to reflood, and then Gas Turbine Generator Number Three tripped offline. The hundreds of added gallons added pressure on the seal surround-ing the starboard shaft. Damaged by the blast, the seal had been reinforced by a series of wooden wedges and okum. The leak rate at the seal increased, causing flood water to begin rising in the Main Engineroom Number Two (MER 2). Commander Lippold recalled: "When the leak rate increased, we were able to keep up with it using the main drainage system, but when the generator quit, we had no way of getting water out of MER 2."

Exhausted *Cole* Sailors scurried down into darkness and waded through rising water in the hope of stopping the inflow and dewatering the space. Because of the amount of pressure needed to get the water out of the deep interior space and over the side, the dewatering effort made little headway.

Thinking through the problem and taking some risk, *Cole* Sailors cut two four-inch holes out of the side just above the waterline. One hole served as an outlet for exhaust from the portable pump and the other for the discharge water. While using the internal-combustion pump in a space that contained spilled fuel was a risk, the flooding posed an even greater danger.

By the time Admiral Fitzgerald arrived early on Sunday morning, the moment of greatest peril had passed. Late that evening *Cole* electricians got the ship's backup generator to kick back in and power was restored. When Fitzgerald first stepped on board, observing the obvious exhaustion and beard growth among the men, he thought they looked as if they had been fighting a war.

As for removing *Cole* from Yemen, the Navy was fortunate that the Norwegian heavy lift-ship *Blue Marlin* was available at Dubai in the United Arab Emirates. Designed to move damaged oil rigs, the *Blue Marlin* featured a flat main deck of 584 feet, enough room to accommodate the damaged 505-foot-long destroyer on welded blocks. To accommodate *Cole*'s sonar dome, Navy engineers determined that the ship would need to be placed at an angle to allow the dome to hang over the side. With the contract signed, workers began modifying the deck in preparation for her unique cargo. With two weeks of work to prepare the deck and a few days to travel to Aden, the crew of the *Cole* would have to sit tight until late October.[8]

For additional support, Moore ordered an Amphibious Ready Group and a salvage rescue ship to the scene. By the following Thursday, Fitzgerald found he had eight ships under his immediate command. To lessen the vulnerable footprint ashore, Moore's deputy checked many of the investigators and support staff out of the hotel and onto one of the amphibious ships. Among those arriving from the States was a team from the Norfolk Naval Shipyard that had the unenviable task of cutting metal away to gain access to the fallen Sailors. As the body of each *Cole* Sailor was recovered, the crew held a brief ceremony in which they would assemble topside as they came to attention and honors were rendered.

Recovery teams eventually recovered the remains of sixteen crewmembers (one Sailor succumbed to his injuries after he had been evacuated off the ship), and Fitzgerald could tell that the effect of seeing former shipmates going over the side in body bags was taking an emotional toll. After Fitzgerald relayed his observations to Moore, the Fifth Fleet commander flew down and gathered the crew from an all-hands talk. "He gave the most incredible speech that I had been a witness to," recalled Fitzgerald. Moore spoke about his past and the war effort in Vietnam that led to his decision to turn in his wings. However, his commander challenged him, asking if he really wanted to give up on his country. He didn't, and he exhorted the crew not to give up on their country, because their survival and recovery of the ship would be seen in the long term as a victory.

Blue Marlin arrived off Yemen around 27 October. The USNS *Catawba* towed the stricken destroyer from Aden on 29 October, and she was raised up on *Blue Marlin* on 30 October. The *Cole*'s crew transferred to USS *Tarawa* late on 30 October to begin their journey home, where they would arrive to a hero's welcome on 5 November.

In the British *Naval Review,* retired Royal Navy Admiral Richard Hill observed that "while the terrorist attacks in the USA on 11 September 2001 changed perceptions all over the world, they were much more profoundly changed in the USA than anywhere else."[9] For the U.S. Navy, the change in perceptions began on 12 October 2000. In the wake of an inquiry into the terrorist attack on *Cole*, the CNO, Adm. Vernon Clark, stated, "We are in the midst of a sea change. . . . We must now make a monumental leap to the attention we pay to this life and death issue."[10]

CHAPTER ELEVEN

Naval Support Activity Bahrain

I n the days following the terrorist attack on *Cole,* the Bahraini–U.S.
Navy relationship once again demonstrated its value—Bahrain served
as an important way station for people en route to and from Yemen. The
Bahrainis cooperated at all levels to ease flight restrictions and offer additional security. For the Sailors stationed in Bahrain, the *Cole* attack was one
in a series of events that would have a strong impact on their daily lives.

Not all of the events made national headlines. For example, in late
January 1999, Admiral Moore headed a group of hundreds of Sailors and
civilians to bid farewell to Hamza A. M. Kaedi. For most of the attendees at
the ceremony, "Mr. Hamza" represented their first memory of their adven-
ture in Bahrain. Debra Stevens recounted a time in the early 1990s when
a planned visit to Bahrain to visit her husband had been blocked by stateside bureaucrats. Calling Kaedi she was told not to worry—that he would be
there to greet her at the airport. Upon her arrival at Bahrain International
Airport: "Mr. Hamza plucked me out of the crowd, whisked me through customs and immigration, put me in a taxi, and sent me on my merry way!"[1]
Expressing his thanks to all those who came to honor him, Kaedi said, "I
will always have the memory of those I've met here and worked with . . .
and the American flag will always fly in my heart."[2]

Six months later, as recounted earlier, Capt. John G. Steele relieved Capt.
Marcia Fulham as commanding officer of the facility that was in the process
of being renamed Naval Support Activity Bahrain.[3] The naval aviator had
served as an executive assistant in the Pentagon to the former NAVCENT
commander Vice Adm. John Scott Redd and, when Steele informed his ex-
boss that he had orders to Bahrain, the admiral responded, "If you don't
take them, I will."[4]

Along with the name, the physical nature of the facility was changing
as hundreds of construction workers fashioned concrete forms and poured
foundations for construction projects costing more than $400 million in
what was considered the largest single site construction program within
the Department of Defense. A month prior to Steele's assuming command,
a ribbon-cutting ceremony was held to open a new chapel and a command training facility. Yards away, progress continued on major military

construction projects funded during 1997 and 1998 and numerous minor construction projects such as windowless reinforced concrete "townhouses" to accommodate several of the forty-two tenant commands. The Army Corps of Engineers oversaw the larger projects with the assistance of the Naval Facilities Engineering Command (NAVFAC) and NSA Bahrain's Public Works Center (PWC). NAVFAC and PWC oversaw minor construction. To coordinate the various construction projects, a naval reserve officer, Cdr. Charles Chandonnet, was recalled to active duty. "If Commander Chandonnet wasn't here we would have to invent him," reflected Captain Steele on the importance of the duties carried out by the commander. Meanwhile, back in Washington, Congress approved funding to construct additional transient quarters, an operational control center, and new housing for the security forces to replace the decades-old Juffair Hilton structure.[5]

The construction and further funding fell in line with a master plan drafted after the Khobar Towers blast to move high-density activities into a triangular area with an adequate standoff zone from the base perimeter. As the region became an even greater focal point for American security interests, the Navy obtained funding for even more structures to support the long-term plan to move offices out of the portion of the property left over from HMS Jufair. So fast-paced was the planning and execution of construction that Captain Steele exclaimed, "The public works office here contracts and executes more construction here in a day than many Navy bases see in a year."[6]

The high tempo of construction not only challenged the public works officer but also the security officer who had to cope with a daily deluge of sometimes more than two thousand third-world-nation workers and dozens of delivery trucks and construction vehicles. With the installation of in excess of one hundred television cameras and other sophisticated sensors providing 360-degree coverage of the perimeter, NSA Bahrain's ability to monitor activity became comparable to the White House. Still, the brunt of the work to keep the facility safe continued to fall on the shoulders of the Gurkhas, Marines, and Sailors who checked the identifications of all incoming visitors, inspected incoming vehicles, stayed alert at their sentry posts, and patrolled the compound in often extreme weather. The security officer at the time, Commander Sheek, was especially impressed with the Gurkhas. "They are the ultimate professionals." How the Marines, Sailors, and Gurkhas fed off of one another's professionalism made the NSA Bahrain security force among the elite in the U.S. military.[7]

Among NSA Bahrain's security headaches remained the Mannai Plaza Hotel—a tempting target with more than five hundred Americans using the facility. To thwart aggressors, a company of Marines, with the cooperation of the Bahrainis, established around the hotel a defensive perimeter that resembled a firebase from the days of Vietnam. A Sailor reporting aboard would be dropped off two hundred yards away, and would then proceed past a maze of large concrete blocks, jersey barriers, and cement-filled oil barrels to an inspection point. There he or she would be told to halt and then slowly come forward to be identified and undergo a search by M-16–toting Marines with other leathernecks observing from a nearby sandbagged guard tower. Once past the Marines, the Sailor still had to walk one hundred yards past checkpoints manned by Bahraini security personnel and other Marines manning sandbag emplacements and bunkers. Looking up at the roof of the nine-story building, the Sailor would see pillboxes. Entering the lobby, the Sailor would be met by additional Bahraini security guards carrying compact machine guns.[8]

With the completion of the transient quarters within the confines of NSA Bahrain in early June 2000, the Mannai Plaza Hotel's days of accommodating Sailors in transit to ships deployed in the Gulf were numbered. Beginning on 1 June newly arriving Sailors were assigned to the new quarters or to hotels in Manama. Through attrition, the population at the Mannai Plaza slowly dwindled. Then on 19 June, the remaining sixty personnel were quietly hustled out. "One day we were there, the next we were gone," reflected Steele about the withdrawal operation. In the war against terrorism, "Mannai Plaza was a victory."[9]

Of course, while the expansion of the facility moved forward, Sailors worked through the sounds of jackhammers and pile drivers to provide support to the fleet. Statistics from 1999 provide some measures regarding the level of activity. In air operations, the Naval Air Logistic Coordination Center at Bahrain International Airport moved some 10,500 military personnel, 1.5 tons of mail, and 3.6 tons of cargo out to the fifteen to twenty ships usually on station in the Gulf. The Surface Operations Department, located on the Mina Sulman pier, coordinated the arrival and departure of forty-six mine countermeasure units, thirty-six frigates, sixteen cruisers, nineteen submarines, eleven patrol craft, twenty-two amphibious ships, and six aircraft carriers. With all of these visiting ships, the Morale Welfare and Recreation office worked hard to schedule events and tours for the two hundred and fifty thousand Sailors and Marines who visited in 1999. To accommodate as many as three thousand men and women stepping ashore, MWR operated ten food service outlets and recreational facilities such as the Inshallah pool. Many of these visitors attended performances featuring top musicians from the United States and from the area.

In addition to the changes occurring at NSA Bahrain, there was a change at the waterfront. Since 1996, the USS *Ardent* (MCM 12) and the USS *Dextrous* (MCM 13) had been rotating crews every six months. After reviewing a 1998 Center for Naval Analyses study that was critical of the rotation program, the CNO, Admiral Johnson, directed Admiral Moore to develop a plan for permanently forward deploying in Bahrain those two minesweepers and the minehunters USS *Cardinal* (MHC 60) and USS *Raven* (MHC 61). In September 1999, Moore received Bahraini permission to homeport U.S. Navy ships in Bahrain again after a gap of twenty-two years. In the spring of 2000, the permanent crews and their families arrived for the two minesweepers. The two minehunters and their crews and families arrived in the fall. Merchants and landlords in Bahrain, seeing the business opportunities that these ships would bring, were ecstatic.[10]

The *Cole* attack sobered everyone. As a well-established location for U.S. Navy ship visits, Bahrain's Mina Sulman pier offered an inviting target to terrorists. As an interim measure, a Coast Guard port security unit was temporarily deployed to Manama. For the long term, the Fifth Fleet Force Protection Board convened, examined the potential threat from several perspectives, and redrafted the security plan. With contingency funds made available, the board recommended that specially designed harbor patrol craft be built locally to augment the in-place security. Kooheji Marine, a reputable Bahraini boat-building firm, began fabrication of the craft on the basis of a handshake and a promise of eventual payment. Within three months the first of several patrol craft entered the harbor's waters.

While Fifth Fleet's Force Protection Board took additional steps to protect Americans in Bahrain, others at higher levels within the Department of Defense moved actions to freeze the transfer to Bahrain of dependents accompanying service personnel reporting aboard. But this seemingly rational edict from above to minimize the American footprint in Bahrain created a scenario with some unfortunate consequences in regard to both turnover and morale.

To the Bahrainis, undergoing a transition to a constitutional monarchy, the Pentagon action overlooked a fifty-plus-year record in which Sailors and dependents lived in a safe environment. Given the low crime rate and other advantages, many Americans enjoyed living in the country, building good relationships with neighbors and shopping in local markets. From the Bahraini perspective, the move may have seemed a vote of non-confidence that would adversely affect their economy.

To the Navy, the switch to allowing Sailors to have only one-year unaccompanied tours as opposed to multi-year accompanied tours would affect readiness adversely because of the continuing turnover and the fact that morale would also suffer. Finally, because strong personal relationships are important when doing business in the Arab world, the shortened tours would hinder efforts to maintain Bahraini and Navy ties.

Finally, as a member of the Bahrain International School Association board, Captain Steele had been projecting the potential impact on the school of newly arriving American dependents expected with the homeported mine-warfare ships, and the board realized that unless the school was expanded, Bahraini and other non-American students could be squeezed out. The board took the initiative to raise capital to expand the school to accommodate the increasing population. The DoD edict threw a monkey wrench into the pro-jected student body population increase. The board reacted by modifying the plan into two phases, with the first phase investing funds to upgrade the existing facility and the second to expand the school in anticipation of the reversal of the DoD edict as Admiral Moore argued up the chain of com-mand for a reconsideration.[11]

The case for resuming accompanied tours suffered a setback in May 2001. Two independent sources agreed with "hair-raising" specificity on the likelihood of a terrorist attack in Bahrain. Reviewing the intelligence at the Fifth Fleet Force Protection Board, Admiral Moore decided to raise the force protection level in the country to "Delta"—an unprecedented step increasing the level of security to respond to an expected attack. Because such a level had previously existed only in theory, the Force Protection Board had to clarify some of the measures. Among the decisions taken was to close the Bahrain International School. Before closing the school and taking other strong measures, Moore and the ambassador called on Crown Prince Shaikh Salman to explain the threat. The crown prince was sup-portive, deploying Bahraini "U" Group Special Forces to the vicinity of the Navy compound. Driving around in black Land Rovers and donning black uniforms and berets, the well-trained and heavily armed "U" Group mem-bers reportedly were recruited from the ranks of retired Pakistani special forces. Additional Bahraini police and coastal patrol craft also moved in to help protect the American facilities.

The school closed, and the Navy community in Bahrain went into a vir-tual lockdown in anticipation of extreme violence. Captain Steele stayed on the base, bunking in his office, and his family moved to a more secure loca-tion in town. As the NSA Bahrain security force peered out over the walls, Moore and Steele walked the perimeter to look for potential vulnerabilities. With additional reinforcements in place, Moore okayed the reopening of the school. "When we reopened the school it was a real gut check to watch your children walk to school," Steele recalled. To eliminate potential car bomb-ers, Steele had ordered restrictions on parking and had moved the students' drop-off point away from the one-story structure.

Instead, the youngsters walked by Marines in full combat gear who were manning machine guns mounted on Humvee vehicles. "You were betting your children's lives that your intel was accurate, and that your presence and security arrangements were such that the bad guys were deterred," reflected Steele. Eventually, other intelligence called into question the valid-ity of the threatening reports. Still, after the brief scare, the NSA Bahrain commander decided to send his family home to Virginia, because he had pending orders to the Pentagon. With his experience in Bahrain, he was ideally suited to take the job on the Navy staff as head of the Navy's physi-cal security program.

To prepare his relief for the turnover, Steele assembled a 145-slide PowerPoint presentation covering all aspects of the job. After a two-week transition period, Steele was relieved on 19 July 2001 and returned to the States to take some well-deserved leave with his family.

Steele reported to his new post in the Pentagon on Thursday, 6 September to begin to check in to his new job. After two days of administra-tive check-in chores inherent in the arrival process, Steele took the weekend off and returned on Monday to undergo a series of briefings that had been arranged by the incumbent, Capt. Marty Erdossey. One area Steele would take charge of was Navy counter-drug operations. On Monday afternoon, six of his counter-drug staffers, who spent most of their time in the new Navy Command Center, called on him to give a pitch on current operations. Steele saw them early the next morning when he entered the Navy Command Center located in the D ring of the recently renovated wedge of the Pentagon facing Arlington Cemetery. Coming into the briefing room, he noted the presence of his new boss, Vice Adm. Timothy Keating, the deputy chief for plans, pol-icy, and operations, and other senior officers who sat in on this daily morn-ing update on world events and the status of the fleet. Whereas Steele had just returned from Bahrain, Keating had been tagged to relieve Moore as NAVCENT/Fifth Fleet and was simply awaiting final orders.

After the briefing, Steele returned to his office and then left the building for a rendezvous with Captain Erdossey at the Naval Criminal Investigative Service office over at the Washington Navy Yard in the southeast part of the District of Columbia to meet more of the people who would soon come under his cognizance. Driving his car from Virginia across the Potomac River on the 14th Street bridge in heavy traffic, the captain listened to National Public Radio news and heard a comment in the course of another report in which the announcer said there were indications that an aircraft may have struck one of the towers of the World Trade Center.

Steele quickly grasped the significance of what had happened. He flipped open his cell phone and dialed Captain Erdossey: "Marty, I think there has been a terrorist attack on the World Trade Center. Could you get down to the MTAC [NCIS Multi-Threat Analysis Center] and check it out?" When Steele arrived, he walked into the MTAC to see the staff staring at TV monitors showing the burning north tower. Suddenly, another passenger plane plowed into the south tower, creating a horrific fireball.

Shortly thereafter, American Airlines Flight 77 plunged into the recently renovated wedge of the Pentagon, destroying the Navy Command Center. "People who had briefed me that previous afternoon were dead—people who were there an hour and a half earlier when I walked out of there were dead. And OPNAV had been rendered deaf, dumb, and blind because they had to evacuate the building." Eventually, the CNO and other key Navy leaders would come over to the Navy Yard to the NCIS headquarters to regain situational awareness of the outside world. Meanwhile Captain Steele and Captain Erdossey took the initiative to issue a message upgrading the threat condition within Naval District Washington to Delta, and elsewhere to Charlie. "We didn't have anybody to tell us what to do."[12]

Throughout the Navy, others were taking initiatives without waiting to be told what to do.[13]

CHAPTER TWELVE

Fifth Fleet Goes to War

T angential to the confrontation with terrorism spurred by the attacks in New York and Washington, the United Nations, the United States, and its coalition partners still had to contend with a belligerent Iraq. In the wake of Operation Desert Fox, the coalition maintained a strategy "to keep low-level pressure and containment on Saddam so that he doesn't get out of his box." American and British aircraft based in Kuwait, Saudi Arabia, and aircraft carriers in the Gulf ensured Iraqi compliance with UN Security Council Resolution 688 by enforcing the no-fly zone over southern Iraq. However, in what amounted to a quasi-war, the Baghdad regime tested the coalition's resolve. In the first two years after Operation Desert Fox, there were between five hundred and six hundred Iraqi provocations including MiG aircraft challenges, surface-to-air missile and anti-air artillery fire, and the placement of anti-ship missiles on the Al Faw peninsula. Coalition force reactions were measured and deliberately unpredictable.[1]

Maintaining at least one carrier on station in the Gulf exposed the United States elsewhere. Moving *Enterprise* back into the Gulf from the Mediterranean in March 1999 made her unavailable for the NATO air war to counter Serbian actions in Kosovo. When USS *Kitty Hawk* (CV 63) relieved the "Big E" a month later, the western Pacific was without a U.S. Navy carrier for the first time in decades. Nor did it help that France had withdrawn from Southern Watch operations after Desert Fox and began to criticize the continuing efforts to enforce the no-fly zones. For example, on 6 April 2000, after a spate of Iraqi violations, British and American aircraft, including those off the USS *John C. Stennis* (CVN 74), launched a series of strikes against Al Kut, Ar Rumaylah, and Basra. French Foreign Ministry spokeswoman Anne-Gazeau-Secret deplored the attacks, exclaiming, "These pointless and deadly bombings are alarming." Responding to French criticism and Iraqi claims of civilian casualties, Admiral Moore countered that the aircraft hit "all military targets, and they were not near any residential areas or any other areas where civilians could possibly be located."[2]

Although Operation Southern Watch was overseen by Joint Task Force–Southwest Asia (JTF-SWA), commanded by an Air Force general based at Prince Sultan Air Base in Saudi Arabia, Fifth Fleet aircraft carriers provided aircraft for a good portion of its missions. Testifying before Congress in early 2000, Admiral Moore stated that the Navy provided 60 percent of the strike aircraft, 100 percent of the electronic combat aircraft, and 100 percent of the U.S. tactical reconnaissance capability when unmanned drones were not deployed in the region. At that time, there were approximately 750 naval air sorties per month. Operation Southern Watch had been under way for a decade, and the coordination between JTF-SWA and Fifth Fleet had become smooth, with an occasional burp when the Navy desired to make a port call for some rest and maintenance while shore-based Air Force squadrons were rotating in and out of the theater.[3]

In the immediate post–Desert Fox era, the CENTCOM commander, General Zinni, established aggressive rules of engagement to inhibit Iraqi movement of military equipment into the southern part of the country. Zinni delegated to the JTF-SWA commander authority to respond to immediate threats. Hardly a week went by without some ordnance being dropped on a radar, gun, or missile site. Occasionally, the cross-Atlantic allies struck back hard. During the early evening hours of 16 February 2001, *Harry S. Truman* (CVN 75) launched a flight of approximately twenty Navy and Marine Corps aircraft to hit anti-aircraft gunnery sites in southern Iraq. The attack represented a jab. The punch came later in the evening when Kuwaiti-based U.S. and Royal Air Force jets joined additional *Truman* planes to go after Iraqi radar and command centers that had been placed above the 33rd Parallel. Armed with the new "Joint Stand Off Weapon" (JSOW), a glide bomb capable of hitting targets some fifty miles from the drop point, many of the attackers struck targets throughout the Baghdad area while avoiding concentrated areas of enemy flak. Fortunately, for the Iraqis, a suspected software problem caused several of the weapons to miss their targets.[4]

Another series of strikes later that year on 10 August, including F/A-18s from *Enterprise*, did succeed in hitting many of the previously spared targets in addition to striking others. At this stage of the ongoing operation, the coalition aviators were dropping ordnance an average of three to four times per month on military targets in response to increasing Iraqi aggression. Ironically, the Iraqis unintentionally were providing the United States and Britain an excellent albeit potentially deadly proving ground to train the dozens of air squadrons that rotated through the theater. Hundreds of aircrews and air controllers became familiar with the hostile skies over Iraq and adept at avoiding threats from the ground.

While the Fifth Fleet contributed aircraft to the ongoing Operation Southern Watch missions, it also oversaw the ongoing Maritime Interdiction Operations (MIO) in support of UN Security Council Resolutions 661, 665,

687, 986, and 1284. The program had three pieces: keeping Iraq from importing weapons of mass destruction or the components to create such devices; monitoring the UN food-for-oil program; and maintaining the embargo on weapons and other banned goods.

This effort involved thousands of sailors from seventeen nations serving aboard dozens of warships. As of the end of February 2000, after a decade of operations, the multinational maritime forces had conducted 28,746 queries, 12,551 boardings, and 695 diversions of suspected smugglers. During 1999 alone, American and allied naval forces made 2,422 queries and 700 boardings, and in nineteen cases they diverted a ship for carrying embargoed goods.[5]

Responding to international criticism that the embargo only denied the Iraqi people food and medicine, the UN food-for-oil program was initiated. Admiral Moore and his staff found it curious that Saddam Hussein did not take full advantage of that program. Instead, rather than looking after the welfare of his people, the Iraqi dictator took advantage of spikes in world oil prices to fill his personal cash coffers through the illegal smuggling of oil. While Hussein's regime smuggled some of the fuel overland by truck, most of it went out to sea. For example, in early 1999 there was little illicit smuggling because oil was fetching only $10 per barrel. But as the year went on, a worldwide oil demand drove prices to more than $30 per barrel. "Concomitantly, we saw a rapid increase in smuggling. By December of 1999, smuggling had reached an all-time high of 400,000 metric tons per month," observed Moore.

To entice the smugglers, the Iraqis offered oil at about $95 per metric ton, well below the market price. Despite paying a tariff fee to the Iranians to allow transit of their territorial waters, the smuggler could still make $50 to $60 per metric ton. With such potential for large profit margins, numerous entrepreneurs jumped into the smuggling game. Iraq assisted the effort by providing experienced former naval officers to serve as pilots. Some smugglers used fairly modern cargo ships, as illustrated by the seizures of the Russian tankers *Volganeft-147* and *Akademik Pustovoyt* in March and April 2000. However, most obtained barely seaworthy vessels to minimize losses in the event of seizure. Besides violating the UN embargo and providing Saddam Hussein funds to maintain his regime, the dilapidated oil carriers presented an environmental danger. For example, in 1998 a suspicious barge sank and spilled thirty thousand barrels of diesel fuel off the United Arab Emirates, causing extensive damage and forcing the closure of several desalination plants.[6]

As implied in the last paragraph, Iran's complicity allowed millions of barrels to escape to the market. Although Iran had not buried the hatchet with Iraq after their eight-year war, Iranian paramilitary organizations allegedly collected "tolls." Admiral Moore brought the problem directly to the attention of the UN Security Council when he traveled to New York on 23 March 2000. Shortly thereafter, Iranian naval forces seized and impounded the *Al-Masru,* a Honduran-registered vessel allegedly carrying illicit oil. For about six weeks, Iran's complicity slacked off.

Occasionally the Iranian navy would drive smugglers (who apparently had not paid any tariffs) out of territorial waters into the arms of the coalition navies. For example, in February 2002, the cruiser *Vella Gulf* (CG 72) radioed an Iranian warship for help after tracking the *Lina* for several days skirting Iranian waters. The Iranian skipper cooperated and forced the suspect vessel clear of the twelve-mile zone. Once in international waters, the *Lina* speeded up to attempt a head-on collision with the American cruiser. The captain of *Vella Gulf,* with its gas turbine engines and reversible-pitch propellers, ordered back full to avoid the oncoming vessel. With the cruiser able to move faster in reverse than the merchantman could go forward, the collision was avoided. The *Vella Gulf* sent over a Visit Boarding Search and Seizure (VBSS) team. Climbing aboard, the armed Sailors climbed to the bridge to find that the structure was heavily armored. Not dissuaded, the Sailors sent for welding torches to cut their way in. Eventually, the plating gave way and the Americans discovered that they had captured a communications ship that had been in business to guide smugglers past the numerous authorities in the Gulf.[7]

Assigned to perform interception operations during the summer of 2000, USS *Hopper* (DDG 70) typified the ongoing effort. To perform its mission, the new Aegis destroyer formed two VBSS teams of eleven members each. Once aboard the suspected merchantman, the boarding officer inspected the ship's registration and paperwork, inquired about the ship's origin, and checked crewmember passports. Meanwhile pairs of search teams verified what was claimed to be below. One boarding officer noted that he was surprised to see that many of the smugglers recorded the loading of the contraband in their deck logs.[8]

A favorite tactic of the VBSS teams was approaching suspected smugglers at night. Electrician's Mate Second Class Lance Howell of USS *Valley Forge* (CG 50) observed, "It's the dark runners that are usually the smugglers, but with NVGs [night-vision goggles] they can't hide from us." As the rigid inflatable boat approached, the boarding officer would order, "Light 'em up!" With light beams bathing the suspected vessel, a member of the VBSS team then yelled in Arabic to announce the boarding. The team then scurried up a rope ladder to begin the inspection.[9]

Loaded down with flak jackets, weapons, radios, and other equipment, Sailors climbing on and off suspected vessels required good physical conditioning and dexterity. As earlier noted, many of these vessels were barely seaworthy. Petty Officer Howell observed, "We've boarded ships that were in such bad shape that water was flowing right past the seal around the shaft, and had to be constantly pumped out."[10] One boarding on 18 November 2001 involving an eight-person VBSS team from the destroyer *Peterson* (DD 969) proved fatal. Finding the merchantman *Samra* low in stormy seas with a list, the *Peterson* dispatched a VBSS team to find some 1,700 tons of Iraqi oil on board. However, during the inspection, the vessel, flying a United Arab Emirates flag, took on water and quickly capsized. *Peterson* was joined by a frigate and a cruiser along with helicopters flying from Bahrain to rescue ten crewmembers from the *Samra* and six American Sailors in fifteen-foot seas. Two Sailors, Vincent Parker of Preston, Mississippi, and Benjamin Johnson, of Rochester, New York, lost their lives.[11]

The MIO effort was multinational, with several nations providing ships to support the inspections. Through such "combined operations," naval commanders were able to learn and exploit the capabilities each navy provided. The Bahraini navy assisted in the effort, escorting suspected smugglers to holding stations and helping with logistics.

Elsewhere in the region, the Fifth Fleet continued to conduct the missions that U.S. Navy ships have always performed. Crown Prince Shaikh Salman noted that the Americans and Bahrainis "were working to maintain a goal of peace and stability so that the world economy doesn't have to suffer setbacks." He added, "It is our duty to protect the oil from the ground to the ships and it is the international community's duty to protect the oil in the international sea lanes."[12] In testimony before Congress, Admiral Moore concurred, stating that the first mission of his command was to keep the Suez Canal, Bab Al-Mandeb, and the Strait of Hormuz chokepoints open. With 43 percent of the world's oil passing through that last chokepoint, it was the one that caused Moore to have the greatest concern. With the continuing presence of a carrier battle group and minesweepers and mine hunters based in Bahrain, Moore felt confident that the Navy could meet any contingency.[13]

Ships and Sailors of the Fifth Fleet also continued to be on call to provide humanitarian assistance when called on. On the Arabian Sea during January 1998, the merchantman *British Harrier* hailed the USS *Gary* (FFG 51) for assistance to treat a burned crewmember. When Hospital Corpsman Chief Clyde Fisher boarded the ship, he discovered that the man had first and third degree burns on his neck, arms, and forehead and had gone into shock.

After initial first aid, Lt. Robert Stanley, the medical officer from USS *Harry W. Hill* (DD 986), arrived and determined that the burns were not life-threatening but needed further medical attention. A short helicopter ride later, the injured seaman was aboard the Gulf-bound USNS *Tippecanoe* (TAO 199) for transfer ashore.[14]

Fourteen months later, the *Gary* again came to the aid of a ship in distress. A small oil tanker was ablaze in the Gulf with the crew trapped on the foc'sle. Hospital Corpsman Patrick Modglin remarked, "We were lucky we got there when we did. We recovered all fourteen crew members without serious injury."[15]

Of course, these operations all fell under the cognizance of Fifth Fleet, based at Naval Support Activity Bahrain. With the departure of Captain Steele, Capt. Lee Holbrook took command of the naval facility. A naval flight officer who flew the EA-6B Prowler, Holbrook had served as the operations officer on the staff of Carrier Group Five, the same staff that had Admiral Moore and his relief Vice Adm. Timothy Keating as alums. He had gained experience operating in the Gulf when the staff embarked on *Independence* and *Kitty Hawk* on successive deployments. Arriving in June 2001, Holbrook had an opportunity to spend three weeks with the man he was to relieve to learn the responsibilities, nuances, and challenges of the job.

Early in his tenure as commanding officer, one of his problems had been resolved when the freeze on dependents was lifted. Admiral Moore and his boss at U.S. Central Command, Gen. Tommy Franks, had prevailed on the secretary of defense to lift the freeze and allow U.S. Central Command to retain authority on this issue for the future. Now plans could go ahead to implement the second phase of the school expansion plan. With this new development, a Bahrain International School Association meeting was scheduled for a September afternoon. Captain Holbrook attended and saw that as the meeting progressed, Tawfeeq Almoyed was looking down at his cell phone, which carried message text of world news. Suddenly a report of a plane flying into the World Trade Center caught Almoyed's eye. He announced this development, and the consensus in the room was that it had to be some wayward small private aircraft. Then the report of the second plane hit came. Captain Holbrook's cell phone rang. He rushed back to his office.

As Americans and Bahrainis in Manama were glued to their television sets in the early evening hours watching the horror of the terrorist attacks play out, Admiral Moore convened an emergency staff meeting to discuss how Fifth Fleet and the Naval Support Activity needed to respond to the breaking news back in the States. "It was classic Vice Admiral Moore,"

Holbrook recounted. With the staff reeling from the shock of the attacks, Moore "took control of the meeting, summed up what we knew and what we didn't know. He quickly took a look at the disposition of naval forces and made some immediate moves and headed forces where they would need to be if Afghanistan became an issue."

With the redirection of homeward-bound *Enterprise* and other Fifth Fleet units, Moore's staff began to discuss the implication of the attacks with regard to local force protection. "Opinions varied quite a bit," recalled Holbrook. Some in the room observed that with Al Qaeda striking at the American homeland, Bahrain might not be high on the terrorism target list. However, before the staff could settle the debate on whether the facility should set condition Charlie or Delta, guidance was received from Washington directing the setting of the latter, more extreme force protection condition.

Since a blueprint for enhanced security had been drawn up earlier in the year because of the terrorist threat, the procedures for going into Condition Delta were well established. Of note, though, the Bahrain International School remained open. Whereas other Department of Defense Schools throughout the world had closed their doors on 12 September, school buses continued to pull up to the Bahrain International School to drop off the youngsters.[16]

Shaikh Hamad quickly condemned the aggression, saying that such acts "violated the spirit of Islam." The Bahraini leader pledged cooperation with the American government and solidarity with the American people. In the days after the attacks in New York and Washington, Bahraini citizens stood in line outside of the American Embassy to sign a condolence book and lay wreaths and flowers. Captain Holbrook recalled, "I received stacks of mail from various folks—friends, businesses—across the board from out in town expressing condolences." Approximately five hundred people attended a memorial service held at the Gulf International Convention and Exhibition Center. Bahraini artist Abbas Al Mousawi was moved by the tragedy to produce an enormous memorial work on canvas featuring "life-size human caricatures rising in a circular motion from piles of flaming debris."[17]

The quick condemnation by the Bahraini government and the sympathy expressed by many Bahrainis contrasted with the many negative images in the area that Americans were seeing of Arabs gleefully celebrating despicable acts that claimed some three thousand lives. Media coverage of such celebratory acts gave the impression that most in the region supported the fundamentalist extremists desiring to take it back to the eleventh century. Crown Prince Shaikh Salman, during an October visit to the United States, worked hard to dispel that notion, appearing on *Larry King Live* and other programs to present an alternative view on Arab perceptions.

As the United States worked with the United Nations and its allies to build a coalition against terrorism, the naval forces at Admiral Moore's disposal rapidly increased. The aircraft carrier *Carl Vinson* (CVN 70) was on station in the region on 11 September, having just relieved *Enterprise*. As noted, the Big "E" and her escorts reversed course and soon rejoined *Carl Vinson* in the northern Arabian Sea. Meanwhile in Japan, Sailors worked around the clock to ready *Kitty Hawk* (CV 63) for deployment and to embark Army helicopters and special operations forces.

Navy carriers and other warships assigned to conduct the strike missions formed Task Force 50, the Fifth Fleet's battle force component in the northern Arabian Sea. This force was commanded by a rear admiral who was embarked on a carrier and who reported to Admiral Moore. With satellite communications, Moore could use video-teleconferencing to conduct dialogues with his Task Force commanders on one hand and with General Franks and CENTCOM staffers on the other.

On 20 September, President Bush addressed Congress, the nation, and the world and demanded that the Taliban leaders in Afghanistan surrender Al Qaeda leaders, close terrorist training facilities, submit to inspections, and release foreigners who were being unjustly held captive. As the president spoke, the Navy was in the process of recalling thousands of reservists to active duty, including those who supported Admiral Moore's Fifth Fleet command, and the some fifty tenant commands. Naval Support Activity Bahrain itself benefited from receiving ten reserve units that provided more than 250 Sailors to furnish additional security, clerical, and logistical support. "We saw a huge upswing in reserve arrivals in Bahrain," recalled Holbrook.

Looking back after completing his tour in 2003, Captain Holbrook reflected, "The reserves were a huge, huge success story in Bahrain. We could not have survived the last two years without our reserves." Overall, the Navy population at Bahrain rose from approximately 2,300 to well over 3,000 Sailors. To find living accommodations for this influx, Chief Warrant Officer Margo Bower worked with local landlords to contract for apartments and homes in town. Eventually, she found shelter for some 900 reservists and arranged for their transportation needs.

With the Taliban refusing to meet the American demands, the president ordered the commencement of Operation Enduring Freedom on 7 October. F-14 Tomcats and F/A-18 Hornets roared off the flight decks of *Enterprise* and *Carl Vinson* laden with ordnance and full fuel tanks for flights that equated to roundtrips from Washington, D.C., to St. Louis. EA-6B Prowlers flew along to suppress enemy air defenses, and a fleet of Air Force tanker aircraft flew in the skies en route to provide the fuel needed for the Navy planes to make the return flight. Flights as long as ten hours tested the endurance of the men and women in the cockpits. Also in the skies over Afghanistan were P-3C Orion maritime patrol planes. Built to counter Soviet submarines, and powered by four turboprop engines, these venerable aircraft proved to be excellent command and communication platforms that provided its sensors to detect enemy positions. If a target of opportunity appeared, the P-3 carried its own ordnance to drop. In addition to Navy jets and P-3C Orion patrol aircraft, Air Force B-1 and B-52 bombers from Diego Garcia, B-2 bombers from Missouri, and AC-130 gunships as well as F-15E and F-16C/D fighters from other bases in the region supported the onslaught against the enemy. The manned sorties were augmented by unmanned drones—some armed, and by cruise missile strikes from American and British surface ships and submarines stationed in the northern Arabian Sea.[18]

Late on 17 October, aircraft flying off *Theodore Roosevelt* (CVN 71) joined the air campaign. Because *Theodore Roosevelt* was on the scene, the Big E could return home from her extended deployment. As "Big Stick" crewmembers readied her attack aircraft for maiden nighttime strikes against the enemy, an American flag recovered from the ruins of the World Trade Center flapped in the breeze on the mast. With the cat shot of the first F/A-18 Hornet, the flag was hauled down and replaced by another flag, the one hung by New York City firefighters at Ground Zero in the days following the attack.

The American air campaign initially focused on the enemy's integrated air defenses, command-and-control facilities, and the remnants of the Afghan air force, and then on military logistics facilities, transportation infrastructure, and armored vehicles. In November, the American pilots, guided by controllers in the air and on the ground, concentrated on Taliban troop emplacements guarding Kabul and other Afghan cities. The attacks demoralized the enemy defenders. With special operations forces joining their ranks, the Northern Alliance commanders finally took the offensive in November and moved forward with surprising swiftness. In December Kabul fell, and U.S. Marines were on the ground in southern Afghanistan.[19]

What made the air campaign unique was that approximately 80 percent of the nearly four thousand sorties flown from 7 October to 16 December had targets assigned as the pilots were inbound. Because more than 90 percent of the ordnance was precision-guided and had a high accuracy rate, one aircraft could eliminate several targets, whereas in the past, it took several aircraft to eliminate one target. By the end of the year the Navy and

Marine pilots based on board Task Force 50 carriers had flown 77 percent of the tactical and strike sorties and could justly claim credit for contributing in a major way to success on the ground.[20]

Back in Bahrain, Captain Holbrook had some trepidation about the local reaction to the air campaign. "I was the most tense on the night we were going to commence the bombing." To prepare for the impending outbreak of American air action over Afghanistan, the Force Protection Board designed ways to increase the robustness of the Naval Support Activity's defenses without tipping off outsiders that combat was imminent. Once the air campaign began, Captain Holbrook shut down the school, and the Bahrain International School closed its doors for five days as a precautionary measure. Looking out from the facility, Holbrook noted that the Bahrainis had also set up additional patrols in the vicinity of the installation.[21]

As the air campaign against the Taliban was helping to turn the tide on the ground, there was a concern that many of the Taliban/Al Qaeda leaders and their followers would escape from central Asia to renew their jihad elsewhere against civilized societies. To prevent this from happening, an effort dubbed Leadership Interception Operations (LIO) was begun in November as Taliban resistance started to collapse under the air-ground campaign. While aircraft were flying night and day from Task Force 50 carriers to support the war on the ground, other warships began to seek out suspicious vessels off the Pakistani and Iranian coastlines.

Twelve countries including Bahrain provided naval forces to augment the Americans. They performed exceedingly well in forming an impromptu combined fleet to assist in leadership interdiction. Because many of these countries had operated with the United States in exercises and in supporting sanctions against Iraq, there was a strong comfort level among the Sailors from the various countries.

Although there were similarities to the ongoing operations in the Gulf, this mission differed in that the targeted cargo was human. Also, the Task Force 50 commander also had to contend with a much larger search area—some eighty thousand square miles covering the northern Arabian Sea over to the Horn of Africa. In addition, each coalition navy operated under different national rules of engagement that had to be considered when assigning ships to perform operations.

Both the Canadians and the Italians took command of sectors in the northern Arabian Sea and helped sort through the hundreds of vessels operating locally and those passing through the region. The Italians, with a strong background in such operations in the Adriatic during the 1990s, were particularly adept at meeting the challenge.[22]

By the time Rear Adm. Mark P. Fitzgerald embarked on *Theodore Roosevelt* and took over as Task Force 50 commander in mid-December, the number of coalition warships involved had topped one hundred. Besides the American flattops, the British, French, and Italians provided carriers and combat aircraft. With each navy assigning liaison officers to Fitzgerald's flagship, the admiral recalled looking at the wardroom and seeing "every different uniform under the sun."

During Fitzgerald's tenure, which lasted into early 2002, there were several take-downs of suspected Al Qaeda ships. What he found particularly challenging was that the smuggling of human cargo in the region had been going on for centuries. "Up in the Straits of Hormuz there was all kinds of human smuggling going on with Pakistanis coming through Iran and across the straits to Oman. You would intercept just dozens of these small boats just packed with people and you had to figure if they were Al Qaeda or just people coming over to try and get jobs." From Oman, Task Force 50 had to contend with fast speedboats that were moving illegal goods clandestinely into Iran.

Both the air war and the leadership interception operations were demanding of the Sailors who made up the multinational armada in the northern Arabian Sea. For example, after her departure from Norfolk, the *Theodore Roosevelt* spent 159 days—more than five months straight—at sea. Keeping Sailors at sea, denying them the opportunity to mingle with the locals and spend dollars on the local economy, yielded a small victory to the terrorists. Yet there was apprehension about conducting port visits in the region and sending thousands of Sailors on liberty ashore in the middle of a war on terrorism. Thus when Admiral Moore asked for and received Bahraini permission to have the *Theodore Roosevelt* make a port call at Bahrain in February 2002, it was understood that some risk was involved.

"There was some trepidation," recalled Admiral Fitzgerald. "There was no animosity on the streets . . . the crew was allowed to go out into town and there were no incidents, the people were just incredibly friendly."[23]

Unfortunately, the warm feelings felt by Bahraini citizens toward American Sailors did not translate into positive attitudes about policies emanating from Washington on the Palestinian-Israeli conflict. Part of the perceived problem was with the American chief executive. As a member of his own party noted, President Bush "is more committed to Israel as a Jewish state than any other president."[24]

In contrast, the Bahrainis strongly supported the Palestinian cause. In a survey of 15,861 people in March 2002, 97 percent argued that the struggle needed to continue, 95 percent wanted Arab leaders to break all ties with Israel, and 96 percent rejected American mediation of the conflict. While Yasser Arafat's headquarters were under siege in Ramallah and the Israeli army was sweeping into cities on the West Bank, Bahrainis marched in the streets in protest, some carrying anti-American as well as anti-Israeli banners.

In the midst of the increased tension over the Israeli-Palestinian situation, the Bahrain Model United Nations Assembly, an Adliya Rotary Club event involving students from across the island, gathered at the Bahrain International Exhibition Center in Manama on 3 April for the opening festivities. During the opening ceremony, a student requested a moment of silence to remember the victims of Israeli aggression, and all stood, including Ambassador Ronald Neumann, who had been invited as the guest of honor, partly in recognition of the U.S. Embassy's contribution of $5,000 to support the event. When all sat, Neumann remained standing and asked for a moment of silence for those on all sides who had been victims of violence. Neumann later reflected: "I believe that mourning for the innocent lives being lost on both sides is the least we owe to our common humanity." The others in attendance strongly disagreed, and he was ruled out of order and asked to sit. Furthermore, the Rotary Club refused to accept the American contribution. "Taking the money would have been like saying to the whole country that what he did was right and that we support the Israelis," stated Redha Faraj, the club president.

Unfortunately, local news accounts of the incident made it seem that Neumann wanted to honor only Israeli dead, which served to inflame passions all over Bahrain. Calls were made to boycott American products. During a candlelight sit-in the following evening, the Al Wefaq National Islam Society issued a communiqué urging Arab nations to recall American ambassadors who "showed scant respect for the feelings of Arab people"—a jab directed at Neumann.

On Friday, 5 April, two days after the Model UN incident, clerics led some two to three thousand protestors to the U.S. Embassy for a peaceful demonstration. The clerics withdrew after some youths began to rampage and hurl stones at the Chancery building. About twenty managed to scale the walls to smash and burn some embassy vehicles. Marines guarding the embassy launched tear gas canisters, and Bahraini security forces also helped push back the protesters. Bahraini hospitals treated injured protesters, including one young man with a critical injury at the Sulmaniya Medical Complex.

With the Saturday holy day, the embassy received a reprieve. During sermons throughout Bahrain, clerics condemned Israel and the American

government's support for the Jewish state, but also urged peaceful protests. Meanwhile, King Hamad ordered an investigation into the riots that
had broken out at the embassy and called on demonstration organizers to
restrain protesters from causing property damage.[25]

On Sunday, the protester with the critical injury died. His funeral, held
on the outskirts of a Shi'ite village just to the north of Manama, attracted
thousands of mourners chanting "No American Base in Islamic Bahrain"
and demanding that the government expel Ambassador Neumann. Mansoor
al-Jamri, a former Bahraini exile who had come home under the government's amnesty program, conceded, "Maybe the ambassador thought what
he was doing was fair, but to Muslim people around the world who feel the
Americans value them at less than zero, this sparked everything."[26]

Although there were calls for the removal of the American naval presence, the rhetoric did not carry over into actual protests at the Naval Support
Activity complex. With Captain Holbrook away on leave, his executive officer, Cdr. Scott Simmons, oversaw the security arrangements and warned
those assigned there to stay clear of the protests.[27]

During the following week, protests continued at Bahrain University, at
the U.S. Embassy, and at other sites on the island. On 11 April King Hamad
called President Bush, urging him to pressure Israel to withdraw from West
Bank villages. Subsequent Israeli withdrawals quelled the ferocity of the
Bahraini demonstrations.

The protests in Bahrain, as well as other demonstrations in capitals
throughout the Arab world, did not bode well for a United States focusing
on combating international terrorism and an increasingly belligerent Iraq.
In the wake of the February protests, the Bush administration sought to
make amends in the region, building on common objectives.

While challenging U.S. policy regarding Israel and Palestine, the
Bahrainis maintained their support for America's war against terrorism. Speaking at an Arab forum earlier in the year, Crown Prince Shaikh
Salman had stated, "Just as surely as we want the U.S. to take some degree
of responsibility for the Israeli attacks on the Palestinians, we should look
to ourselves for September 11. We must address what is wrong in our societies that caused this misinterpretation of Islam."[28]

While the Northern Alliance and allied forces were completing operations against remaining Taliban and Al Qaeda strongholds in Afghanistan,
Washington turned its attention toward Iraq. The Iraqis had received a slight
reprieve in the fall of 2001 and the winter of 2002 as the air campaign over
central Asia drew aircraft away from Iraq. However, with the situation in
Afghanistan stabilized, coalition air forces resumed their aggressive posture

on 20 May 2002 and hit Iraqi military targets three more times before the close of the month. By the end of the year, coalition aircraft had conducted more than fifty strikes in response to Iraqi non-compliance with UN Security Council Resolution 688. There was continuing pressure to urge nations in the region to support the UN resolutions fully, accompanied by a redoubling of the boarding effort that helped to slowly turn off the oil spigot. During 2002, there were 3,016 boardings, more than twice the number from the previous year.[29]

There was also an escalation in the rhetoric. Visiting Bahrain on 11 June 2002, Secretary of Defense Donald H. Rumsfeld addressed some of the 4,225 Sailors and Marines present at the Naval Support Activity Complex. Standing on a platform outside the Desert Dome in the early evening, Rumsfeld emphasized, "If you want to know who is a world-class liar, it's Saddam Hussein," in the wake of recent Iraqi denials about possessing weapons of mass destruction. To many Sailors and Marines, Rumsfeld held "rock-star" status. Ignoring plans to have him quickly exit from the stage, the defense secretary plunged into the crowd to shake hands and chat with the young men and women posted in Bahrain. Besides meeting with service personnel, the American defense secretary met with Bahrain's king and crown prince to discuss the war on terrorism and mutual concerns about Iraq.[30]

Through its public statements, the American administration signaled its intent to bring the confrontation with Iraq to a conclusion, unilaterally if necessary. However, although there was no love for the Baghdad regime in Manama, the prospect of a major American-led military operation against an Arab nation was clearly uninviting. In August, a "National Committee for Supporting Iraqi People" gathered representatives from some thirty-five societies and institutions with the goal of collecting food and medicine for the citizens of Iraq. So, in the aftermath of a tumultuous spring, given the sentiments supporting the Iraqi people within the population, and in view of the forthcoming October legislative elections, the government was loath to embrace Washington's aggressive tact publicly. Public statements from Bahraini officials as well as from other world leaders urged America to work through the United Nations for a peaceful solution.

Heeding the international sentiment and the advice of Secretary of State Colin Powell, President Bush traveled to New York on 12 September to address a special session of the United Nations and call for multilateral action. Four days later, the Baghdad regime announced it would allow the return of weapons inspectors. Bahraini leaders still urged caution. On 21 September, Prime Minister Shaikh Khalifa bin Salman al Khalifa argued that an attack against Iraq "would harm the whole region."[31]

Throughout October, the UN Security Council debated on how to resolve the issues pertaining to Iraq. Adding to the urgency of the debate was a vote on 11 October by Congress authorizing President Bush to use military force against Saddam Hussein's regime. On 8 November, the Security Council adopted Resolution 1441, deploring Iraq's record of non-compliance with previous resolutions and affording Baghdad one more opportunity to comply. Specifically, Iraq was given thirty days to produce a "currently accurate, full, and complete declaration of all aspects of its programmes to develop chemical, biological, and nuclear weapons, ballistic missiles, and other delivery systems." The resolution also ordered that there be complete access for the UN Monitoring, Verification, and Inspection Commission (UNMOVIC) to sites throughout Iraq and that interviews of knowledgeable Iraqis be allowed to occur without government observers, outside the country if necessary.[32]

Despite protestations from Iraqi officials, the Baghdad regime agreed to the binding resolution. On 7 December, the Iraqi government provided UNMOVIC and the International Atomic Agency Commission a document of approximately twelve thousand pages in an attempt to fulfill its obligations under Resolution 1441. Meanwhile, UNMOVIC inspection teams under Executive Chairman Hans Blix fanned out around Iraq to verify Iraqi's claims that they were in compliance.

As the world entered 2003, tensions mounted in the region and in Bahrain. An unfortunate predawn event on the first day of the New Year illustrated the potential volatility. In recent years, there had been incidents of teenage youths committing acts of vandalism during New Year's festivities, so Captain Holbrook warned his people to be cautious. However, the 2003 misbehavior well exceeded that of past years as young male revelers turned into rioters on Exhibition Avenue and went on a rampage smashing hotel and shop windows and burning more than one hundred vehicles. Of note, many of the businesses that were attacked catered to Saudi clientele and many of the sedans burned had Saudi tags. Captain Holbrook looked out from his house and saw that the six-lane highway leading downtown from the Al Fetah Grand Mosque was gridlocked. Although the New Year's riots had no overt political overtones, two days later hundreds of demonstrators met near the Al Fetah Grand Mosque to call for the end of U.S. threats against Iraq.[33]

On 13 January, Shura Council members sent King Hamad a letter reasserting the concern that war would be catastrophic for the region and urging solidarity among Arabs in standing up for Iraq. A week later, in the wake of UNMOVIC discoveries of empty chemical warheads in Iraq, King

Hamad relayed the Shura Council's concerns to visiting American Assistant Secretary of State William Burns, emphasizing that Bahrain wanted to see regional security and stability maintained with a peaceful solution to the Iraqi situation. The king, however, emphasized his support for the international effort to disarm Iraq.

In the meantime, the buildup of American and allied forces in the region caused the Bahraini government to take precautionary measures. Government agencies conducted emergency training for school administrators, set up a community warden scheme, established a national command center, and trained women police officers to decontaminate women affected by any bio-chem attacks.

In Iraq, except for the empty chemical warheads, the UNMOVIC inspectors were not finding any "smoking guns." The Americans and British were becoming increasingly frustrated by what appeared to be an Iraqi shell game. In his 28 January State of the Union address, the president emphasized that the 108 UN inspectors "were not sent to conduct a scavenger hunt for hidden materials across a country the size of California." Earlier that day, in Bahrain more than one hundred protesters met outside the UN House at Hoora to shout anti-Israeli and anti-American slogans for an hour and then release balloons and white doves. Captain Holbrook recounted, "What we saw was on Friday, sometimes on other nights, but typically Friday after prayers there were large but peaceful processions demonstrating in support of the people of Iraq. Again, you found out in town a large concern of what was going to happen to innocent civilians."[34]

Three days after the State of the Union address, the president met with British prime minister Tony Blair. Speaking at a joint press conference, the two leaders underlined the dangers that Saddam Hussein posed to the world and stated that if he did not comply with Resolution 1441, action would be taken within "a matter of weeks, not months." Responding to a question about the need for a second resolution, Bush said he would welcome such if it reinforced the intent to disarm Iraq but he reemphasized that Resolution 1441 provided the authority to act if Iraq did not comply.[35]

On 3 February King Hamad met with President Bush in Washington to discuss the Iraqi situation and other regional issues. Landing at Andrews Air Force Base, the king urged Saddam Hussein to extend full cooperation to UNMOVIC to avoid war, again stressing that such a war "will only create danger and instability and have a negative impact on the nation's economy." In his meeting with President Bush, King Hamad urged him to go back to the United Nations to seek peace on all fronts. On the following day, the king, along with Bahrain's deputy prime minister, minister of state for foreign affairs, and the chief of staff of the armed forces, had a lunchtime meeting with Secretary of Defense Rumsfeld to discuss regional security issues. Speaking with reporters afterward, King Hamad referred to the military cooperation between Bahrain and the United States as "a key element in the defense system of the Arabian Gulf." Speaking at the podium with the king at his side, Rumsfeld extended his deep-felt appreciation for the assistance and support that Bahrain had long been providing the United States.[36]

With King Hamad and his delegation departing from Andrews Air Force Base for the long flight home late on 5 February, Secretary of State Colin Powell prepared to leave for New York to address the UN General Assembly and to lay out the case against Iraq. Before the world body the next day, the American secretary of state offered intelligence to support claims that Saddam Hussein was a danger to the region and detailed the rationale for military action. Although he made a strong argument for immediate action, some members of the Security Council, led by France and Russia, countered that the UNMOVIC teams should be given more time to verify Iraq's claims on its weapons of mass destruction programs.

While some countries sought to delay or prevent war, the United States, Britain, and other nations moved additional forces into the region. Over the skies of southern and northern Iraq, the number of air missions ratcheted up in early 2003 as additional aircraft from new carriers and from air bases in the region dropped ordnance in response to no-fly zone violations. Leaflets also fell from the skies as a measure to dissuade Saddam's military from fighting for their dictator.

While the majority of forces being sent to the region were destined for Kuwait, Bahrain also served as an important base for coalition operations. Whereas the American military population had jumped approximately 50 percent to support Operation Enduring Freedom operations in central Asia, Captain Holbrook found he had to accommodate more than five thousand Sailors, Marines, and other support personnel assigned to his facility. Again, most of these people were berthed in rental units in Manama. Holbrook worried that some apartment complexes with large concentrations of Americans could be vulnerable to terrorist activity. However, the Bahrainis eased his concern by establishing a highly visible security presence in these neighborhoods. "They were all over—all over," he recalled.[37]

Included in the buildup for what would become known as Operation Iraqi Freedom was the relocation of the U.S. Marine Forces Central Command (MARCENT) from Hawaii to Bahrain. Suddenly, a small city consisting of several large cloth-covered buildings nicknamed "Sprungs" as well as smaller tents appeared on the Naval Support Activity softball field as Lt. Gen. Earl B. Hailston co-located his headquarters with Admiral Keating's NAVCENT/Fifth Fleet command.

Again Shaikh Essa Air Base located on the southern portion of the island would play an important role as the U.S. Air Force and Marines based tanker and cargo aircraft there.

Bahrain added firepower to forces assembling in the northern Gulf by deploying F-16 fighters to Kuwait along with ground troops and rocket launchers to support a GCC Peninsula Shield force designed to defend the area against a pre-emptive Iraqi attack. The BRNS* *Sabha* also deployed from Mina Sulman pier to join the allied naval armada off the Kuwaiti coast. The departure of the Bahraini Defense Force jets provided additional facilities for the stationing of U.S. Marine Corps F/A-18 Hornets and support aircraft in the region.[38]

With the prospect of war, and given the anti-American sentiment in the Arab world, the State Department issued warnings to Americans living in the region to return to the United States. However, as in 1990, most Americans chose to ignore the admonition. American Association of Bahrain president Jeff Jones said, "I don't feel any sense of danger whatsoever. People over here have been very friendly."[39]

Back in New York, the United States and Britain tabled a second resolution finding Iraq in non-compliance and authorizing military action. However, permanent members France and Russia threatened to veto the measure. In the Middle East, Saddam Hussein ignored messages from fellow Arab leaders explaining the gravity of the situation and urging him to step down. Finally, on 14 March, President Bush addressed the nation and the world to state that military action was imminent and that Hussein and his two sons had forty-eight hours to leave the country. With only bellicose rhetoric as a response, the United States and its coalition partners launched Operation Iraqi Freedom on 17 March 2003.

---

* When Bahrain became a kingdom "Bahrain Royal Navy Ship" (BRNS) replaced Bahrain Amiri Navy Ship (BANS).

Notes

INTRODUCTION

1. This information was gathered by Capt. James A. Noone, USNR, and the author, who visited *Enterprise* in April 1999, and refined in subsequent correspondence with several of the participants. Comments by Capt. Kevin Miller, USN (Ret.), were particularly helpful.

CHAPTER 1

1. J. B. Kelly, *Britain and the Persian Gulf, 1795–1880* (London: Oxford University Press, 1968), 28–29.
2. J. B. Kelly, *Arabia, the Gulf and the West* (New York: Basic Books, 1980), 178–79, 181–82; Peter Mansfield, *A History of the Middle East* (New York: Viking, 1991), 120; Peter Mansfield, ed., *The Middle East: A Political and Economic Survey* (London: Oxford University Press, 1973), 128.
3. Kelly, *Britain and the Persian Gulf,* 103.
4. Ibid., 165.
5. Ibid., 221–22.
6. Ibid., 236–37; Michael A. Palmer, *On Course to Desert Storm: The United States Navy and the Persian Gulf* (Washington, DC: Naval Historical Center, 1992), 3.
7. Kelly, *Britain and the Persian Gulf,* 361–62; Sami A. Hanna, *A Modern Cultural History of Bahrain* (Bahrain: Ministry of Information, 1991), 27, 30.
8. Kelly, *Britain and the Persian Gulf,* 382–83.
9. Ibid., 458.
10. Ibid., 472–93.
11. Ibid., 525, 672–75; Anthony H. Cordesman, *Bahrain, Oman, Qatar, and the UAE: Challenges of Security* (Boulder, CO: Westview Press, 1997), 34–36, 46; Angela Clarke, *Bahrain: A Heritage Explored* (Bahrain: Public Relations Group, 1991), 19–21.
12. Clarke, *A Heritage Explored,* 22.
13. Andrew Wheatcroft, *Bahrain in Original Photographs: 1880–1961* (London: Kegan Paul International, 1988), 7.
14. Clarke, *A Heritage Explored,* 22; Wheatcroft, *Bahrain in Original Photographs,* 7.

15. Mansfield, *The Middle East: A Political and Economic Survey,* 130; John Marlowe, *The Persian Gulf in the Twentieth Century* (New York: Frederick A. Praeger Publishers, 1962), 133; Angela Clarke, *Bahrain Oil and Development, 1929–1989* (London: Immel Publishing, 1990), 136. Marlowe referred to Belgrave as "a virtual Prime Minister." Clarke stated that many American oil workers and Bahrainis considered Belgrave to be a "typical imperialist."

16. Charles Belgrave, *Personal Column* (London: Hutchinson, 1960), 214. Eventually Belgrave visited the American ship in Boston and was invited to join the *Guerriere* Dinner Club, consisting of direct descendents of those on the *Constitution* who had triumphed over the British warship.

17. Ibid., 7–10.

18. Mansfield, *The Middle East: A Political and Economic Survey,* 128, 130. Belgrave, *Personal Column,* 76, 106.

19. Belgrave, *Personal Column,* 76, 106. The establishment date was found in a 1991 ASU Welcome Aboard booklet.

20. Palmer, *On Course to Desert Storm,* 5.

21. Paul Armerding, "The American Mission Hospital: A Century of Progress in Medicine," in *The American-Bahraini Relationship: A Special Report* (Washington, DC: National Council on U.S.-Arab relations, no date), 20–22. For a detailed history of the American Mission Hospital see Angela Clarke, *The American Mission Hospital Bahrain: Through Changing Scenes of Life, 1893–1993* (Bahrain: American Mission Hospital Society, 1993).

22. Donald Hepburn, "BAPCO-CALTEX: Oil Pioneers in the Arabian Gulf," in *The American-Bahraini Relationship: A Special Report* (Washington, DC: National Council on U.S.-Arab Relations, no date), 13–16.

23. Belgrave, *Personal Column*, 81.

24. Clarke, *Bahrain Oil and Development,* 167–71; Belgrave, *Personal Column,* 121.

25. Clarke, *Bahrain Oil and Development,* 176.

26. Palmer, *On Course to Desert Storm,* 11.

27. Ibid., 12–13; Marlowe, *The Persian Gulf in the 20th Century*, p. 133; T. H. Vail Motter, *The Persian Corridor and Aid to Russia: The United States Army in World War II* (Washington, DC: Center for Military History, 1952), 291–95.

28. Motter, *The Persian Corridor,* 298–302.

29. Clarke, *Bahrain Oil and Development,* 184, 186.

30. Ibid., 180; Hamza A. M. Kaedi interview by author, 12 Nov. 1998.

31. Belgrave, *Personal Column*, 124, 133.

CHAPTER 2

1. Palmer, *On Course to Desert Storm,* 21–28; David Alan Rosenberg, "The U.S. Navy and the Problem of Oil in a Future War: The Outline of a Strategic Dilemma, 1945–1950," *Naval War College Review* (Summer 1976): 54–55.

4

2. Palmer, *On Course to Desert Storm,* 30–32; Rosenberg, "The U.S. Navy and the Problem of Oil in a Future War," 55–56.

3. Rosenberg, "The U.S. Navy and the Problem of Oil in a Future War," 56–57; CINCNELM Semi-Annual Summary, 1 Oct. 1947–31 Mar. 1948, Operational Archives, Naval Historical Center (NHC).

4. Palmer, *On Course to Desert Storm,* 36.

5. W. Seth Carus, Barry McCoy, and John R. Hafey, *From MIDEASTFOR to Fifth Fleet: Forward Naval Presence in Southwest Asia* (Alexandria, VA: Center for Naval Analyses, 1995), 31.

6. Rosenberg, "The U.S. Navy and the Problem of Oil in a Future War," 57.

7. USS *Rendova* Round the World Cruise Report, Operational Archives, NHC.

8. Ibid.; Belgrave, *Personal Column,* 163.

9. CO *Greenwich Bay* (AVP 41) to Chief of Bureau of Ships letter dated 11 August 1948, CINCNELM General Admin. Files, R.G. 313—Naval Operating Forces, National Archives; CINCNELM Semi-Annual Summary, 1 April–30 Sept. 1948, Operational Archives, NHC.

10. Ibid.; Belgrave, *Personal Column,* 163.

11. CINCNELM Semi-Annual Summary, 1 April–30 Sept. 1948; CINCNELM Operations Report, 1 July 1948–30 July 1949; CINCNELM Operations Report, 1 July–1 Nov. 1950, Operational Archives, NHC; Rosenberg, "The U.S. Navy and the Problem of Oil in a Future War," 59.

12. Carus, McCoy, and Hafey, *From MIDEASTFOR to Fifth Fleet,* 36. Although not mentioned in the CINCNELM Operations Summaries, the Bahrain visit is noted under the individual ship entries in the *Dictionary of American Naval Fighting Ships* series.

13. USS *Rendova* Round the World Cruise Report; CINCNELM Annual Report 30 Nov. 1949 Operational Archives, NHC; Palmer, *On Course to Desert Storm,* 35–36.

14. CINCNELM Semi-Annual Summary, 1 April–30 Sept. 1948.

15. Carus, McCoy, and Hafey, *From MIDEASTFOR to Fifth Fleet,* 31–32; Rosenberg, "The U.S. Navy and the Problem of Oil in a Future War," 60.

CHAPTER 3

1. John Lewis Gaddis, *Strategies of Containment: A Critical Appraisal of Postwar American National Security Policy* (New York: Oxford, 1982), 25–26, 50.

2. CINCNELM Report of Operations, 1 July 1948–30 July 1949; CINCNELM Report of Operations, 1 July–1 Nov. 1950; Transcript of interview with Rear Adm. Ernest M. Eller, USN (Ret.), 15 May 1979, U.S. Naval Institute Oral History Program.

3. Eller interview.

4. Ibid.

5. Ibid.

6. Ibid.

7. From *Valcour, Duxbury Bay,* and *Greenwich Bay* entries in *Dictionary of American Naval Fighting Ships,* series.

8. YNC Jim Lee, USN (Ret.), memorandum to author, 10 Nov. 1998.

9. COMIDEASTFOR Command History, 1960, Operational Archives, NHC.

10. *Duxbury Bay* Command History, 1951, Ships History Branch, NHC.

11. Ibid.

12. Ibid.

13. Ibid.

14. *Duxbury Bay,* Command History, 1952, Ships History Branch, NHC.

15. Lee memorandum.

16. Transcript of interview with Adm. Harry D. Felt, USN (Ret.), 1974, U.S. Naval Institute Oral History Program.

17. Transcript of interview with Adm. Noel A. M. Gayler, USN (Ret.), 7 Feb. 1984, U.S. Naval Institute Oral History Program.

18. Felt interview; Lee memorandum.

19. Gayler interview.

20. Carus, McCoy, and Hafey, *From MIDEASTFOR to Fifth Fleet,* 41–42.

21. Transcript of interview with Vice Adm. William P. Mack, USN (Ret.), 1980, U.S. Naval Institute Oral History Program.

22. Walter LeFeber, *America, Russia, and the Cold War: 1945–1990,* 6th ed. (New York: McGraw-Hill, 1991), 184–189.

23. Gayler interview.

24. Senator James M. Jeffords interview by author, 26 July 2003, Washington, DC.

25. *Duxbury Bay* Command History, 1953, Ships History Branch, NHC; *Greenwich Bay* entry in *Dictionary of American Naval Fighting Ships,* series.

26. Carus, McCoy, and Hafey, *From MIDEASTFOR to Fifth Fleet,* 45.

27. COMIDEASTFOR Command History, 1958, Operational Archives, NHC.

28. *Duxbury Bay* Command History, 1962; *Duxbury Bay* Command History, 1963, Ships History Branch, NHC.

29. As told by Framarz Brandran to author, 13 Nov. 1998.

30. COMIDEASTFOR Command History, 1958, Operational Archives, NHC.

31. Assorted *Duxbury Bay, Greenwich Bay,* and *Valcour* cruisebooks are in the Navy Department Library at the Washington Navy Yard.

32. *Valcour* Command History, 1966, Ships History Branch, NHC.

33. *Valcour* Command History, 1966, Ships History Branch, NHC.

34. Kaedi interview.

35. Transcript of interview with MCPON William Plackett, 1997, Naval Historical Foundation Oral History Program.

36. Ibid.

37. Ibid.
38. Ibid.
39. Kaedi interview.
40. Eller interview.
41. Ibid.
42. Ibid.
43. Felt interview.
44. Ibid.
45. Belgrave, *Personal Column,* 164–65.
46. Transcript of interview with Vice Adm. Benedict J. Semmes, USN (Ret.), 1 Sept. 1988, U.S. Naval Institute Oral History Program; Katharine Ainsworth Semmes, "Bahrain: Pearl of the Persian Gulf," U.S. Naval Institute *Proceedings* (May 1966): 93.
47. COMIDEASTFOR Command History, 1960.
48. Semmes, "Bahrain," 96–97.
49. Ronald H. Cole, Walter S. Poole, James F. Schnabel, Robert J. Watson, and Willard J. Webb, *The History of the Unified Command Plan, 1946–1993* (Washington, DC: Joint History Office, 1995), 29–30.
50. Ibid., 33–34; COMIDEASTFOR Command History, 1963, Operational Archives, NHC.
51. Carus, McCoy, and Hafey, *From MIDEASTFOR to Fifth Fleet,* 33–34; Palmer, *On Course to Desert Storm,* 147; CINCUSNAVMEAAFSA 231932Z Dec. 71, Operational Archives, NHC.

CHAPTER 4

1. For an excellent chronology of events in the Middle East, see *The Middle East: U.S. Policy, Israel, Oil and the Arabs* (Washington, DC: Congressional Quarterly, 1974).
2. Lt. Cdr. James Stewart, RN, "East of Suez," U.S. Naval Institute *Proceedings* (March 1966): 41–51.
3. COMIDEASTFOR 22 July 1967, Status of Forces memorandum, Operational Archives, NHC.
4. Rear Adm. Walter S. Small, USN (Ret.), letter to author, 18 Apr. 1999.
5. Ibid.; COMIDEASTFOR Command History, 1967, Operational Archives, NHC; Kaedi interview.
6. Kelly, *Arabia, the Gulf, and the West,* 25–26.
7. Ibid., 47–48.
8. Ibid., 51–52.
9. Ibid., 54–56.
10. Ibid., 59.
11. Transcript of interview with Vice Adm. Marmaduke G. Bayne, USN (Ret.), 1998, Naval Historical Foundation Oral History Program.

12. COMIDEASTFOR to CINCUSNAVEUR 050954Z Jun 68, Operational Archives, NHC.

13. Kelly, *Arabia, the Gulf, and the West,* 54.

14. CNO to CINCLANTFLT letter 29 March 1969, Operational Archives, NHC.

15. Palmer, *On Course to Desert Storm,* 82–83.

16. Carus, McCoy, and Hafey, *From MIDEASTFOR to Fifth Fleet,* 53–56; Palmer, *On Course to Desert Storm,* 75–77.

17. Bayne e-mail to author, 27 Oct. 1998.

18. Bayne e-mail to author, 30 Oct. 1998.

19. *Valcour* Command History, 1968, Ships History Branch, NHC.

20. *Valcour* Command History, 1969, Ships History Branch, NHC.

21. Bayne e-mail to author, 30 Oct. 1998.

22. Bayne interview.

23. Bayne e-mail to author, 17 Nov. 1998; COMIDEASTFOR Command History, 1971, Operational Archives, NHC.

24. CNO to CINCUSNAVEUR 041746Z Aug 71, Operational Archives, NHC.

25. Bayne e-mail to author, 17 Nov. 1998.

26. Yousuf Ahmed Al Shirawi, interview by author and Cdr. James Wombwell, 24 Nov. 1998, Bahrain.

27. *Valcour* Command History, 1971, Ships History Branch, NHC.

28. Bayne e-mail to author, 17 Nov. 1998; Al-Shirawi interview; Carus, McCoy, and Hafey, *From MIDEASTFOR to Fifth Fleet,* 68–69.

29. Ibid., Kelly, *Arabia, the Gulf, and the West,* 317.

30. Kaedi interview; *Valcour* Command History, 1972, Ships History Branch, NHC.

31. COMIDEASTFOR Command History, 1972, Operational Archives, NHC; *Valcour* Command History, 1972, Ships History Branch, NHC.

32. COMIDEASTFOR Command History, 1972, Operational Archives, NHC.

33. *Valcour* Command History, 1972, Ships History Branch, NHC.

34. Semmes interview.

35. COMIDEASTFOR Command History, 1967; Small letter.

36. DIRECTOR USDESEA KARLSRUHE GERMANY to COMIDEASTFOR 041300Z Jun. 68, Operational Archives, NHC.

37. Bayne e-mail to author, 27 Oct. 1998.

38. Ibid.

39. Al Shirawi interview.

40. Frithjof R. Wannebo e-mail to author, 12 Aug. 2000; COMIDEASTFOR Command History, 1972, Operational Archives, NHC.

41. Bayne e-mail, 27 Oct 1998.

42. H. H. Shaikh Salman bin Hamad Al Khalifa interview by author, 23 Aug. 2000.

43. COMIDEASTFOR Command History, 1971, Operational Archives, NHC.

44. *Valcour* Command History, 1972; *La Salle* Command History, 1972, Ships History Branch, NHC.
45. Clarke, *Bahrain Oil and Development,* 324; Kacdi interview.
46. COMIDEASTFOR Command History, 1972, Operational Archive, NHC.
47. Hanks to Stolz, 27 March 1973, *La Salle* Folder, Ships History Branch, NHC.
48. COMIDEASTFOR Command History, 1973, Operational Archives, NHC.
49. Cole, Poole, Schnabel, Watson, and Webb, *The History of the Unified Command Plan,* 38–41.
50. COMIDEASTFOR Command History, 1973, Operational Archives, NHC; CINCUSNAVMEAFSA 231932Z Dec 71, Operational Archives, NHC.
51. CINCLANT to JCS 011450Z Sep 72; COMIDEASTFOR to CINCUSNAVEUR 201524Z Nov. 72, Operational Archives, NHC.
52. Commander Middle East Force to Chief of Naval Operations, letter 19 May 1973, Operational Archives, NHC; Factsheet provided by Defense Energy Region Middle East stated that the "Navy Petroleum Products Middle East" office was established in 1939, but the author has not found corroborating evidence.

Chapter 5

1. Quoted in Palmer, *On Course to Desert Storm,* 76
2. Ibid., 79.
3. Ibid., 89. During the period Sept. 1973–Jan. 1974, the cost of oil rose from $3 to $11 per barrel.
4. Bruce R. Kuniholm, *The Persian Gulf and United States Policy: A Guide to Issues and References* (Claremont, CA: Regina Books, 1984), 26.
5. Palmer, *On Course to Desert Storm,* 80–81.
6. Edward J. Marolda and Robert J. Schneller Jr., *Shield and Sword: The United States Navy and the Persian Gulf War* (Washington, DC: Naval Historical Center, 1999), 16.
7. Carus, McCoy, and Hafey, *From MIDEASTFOR to Fifth Fleet,* 59; 1973 MEF Command History, MEF Command File, Operational Archives, NHC; and 1975 MEF Command History, MEF Command File, Operational Archives, NHC.
8. Robert Hanks, *Middle East Journal* (unpublished, 1994), 181–84, 196.
9. Marolda and Schneller, *Shield and Sword*, 15; Hanks, *Middle East Journal,* 193–94, 196–98.
10. Hanks, *Middle East Journal,* 199.
11. Marvin Kalb and Bernard Kalb, *Kissinger* (Boston: Little and Brown, 1974), 470–71, 477–78.
12. Ibid., 480; Hanks, *Middle East Journal,* 207.
13. Hanks, *Middle East Journal,* 208

14. Ibid., 206.
15. Ibid., 216–19.
16. Ibid., 224–26.
17. Adm. Thomas H. Moorer, USN (Ret.), oral interview, Vol. III, U.S. Naval Institute, Annapolis, MD, 1984.
18. Hanks, *Middle East Journal,* 228, 246–47.
19. Ibid., 257–59.
20. COMIDEASTFOR TO CINCUSNAVEUR, message dated 111104Z Nov 73, MEF Admin. Correspondence, 1967–1987, Box 256A: Post 74 Command File, MEF Chron-Plans, Operational Archives NHC.
21. Ibid.
22. Hanks, *Middle East Journal,* 265–66.
23. Daniel Wyckoff interview by Commander Wombwell, 17 Nov. 1998.
24. Hanks, *Middle East Journal,* 272–74; Palmer, *On Course to Desert Storm,* 88.
25. Hanks, *Middle East Journal,* 287–88.
26. Ibid., 295–98.
27. Ibid., 299.
28. 1974 Naval Control of Shipping Office (NCSO), Bahrain Command History, Administrative Support Unit, Bahrain Command File, Operational Archives, NHC; Moorer interview.
29. 1974 MEF Command History, Operational Archives, NHC.
30. Hanks, *Middle East Journal,* 326–28.
31. Ibid., 330.
32. Tariq A. Almoayed interview by author and Commander Wombwell, 25 Nov. 1998.
33. 1973 MEF Command History, MEF Command File, Operational Archives, NHC.
34. Hanks, *Middle East Journal,* 350.
35. Ibid., 351.
36. Vice Adm. Thomas J. Bigley, USN (Ret.), interview by author and Commander Wombwell, 26 Oct. 1998.
37. 1975 MEF Command History, Operational Archives, NHC.
38. Cordesman, *Bahrain, Oman, Qatar, and the UAE,* 51–52; Adm. William J. Crowe Jr., USN (Ret.), with David Chanoff, *The Line of Fire* (New York: Simon and Schuster, 1993), 163–63.
39. Crowe, *The Line of Fire,* 163–64.
40. COMIDEASTFOR to CINCUSNAVEUR, message dated 131444Z Jun 76, MEF Admin. Correspondence, 1967–1987, Box 256A: Post 74 Command File, MEF Chron-Plans, Operational Archives, NHC.
41. COMIDEASTFOR to CINCUSNAVEUR, message dated 130803Z Mar 76, MEF Admin. Correspondence, 1967–1987, Box 256A: Post 74 Command File, MEF Chron-Plans, Operational Archives, NHC.
42. Bigley interview.

43. Ibid.

44. Wannebo e-mail to author, 12 Aug. 2000. In the e-mail Wannebo notes that Twinan even had a new superintendent hired and sent to Bahrain to await his departure.

45. Col. G. D. Rawlings, MEAF Division, J5, to CJCS, "MIDEASTFOR Stationing in Bahrain," memo dated 23 June 1976, states that the "State Department desk officers are holding out for a slow deliberate process which would permit the U.S. Ambassador to weigh in and take the lead in future exchanges between the two governments. Some lower ranking State officials are somewhat miffed over the fact that the Bahraini Amir and Prime Minister approached COMIDEASTFOR rather than the U.S. Ambassador."

46. COMIDEASTFOR to CINCUSNAVEUR, message dated 131444Z Jun 76, MEF Admin. Correspondence, 1967–1987, Box 256A: Post 74 Command file, MEF Chron-Plans, Operational Archives, NHC.

47. Ibid.; The amount of the annual payment had increased by 1974 from $800,000 to $4,000,000. See 1974 MEF Command History, MEF Command File, Operational Archives, NHC.

48. Crowe, *The Line of Fire,* 164; 1976 MEF Command History, MEF Command File, Operational Archives, NHC.

49. Crowe, *The Line of Fire,* 165.

50. J-5 Point Paper to CJCS dated 23 June 1976 provided by Vice Admiral Bigley.

51. COMIDEASTFOR to CINCUSNAVEUR, message dated 131444Z Jun 76, MEF Admin. Correspondence, 1967–1987, Box 256A: Post 74 Command file, MEF Chron-Plans, Operational Archives, NHC.

52. 1976 MEF Command History, MEF Command File, Operational Archives, NHC.

53. Crowe, *In Line of Fire,* 165.

54. Almoayed interview.

55. COMIDEASTFOR to CINCUSNAVEUR, message dated 101410Z Aug 76, MEF Admin. Correspondence, 1967–1987, Box 256A: Post 74 Command file, MEF Chron-Plans, Operational Archives, NHC.

56. CINCPACFLT to CNO, message dated 060627Z Jan. 77, MEF Admin. Correspondence, 1967–1987, Box 256A: Post 74 Command file, MEF Chron-Plans, Operational Archives, NHC.

57. Crowe, *The Line of Fire,* 167–68; 1976 MEF Command History, MEF Command File, Operational Archives, NHC.

58. "Defense Requirements Survey Team for Bahrain, 22–30 Nov. 1976; trip report," dated 6 Dec. 1976; CINCUSNAVEUR to CNO, message dated 041101Z Jan 77, MEF Admin. Correspondence, 1967–1987, Box 256A: Post 74 Command file, MEF Chron-Plans, Operational Archives, NHC.

59. Bigley interview.

60. Dr. F. R. Wannebo e-mail to Commander Wombwell, 28 Nov. 1998 and 1 Dec. 1998.

61. Almoayed interview; Wannebo e-mail, 1 Dec. 1998.
62. AMEMBASSY MANAMA to SECSTATE, message dated 291305Z Jan 77, MEF Admin. Correspondence, 1967–1987, Box 256A: Post 74 Command file, MEF Chron-Plans, Operational Archives, NHC.
63. Crowe, *The Line of Fire*. 168–69.
64. Ibid., 169; 1977 MEF Command History, MEF Command File, Operational Archives, NHC.
65. COMIDEASTFOR to CINCUSNAVEUR, message dated 081510Z Apr 77, MEF Admin. Correspondence, 1967–1987, Box 256A: Post 74 Command file, MEF Chron-Plans, Operational Archives, NHC.
66. COMIDEASTFOR to CINCUSNAVEUR, message dated 081200Z Jun 77, MEF Admin. Correspondence, 1967–1987, Box 256A: Post 74 Command file, MEF Chron-Plans; 1977 MEF Command History, MEF Command file, Operational Archives, NHC.
67. Crowe, *Line of Fire*, 171.
68. Ibid.

CHAPTER 6

1. 1977 Middle East Force Command History, Operational Archives, NHC.
2. Rear Adm. Samuel Packer, USN (Ret.), interview by author, 8 Aug. 2000.
3. 1977 Middle East Force Command History; 1977–1978 ASU Bahrain Command History, Operational Archives, NHC; Capt. Marcia Fulham, USN, e-mail to author, 25 July 2000.
4. Don Hepburn interview by author, 1 Feb. 2001.
5. Palmer, *On Course to Desert Storm,* 90.
6. Ibid., 92–93; Rear Adm. Samuel Packer, USN (Ret.), interview by Commander Wombwell, 26 Feb. 1999.
7. David B. Crist, *Operation Earnest Will: The United States in the Persian Gulf, 1986–1989* (Ph.D. Diss., Florida State University, 1998), 34–35; Lawrence R. Benson, "A Survey of Bases and Forces," *The United States Military in North Africa and Southwest Asia Since World War II* (Tampa, FL: U.S. Central Command History Office, 1988), 33.
8. Packer interview by Wombwell; Rear Adm. Harold Bernsen, USN (Ret.), interview by Commander Wombwell, 22 Mar. 1999.
9. Jay E. Hines, "American Eagle in the Sand: The Story of the United States Central Command," *The Political Chronicle* (Spring/Summer 1996), 1–2.
10. Ibid., 3; Crist, *Operation Earnest Will,* 47–48; Adm. James "Ace" Lyons interview with author and Commander Wombwell, 8 Mar. 1999; Vice Adm. Thomas Bigley interview with author, 12 Sept. 2000.
11. Marolda and Schneller, *Shield and Sword,* 35.
12. Ibid., 35–36; Lyons interview; Rear Adm. Harold Bernsen e-mail to author, 30 Apr. 2001.

13. Packer interview by Wombwell.

14. Carus, McCoy, and Hafey, *From MIDEASTFOR to Fifth Fleet*, 113; Capt. Evan Robinson, USN, interview by Cdr. Wombwell, 17 Mar. 1999.

15. Ambassador Robert H. Pelletreau interview by author, 13 Sept. 2000.

16. Carus, McCoy, and Hafey, *From MIDEASTFOR to Fifth Fleet,* 113.

17. Palmer, *On Course to Desert Storm,* 96.

18. Pelletreau interview.

19. Bernsen interview.

20. Crist, *Operation Earnest Will,* 40–41; Palmer, *On Course to Desert Storm,* 99.

21. Cordesman, *Bahrain, Oman, Qatar and the UAE,* 41–42; Bernsen e-mail.

22. Crist, *Operation Earnest Will,* 44.

23. "The Holy War in the Persian Gulf," *Newsweek* (12 March 1984); "Oil Wars: A Test for Reagan," *Newsweek* (28 May 1984); Capt. Thomas Daly, "The Enduring Gulf War," U.S. Naval Institute *Proceedings* (May 1985), 151–54.

24. Crist, *Operation Earnest Will,* 41–45; "Stop the Aggression League Tells Iran," *Emirate News,* 21 May 1984, 1–2; Ronald O Rourke, "The Tanker War." U.S. Naval Institute *Proceedings* (May 1988), 30.

25. Rear Adm. John F. Addams, USN (Ret.), interview by author and Commander Wombwell, 2 Mar. 1999; Crist, *Operation Earnest Will,* 45–46.

26. Daly, "The Enduring Gulf War," 159.

27. Addams interview; 1984 ASU Bahrain Command History, Operational Archives, NHC.

28. Addams interview.

29. 1985 Middle East Force Command History, Operational Archives, NHC.

30. Bernsen e-mail.

31. Crist, *Operation Earnest Will,* 53–54.

32. 1986 Middle East Force Command History, Operational Archives, NHC.

33. Palmer, *On Course to Desert Storm,* 112; Crist, *Operation Earnest Will,* 59–60.

34. Palmer, *On Course to Desert Storm,* 110–11.

35. Shaikh Salman interview.

36. Cordesman, *Bahrain, Oman, Qatar and the UAE,* 47.

37. Adm. James L. Holloway III, USN (Ret.), facsimile to author, 26 Feb. 2000.

38. Carus, McCoy, and Hafey, *From MIDEASTFOR to Fifth Fleet,* 115.

39. Crist, *Operation Earnest Will,* 55.

40. Crowe, *The Line of Fire,* 176; Crist, *Operation Earnest Will,* 78; Palmer, *On Course to Desert Storm,* 112.

41. Shaikh Salman interview.

42. Bernsen e-mail. When asked if the Kuwaitis would make arrangements to provide fuel for the U.S. escort ships, the prime minister enthusiastically agreed, a pledge that later became the basis for a significant transfer of fuel from Kuwait to the U.S. Navy during Operation Earnest Will.

43. 1980 USS *La Salle* Command History, Ships History Branch, NHC; Crist, *Operation Earnest Will,* 65, 89–93; Bernsen e-mail.
44. John Partin, *Special Operations Forces in Operation Earnest Will / Prime Chance I* (Tampa, FL: U.S. Special Operations Command History and Research Office, April 1998), 9.
45. Crist, *Operation Earnest Will,* 101.
46. 1987 Middle East Force Command History, Operational Archives, NHC; Crist, *Operation Earnest Will,* 99–101.
47. Jeffrey L. Levinson and Randy L. Edwards, *Missile Inbound: The Attack on the Stark in the Persian Gulf* (Annapolis, MD: Naval Institute Press, 1997), 21.
48. Shaikh Salman interview; Levinson and Edwards, *Missile Inbound,* 35.
49. Crist, *Operation Earnest Will,* 102; 1987 Middle East Force Command History; 1987 ASU Bahrain Command History, Operational Archives, NHC: Transcript of Rear Adm. Anthony A. Less, USN, speech to Manama Rotary Club, 5 March 1989, NavCent PAO archives, Bahrain.
50. Crist, *Operation Earnest Will,* 106.
51. Less, speech to Manama Rotary Club; Crist, *Operation Earnest Will,* 124–29.
52. Crist, *Operation Earnest Will,* 131.
53. Crowe, *The Line of Fire,* 192–93; Crist, *Operation Earnest Will,* 132.
54. Crist, *Operation Earnest Will,* 138–39.
55. Ibid., 147–53, 157.
56. Partin, *Special Operations Forces in Operation Earnest Will,* 13–15, 25–30. These were small quiet helicopters. The MH-6 was equipped with a forward-looking infrared radar videotape system to identify targets for the heavily armed AH-6 birds. Their deployment was named Prime Chance I.
57. Cdr. Greg Hawkins, USN (Ret.), interview by Commmander Wombwell, 12 Nov. 1998.
58. Bernsen e-mail.
59. Crist, *Operation Earnest Will,* 160–63.
60. Crowe, *The Line of Fire,* 97–199; 1987 Middle East Force Command History, Operational Archives, NHC. Bernsen had permission previously authorized by the chain of command. Partin, *SpecialOperations Forces in Operation Earnest Will*, 51–64.
61. Cdr. Charles Allen Gerringer, USN, interview by Commander Wombwell, 16 Nov. 1998; AMSC Timothy Walters, USN, interview by Commander Wombwell, 13 Dec. 1998; "New Navy Helicopter Squadron Sees Action," *Rotor & Wing International* (October 1987): 81; PH1 Chuck Mussi, "Desert Ducks: Deliverymen of the Persian Gulf," *All Hands* (March 1988): 14–15.
62. AT1 Kevin Secord, USN, interview by Commander Wombwell, 13 Dec. 1998.
63. Hepburn interview; Crist, *Operation Earnest Will,* 170–71.
64. Maritime Liaison Office Bahrain briefing sheet provided to Commander Wombwell, Nov. 1998.

65. Bernsen e-mail. Partin, *Special Operations Forces in Operation Earnest Will,* 39–41. The projected leasing cost for six months was $6 million.

66. Crist, *Operation Earnest Will,* 179–83; Partin, *Special Operations Forces in Operation Earnest Will,* 43–44.

67. Bernsen e-mail. Partin, *Special Operations Forces in Operation Earnest Will,* 41–42; According to Partin the barge conversion supervisors and eventual commanders were SEALs as Bernsen was impressed with their "can do" attitude.

68. 1987 Middle East Force Command History, Operational Archives, NHC; Crist, *Operation Earnest Will,* 194. Partin, *Special Operations Forces in Operation Earnest Will,* 67–74.

69. Crist, *Operation Earnest Will,* 195–96; Capt. Gerald J. O'Donnell, USN, interview by Commander Wombwell, 16 Nov. 1998.

70. 1987 Middle East Force Command History, Operational Archives, NHC; Crist, *Operation Earnest Will,* 205; Partin, *Special Operations Forces in Operation Earnest Will,* 79–82.

71. 1987 Middle East Force Command History, Operational Archives, NHC; Bernsen e-mail.

72. Crist, *Operation Earnest Will,* 211.

73. Anoushiravan Ehteshami, "Strategic Survey of the Near East 1988/89," *Middle East Strategic Studies Quarterly* (Spring/Summer 1989): 3–6.

74. Crowe, *The Line of Fire,* 200; Crist, *Operation Earnest Will,* 212–13.

75. Crowe, *The Line of Fire,* 201; Crist, *Operation Earnest Will,* 217.

76. Robert George e-mail to author, 28 Dec. 2004. George was the missile plot supervisor on *Wainwright.*

77. Crist, *Operation Earnest Will,* 224–28.

78. Crowe, *The Line of Fire,* 202; Crist, *Operation Earnest Will,* 231.

79. Crist, *Operation Earnest Will,* 235.

80. Ibid., 241–42; Adm. William Fogarty, USN (Ret.), e-mail to author, 10 July 2000.

81. Crist, *Operation Earnest Will,* 243.

82. Ibid., 252–53, 257.

83. Less, speech to Manama Rotary Club.

84. Crist, *Operation Earnest Will,* 266; 1989 Joint Task Force Middle East Command History, Operational Archives, NHC. The Joint Chiefs of Staff had selected Vice Adm. Henry C. Mustin to relieve General Crist as CINCCENT, but Secretary of Defense Carlucci changed the nominee to Schwarzkopf after National Security Advisor Gen. Colin Powell objected. In a 21 March 2001 Naval Historical Foundation interview with the author, Mustin indicated he would have complemented the end-around ground campaign by landing Marines at Basra in a move reminiscent of Inchon.

85. Fogarty e-mail; 1989 Middle East Force Command History, Operational Archives, NHC.

86. Fogarty e-mail.
87. Shaikh Salman interview.

CHAPTER 7

1. Fogarty e-mail to author.
2. Jay E. Hines, "Forged in the Desert: United States Central Command from Desert Shield to Today," *Desert Shield, Desert Storm, The 10th Anniversary of the Gulf War* (Tampa, FL: Faircount LLC, 2001), 46–47.
3. Marolda and Schneller, *Shield and Sword,* 3–4.
4. Ibid., 64; Rear Adm. Robert Sutton, USN (Ret.), letter to author, 16 Mar. 2001.
5. JO1 Lee Bosco, "Making Things Happen in the Persian Gulf," *All Hands* (June 1991): 32. Marvin Pokant, *Desert Shield at Sea: What the Navy Really Did* (Westport, CT: Greenwood Press,1998), 106.
6. Vice Adm. Henry H. Mauz Jr., USN (Ret.), e-mail to author, 7 May 2000.
7. Pokant, *Desert Shield at Sea,* 58; Cordesman, *Bahrain, Oman, Qatar and the UAE,* 115.
8. Marolda and Schneller, *Shield and Sword,* 82; Pokant, *Desert Shield at Sea,* 22.
9. Pokant, *Desert Shield at Sea,* 25.
10. Ibid., 33–36.
11. Ibid., 43–46, 121–22.
12. Gen. H. Norman Schwarzkopf, *It Doesn't Take a Hero* (New York: Bantam, 1992), 351–52.
13. QM1 Timothy E. Smith, USN, interview by Commander Wombwell, 17 Nov. 1998; 1990 ASU Bahrain Command History, Operational Archives, NHC.
14. 1990 ASU Bahrain Command History.
15. Ibid.
16. Bosco, "Making Things Happen in the Persian Gulf," 33.
17. 1990 ASU Bahrain Command History; Rear Adm. R. A. K. Taylor e-mail to author, 10 Sept. 2000.
18. Bosco, "Making Things Happen in the Persian Gulf," 34–35; 1990 ASU Bahrain Command History; Admiral Sutton letter to author.
19. Pokant, *Desert Shield at Sea,* 211–12; Smith interview; 1990 ASU Bahrain Command History; Hepburn interview; Admiral Sutton letter to author.
20. Hepburn interview.
21. Master Chief Timothy Moes e-mail to author, 13 Sept. 2004.
22. John Burlage, "Paddling above Water," *Navy Times* (26 Nov. 1990): 14; Secord interview.
23. Pokant, *Desert Shield at Sea,* 158–59.
24. Smith interview; 1990 ASU Bahrain Command History; Nick Kuriger e-mail to author, 30 May 2003.

25. Ibid. (3 sources); Schwarzkopf, *It Doesn't Take a Hero,* 197.

26. 1990 ASU Bahrain Command History.

27. Admiral Sutton letter to author; Paul Miller e-mail to author, 22 Nov. 2000.

28. Marolda and Schneller, *Shield and Sword,* 146; Pokant, *Desert Shield at Sea,* 144.

29. Marolda and Schneller, *Shield and Sword,* 137.

30. Ibid., 203–04.

31. May 1991 MIUW Group TWO Memorandum: Subject, "Group Grope #5"; Marolda and Schneller, *Shield and Sword,* 361.

32. Marolda and Schneller, *Shield and Sword,* 167.

33. Shaikh Salman interview.

34. Cordesman, *Bahrain, Oman, Qatar and the UAE,* 116.

35. Smith interview.

36. Ibid.; Shaikh Salman interview.

37. "Group Grope #5."

38. Marolda and Schneller, *Shield and Sword,* 235.

39. Ibid., 264–68; Admiral Sutton letter to author.

40. Cordesman, *Bahrain, Oman, Qatar and the UAE,* 116.

41. 1990 ASU Bahrain Command History.

42. Adm. Stanley R. Arthur, USN (Ret.), interview in *Desert Shield, Desert Storm: The 10th Anniversary of the Gulf War* (Tampa, FL: Faircount LLC, 2001), 111.

43. Shaik Salman interview.

CHAPTER 8

1. Marolda and Schneller, *Shield and Sword,* 310–11.

2. Dennis Merkel interview by Commander Wombwell, 18 Nov. 1998.

3. Marolda and Schneller, *Shield and Sword,* 359.

4. Rear Adm. R. A. K. Taylor, USN (Ret.), e-mail to author, 10 Sept. 2000.

5. Marolda and Schneller, *Shield and Sword,* 325–29; Admiral Sutton letter to author.

6. 1991 ASU Bahrain Command History, Operational Archives, NHC.

7. Marolda and Schneller, *Shield and Sword,* 330–31.

8. Ibid., 317–18.

9. Taylor e-mail; Marolda and Schneller, *Shield and Sword,* 322.

10. Marolda and Schneller, *Shield and Sword,* 334–36.

11. Ibid., 336–37; Rear Adm. David Rogers, USN (Ret.), letter to author, 31 July 2000.

12. Ibid., 312: UNSCOM Chronology from United Nations webpage www.un.org.

13. Marolda and Schneller, *Shield and Sword,* 337–40.

14. Ibid., 342; UNSCOM Chronology.
15. Marolda and Schneller, *Shield and Sword,* 342.
16. Ibid., 34–346.
17. Capt. Thomas Feeks, USN, written statement to Commander Wombwell (undated).
18. UNSCOM Chronology.
19. Rogers letter.
20. Marolda and Schneller, *Shield and Sword,* 347–49.
21. 1992 ASU-SWA Command History, COMUSNAVCENT Command History, NHC.
22. 1992 COMNAVCENT Command History; JO2 Kevin Stephens Press Release.
23. Cdr. Victoria M. Smith, USN, interview by Commander Wombwell, 18 Nov. 1998.
24. 1992 COMNAVCENT Command History; Stephens Press Release.
25. 1992 ASU-SWA Command History; Marolda and Schneller, *Shield and Sword,* 350.
26. Rogers letter.
27. UNSCOM Chronology; Vice Adm. Douglas Katz, USN (Ret.), interview by author, 25 Feb. 1999; Marolda and Schneller, *Shield and Sword,* 352.
28. Katz interview.
29. Ibid.
30. 1993 ASU-SWA Command History; 1994 ASU-SWA Command History; UNSCOM Chronology.
31. UNSCOM Chronology; Marolda and Schneller, *Sword and Shield,* 352–53.
32. NAVCENT PAO Press Release, 13 April 95.
33. Cdr. Joseph Thomas, USNR, "Fifth Fleet Stands Up," *Pull Together* (Spring/Summer 1997): 6–9.
34. Ibid., 9.
35. Ibid., Perry Memorandum to SecNav, 4 May 1995; CNO Memorandum to SecNav, 10 March 95.
36. Feeks phone conversation with author, 29 Jan. 2000.
37. Thomas, "Fifth Fleet"; U.S. Fifth Fleet Press Release, 29 Feb. 1996.
38. NAVCENT Press Release, 25 May 1995.
39. NAVCENT Press Release, 27 March 1995.
40. NAVCENT Press Release, 1 Sept. 1995.
41. Fifth Fleet Press Release, 29 Feb. 1996; Shaikh Salman interview.
42. UNSCOM Chronology.
43. Feeks written statement.
44. Feeks phone conversation with author; Bahraini Advertisement, *Washington Times,* 21 March 2000; Cordesman, *Bahrain, Oman, Qatar and the UAE,* 81.
45. Feeks written statement.

46. Fargo Recommendation for Ransom to receive DoD Public Service Award, undated.
47. NAVCENT Press Release, 1 Feb. 1996; Fifth Fleet Press Release, 5 Feb. 1996.
48. Fifth Fleet Press Release, 29 April 1996.
49. Fifth Fleet Press Release, 24 March 1996.
50. UNSCOM Chronology.
51. Feeks written statement; 1996 ASU-SWA Command History, NHC.
52. Capt. John G. Steele, USN, interview by author, 17 Aug. 2000.
53. Lt. Cdr. Gordan Sheek, USN, interview by author, 18 Aug. 2000.
54. Feeks written statement; Vice Adm. Thomas B. Fargo, USN, interview by Commander Wombwell, 13 Sept. 1996; 1996 ASU-SWA Command History; NSA Bahrain Facilities, 12 Aug. 2000, PowerPoint presentation.
55. Fargo interview; Joe Vann interview by Commander Wombwell, 18 Nov. 1998.
56. Hines, "Forged in the Desert," 59–60; Fargo interview.
57. Navy News Wire Service.
58. CTF50 message to Fifth Fleet 131216Z OCT 96.
59. Port visit history matrix provided by ASU-Operations.
60. J03 Hien Vu, "New Parking Lot Opening Planned, Pedestrian Facility on the Horizon," USNAVCENT *Connection*, 9 May 1998, 1; JOSN John Baughman, "Main Street Project Underway," USNAVCENT *Connection*, 2 July 1998, 1.
61. Cdr. Charles Chandonnet, USNR, interview by author, 22 Aug. 2000.
62. Capt. Marcia Fulham, USN, interview with Capt. James A. Noone, USNR, and author, 11 Apr. 1999; Fifth Fleet News Release, 23 July 1997.
63. UNSCOM Chronology.
64. Ibid.
65. Fargo interview.
66. UNSCOM Chronology; Tom Clancy with Gen. Tony Zinni (Ret.) and Tony Koltz, *Battle Ready* (New York: G. P. Putnam's Sons, 2004), 9; Vice Adm. Charles W. Moore, USN, interview by author, 27 Aug. 2000.
67. Lt. Jason Gilbert, USN, interview by Commander Wombwell, 11 Nov. 1998. The detachment was administratively transferred to EODMU-8 based at Sigonella Sicily as of 1 October 1998.
68. Lt. Cdr. John Bowie, USN, interview by author, 28 Nov. 1998.
69. 1997 ASU-SWA Command History, NHC.
70. Shaikh Salman interview.
71. "New U.S. Forces Chief Welcomed," *Gulf Daily News,* 26 July 1998.
72. "Fargo Praises Bahrain," *Bahrain Tribune,* 28 July 1999.
73. UNSCOM Chronology.
74. Scott Truver, "U.S. Navy Year in Review," U.S. Naval Institute *Proceedings* (May 1999): 79; Zinni quote in Clancy, *Battle Ready*, 340.
75. Moore interview.

76. Sheek interview. After 1998 more than two dozen of these young men would reapply and successfully complete the BUDS course.
77. Clancy, *Battle Ready,* 12–14.
78. UNSCOM Chronology; Clancy, *Battle Ready,* 1–3, 14–15.
79. Clancy, *Battle Ready,* 16.
80. Moore interview.

CHAPTER 9

1. *American Bahraini Friendship Society Newsletter,* Spring 1999, 2.
2. Douglas Jehl, "Sheik Isa, 65, Emir of Bahrain Who Built Non-Oil Economy," *New York Times,* 7 March 1999, A49.
3. "U.S. Leaders Praise Amir," USNAVCENT *Connection,* 12 March 1999, 1: Moore interview.
4. Ibid. Commander Wombwell deserves credit for finding the photograph and locating the deck plank for the presentation. In a meeting with the amir shortly after the CNO's departure, the amir expressed delight to Wombwell about the thoughtful presentations.
5. Fulham interview.
6. "Shaikh Isa Hailed by U.S. Navy," *Gulf Daily News,* 8 July 1999, 8; "Amir Praises U.S. Role in Helping to Maintain Regional Peace, Stability," *Bahrain Tribune,* 8 July 1999, 1.
7. *American Bahraini Friendship Society Newsletter,* Spring 1999, 4.
8. For example, during 1999 Shaikh Hamad visited the UAE, Jordan, Egypt, France, Syria, Morocco, England, Saudi Arabia, Italy, and the Vatican and received calls from several heads of state. Shaikh Hamad visited Oman, Kuwait, Qatar, South Africa, and Algeria. *American Bahraini Friendship Society Newsletter,* Summer, Autumn 1999, Winter, Spring 2000.
9. *American Bahraini Friendship Society Newsletter,* Winter 2000, 5.
10. *American Bahraini Friendship Society Newsletter,* Autumn 1996, 4.
11. Included in the documents was "official correspondence" signed by individuals who were deceased or ten years old at the reputed time and an 1873 Ottoman Survey map marked with seals that Bahraini investigators discovered were available at a novelty shop at The Hague. Testimony published online at www.bahraintribune.com; *American Bahraini Friendship Society Newsletter,* Spring 1997, Spring/Summer 1999.
12. *American Bahraini Friendship Society Newsletter,* Winter 2000.
13. Testimony published online at www.bahraintribune.com.
14. *American Bahraini Friendship Society Newsletter,* Summer 2000, 6–8.
15. *American Bahraini Friendship Society Newsletter,* Spring 2001, 3–4.
16. *CIA Factbook* (www.cia.gov/cia/publications/factbook); "Qatar in Dilemma over U.S. Threat to Iraq," *Gulf News Online Edition* (www.gulf-news.com), 15 July 2002.

17. *American Bahraini Friendship Society Newsletter,* Autumn 2000, Spring 2001; Capt. John G. Steele, USN (Ret.), interview by author, 19 June 2003.

18. "Iran and Bahrain Oppose Iraq Attack," *BBC NEWS World Edition*, 18 August 2002, http://news.bbc.co.uk/2/hi/middle_east/2201390.stm; "King, Khatami Stress Regional Stability," *Bahrain Tribune,* 17 May 2001, 1; "Agreement to Bolster Security in Region," *Bahrain Tribune,* 18 May 2003, 1. Given that the accord was signed in the wake of a bloody terrorist attack in Saudi Arabia allegedly directed by an al Qaeda operative working from Iran, some observers were led to question the sincerity of the document.

19. *American Bahraini Friendship Society Newsletter,* Summer 1999, 7; Autumn 1999, 3.

20. *American Bahraini Friendship Society Newsletter,* Autumn 1996, 6.

21. *American Bahraini Friendship Society Newsletter,* Winter 2001, 2–3.

22. "A Gesture in Bahrain to Ease Referendum," *New York Times*, 6 February 2001, 6; "Bahrain: Vote on Charter," *New York Times,* 15 February 2001, 6; *American Bahraini Friendship Society Newsletter,* Spring 2001, 2–3, 7.

23. "Bahrain, A Constitutional Monarchy," *Bahrain News and Information* (Spring 2002), 1, 6; *American Bahraini Friendship Society Newsletter,* Spring 2002, 2–3.

24. *American Bahraini Friendship Society Newsletter,* Summer 2002, 5.

25. Neil MacFarquhar, "In Bahrain, Women Run, Women Vote, Women Lose," *New York Times,* 22 May 2002, A3.

26. *American Bahraini Friendship Society Newsletter,* Summer 2002, 5.

27. Neil MacFarquhar, "Bahrain Tries to Fill in Potholes on Road to New Government," *New York Times*, 18 June 2002, A10.

28. Mohammed Almezel, "Bahrain King Urged to Postpone Elections," *Gulf News Online Edition* (www.gulf-news.com), 10 October 2002.

29. Thomas L. Friedman, "There Is Hope," *New York Times*, 27 October 2002, Op-Ed 13.

30. Ibid., Somini Sengupta, "Bahrain Says 52% Vote Turnout Meets Democratic Goals," *New York Times*, 25 October 2002, A6.

31. *American Bahraini Friendship Society Newsletter,* Winter 2003, 2; Jean-Francois Seznec speech at Bahraini Embassy, Washington, DC, 2 April 2003; www.pogar.org/countries/bahrain/elections.html.

32. www.pogar.org/countries/bahrain/elections.html.

33. *American Bahraini Friendship Society Newsletter,* Autumn 2000, 6–8.

34. Rear Adm. Mark Fitzgerald, USN, interview by author, 18 June 2003; Sara Horton, "People Government and Services Pull Together," *Gulf Daily News,* 25 August 2000, 4–5.

35. Ibid.; Amira Al Hussaini, "Surgeons Shocked at Mutilations," *Gulf Daily News,* 25 Aug 2000, 7; Navy News Wire Service, 1 Sept. 2000; *American Bahraini Friendship Society Newsletter,* Autumn 2000, 6.

36. Horton, "People Government and Services Pull Together."
37. Shaikh Salman interview.

CHAPTER 10

1. "U.S. Senate Armed Services Committee Hearing on the Recent Attack in Yemen on the USS *Cole*," 19 Oct. 2000. Actually *Cole* was the twenty-fifth ship to refuel under this contract. Three ships were refueled prior to the contract, and there were two other ships that called on Aden but didn't refuel.
2. Cdr. Hal Pittman, "In the Presence of Heroes," *All Hands* (May 2001); 24–42; Admiral Moore phone conversation with author, 4 June 2004; Capt. Kirk Lippold e-mail to author, 20 June 2004; Clancy, *Battle Ready*, 337–38.
3. Steele interview, June 2003.
4. Fitzgerald interview.
5. Pittman, "In the Presence of Heroes," 36–39.
6. Command Histories from 2000 of USS *Donald Cook* and USS *Hawes*, NHC Warfare History Division.
7. Fitzgerald interview.
8. "U.S. Navy Strikes Deal for *Blue Marlin* to Transport USS *Cole* to Virginia," CNN.com, 16 Oct. 2000.
9. Richard Hill, "United States Naval Institute *Proceedings,* July 2002, January 2003," *The Naval Review,* May 2003, 167.
10. Scott C. Truver, "The U.S. Navy Year in Review," U.S. Naval Institute *Proceedings* (May 2001): 84.

CHAPTER 11

1. Debra Stevens, "Mr. Hamza's Smiles Will Be Missed on ASU," USNAVCENT *Connection,* 29 Jan. 1999, 2.
2. JO2 Joseph Rehana, "Hamza Retires after Half Century of Service to U.S. Navy in Bahrain," USNAVCENT *Connection,* 29 Jan. 1999, 1.
3. Taimour Raouf, "Bahrain and U.S. Friendship Hailed," *Bahrain Tribune,* 16 July 1999, 1; Richard Moore, "Change of Command at Unit," *Gulf Daily News,* 16 July 1999, 3. Shortly after taking the helm, Steele was notified that effective 5 August 1999, Administrative Support Unit–Southwest Asia would be redesignated as Naval Support Activity Bahrain. The push to change the name came from Steele's predecessor, who felt the generic ASU-SWA moniker provided no clue as to the types of activities provided by the Navy facility in Bahrain. In contrast, *Naval Support Activity* is a common term used throughout the world denoting facilities that provide direct support to the fleet. With the ASU term created two decades earlier as a counter to those who claimed that Bahrain was hosting a U.S. military

base, the fiction of a non-U.S. presence could hardly be maintained in light of the massive ongoing construction. After Steele informed Moore of this development, the admiral sent a letter to the Bahraini government via the embassy to explain the change.

4. G. Steele interview by author, 19 June 2003.
5. NSA Bahrain Facilities, 12 Aug. 2000, PowerPoint presentation; Steele interview, 19 June 2003.
6. Steele interview, 19 June 2003.
7. Indeed, after being recognized as having the Navy's top overseas security protection program on 1997 and 1998, NSA Bahrain won the Department of Defense award for the best Antiterrorism/Force Protection program for any DoD installation in the world for 1999. Sheek interview; JO3 Traci Feibel, "NSA Security Captures World-Wide Honor," USNAVCENT *Scimitar,* 28 June 2000, 1–2.
8. Author stayed at the Mannai Plaza Hotel in November 1998 and April 1999.
9. Steele and Sheek interviews.
10. JO3 Traci Feibel, "Rotational Crews Turn Permanent in Bahrain," COMNAVCENT *Scimitar,* 3 May 2000, 1, 3.
11. Cdr. David F. Winkler, point paper, "Unaccompanied Duty in Bahrain: Historical Overview," May 2001; Steele interview, 19 June 2003 ; Capt. Lee Holcomb, USN, interview with author, 8 Sept. 2003.
12. Steele interview, 19 June 2003.
13. Vice Adm. John B. Nathman, USN, "We Were Great: Navy Air in Afghanistan," U.S. Naval Institute *Proceedings* (March 2002): 94.

CHAPTER 12

1. Fitzgerald interview.
2. "France Condemns Raids on Iraq," *BBC News,* 7 Apr. 2000.
3. "Statement of Charles W. Moore Jr., Vice Admiral, U.S. Naval Forces Central Command, Commander Fifth Fleet," to the House Military Procurement Sub-committee on 29 February 2000; Fitzgerald interview.
4. Maj. Fred H. Allison, USMC (Ret.), "Midnight in Baghdad," U.S. Naval Institute *Proceedings* (February 2002): 32–35; Scott C. Truver, "The U.S. Navy Year in Review," U.S. Naval Institute *Proceedings* (May 2002): 74–75.
5. Ibid., 1999 Draft USNAVCENT Command History, Fifth Fleet PAO.
6. Charles Recknagel, "Iraq: Oil Smuggling Produces High Profits," *Radio Free Europe/Radio Liberty* broadcast, 21 June 2000.
7. Fitzgerald interview; "*Vella Gulf*: 2002 Annual History," Warfare History Branch, Naval Historical Center.
8. JO3 Traci Feibel, "Patrolling the Oceans with USS *Hopper,*" USNAVCENT *Scimitar,* 9 Aug. 2000.

9. Bob Houlihan, "Policing the Gulf," *All Hands* (March 2003): 26.

10. Ibid. 22.

11. "Oil Ship Sink, U.S. Sailors Missing in Persian Gulf," cnn.com, 18 November 2001.

12. Shaikh Salman interview.

13. "Statement of Charles W. Moore Jr., Vice Admiral, U.S. Naval Forces Central Command, Commander Fifth Fleet," to the House Military Procurement Sub-committee on 29 February 2000.

14. "Around the Fleet," USNAVCENT *Connection,* 15 Jan. 1998, 3.

15. Lt. (jg) Michael Atwell, "Gary Rescues Crew of Burning Tanker," USNAVCENT *Scimitar,* 15 March 2000, 2.

16. Capt. Lee Holbrook interview by author, 8 Sept. 2003.

17. Holbrook interview; *American Bahraini Friendship Society Newsletter,* Autumn 2001, 2–3.

18. John D. Gresham, "Forces Fighting for Enduring Freedom," U.S. Naval Institute *Proceedings* (November 2001): 45–46.

19. "USS *Theodore Roosevelt* Pounds Taliban and Terrorist Targets," *Seapower* (December 2001): 24; Richard R. Burgess, "Air Strikes Hit Afghan Front Lines," *Seapower* (December 2001): 25.

20. Nathman, "We Were Great," 94–96; Truver, "The U.S. Navy Year in Review," May 2002, 76.

21. Holbrook interview.

22. Capt. Phil Wisecup, USN, and Lt. Tom Williams, USN, "Making Coalition Naval Warfare Work," U.S. Naval Institute *Proceedings* (September 2002): 52–55.

23. Fitzgerald interview.

24. Quote of Rep. Eric Cantor to Ralph Z. Hallow, "Lieberman a Tough Sell Among Jewish Donors," *The Washington Times,* 8 July 2003, A1.

25. *American Bahraini Friendship Society Newsletter,* Summer 2002, 3–4; Neil MacFarquhar, "Arab Protesters Focus Ire on U.S.," *New York Times,* 6 April 2002, A1, A9.

26. Neil MacFarquhar, "Death in Bahrain Brings Demand That U.S. Leave," *New York Times,* 8 April 2002, A9.

27. Holbrook interview.

28. *American Bahraini Friendship Society Newsletter,* Spring 2002, 4.

29. www.glogalsecurity.org, annual Southern Watch chronologies.

30. Thom Shanker, "Rumsfeld Says Iraq Has Chemical Arms Ready," *New York Times,* 11 June 2002, A14; Holbrook interview.

31. ABCNEWS.COM, "Iraq Special Report: Timeline"; *American Bahraini Friendship Society Newsletter,* Autumn 2002, 8.

32. United Nations Security Council Resolution 1441 (2002) at www.un.org.

33. Holbrook interview.

34. Ibid.

35. "President Bush Meets with Prime Minister Blair," remarks on www.white-house.gov.

36. *American Bahraini Friendship Society Newsletter,* Spring 2003, 7; *Bahrain News and Information,* No. 30, Spring 2003, 1, 2, 6.

37. Holbrook interview.

38. *American Bahraini Friendship Society Newsletter,* Spring 2003, 2.

39. Ibid.

Glossary

AFB	Air Force Base
AGF	Command Ship
ASU Bahrain	Administrative Support Unit Bahrain
ASU-SWA	Administrative Support Unit Southwest Asia
AO	Oiler
AOR	Area of Responsibility
AVP	Airplane Tender
BANS	Bahrain Amiri Navy Ship
BAPCO	Bahrain Petroleum Company
BISA	Bahrain International School Association
CENTAF	Central Command Air Force
CENTCOM	Central Command
CENTO	Central Treaty Organization
CINC	Commander in Chief
CINCEUR	Commander in Chief, Europe
CINCLANT	Commander in Chief, Atlantic
CINCLANTFLT	Commander in Chief, Atlantic Fleet
CINCNELM	Commander in Chief, Northeastern Atlantic and Mediterranean
CINCPAC	Commander in Chief, Pacific
CINCPACFLT	Commander in Chief, Pacific Fleet
CINCUSNAVEUR	Commander in Chief, U.S. Naval Forces Europe
CJTFME	Commander Joint Task Force, Middle East
CMEF	Commander, Middle East Force
CNO	Chief of Naval Operations
CO	Commanding Officer
COMFIFTHFLT	Commander Fifth Fleet
COMIDEASTFOR	Commander Middle East Force
COMSEVENTHFLT	Commander Seventh Fleet
COMUSNAVCENT	Commander, U.S. Naval Forces, Central Command

COMUSNAV-LOGSUPFOR	Commander, U.S. Naval Logistics Support Force
DODDS	Department of Defense Dependents Schools
GCC	Gulf Cooperation Council
HMS	Her Majesty's Ship/Her Majesty's Station
JCS	Joint Chiefs of Staff
JSSC	Joint Strategic Survey Committee
JTFME	Joint Task Force, Middle East
JTF-SWA	Joint Task Force, Southwest Asia
JWPC	Joint Warfare Plans Committee
LEDet	Law Enforcement Detachment
LSM	Landing Ship Medium
LST	Landing Ship Tank
MCM	Mine Countermeasures
MEF	Middle East Force
MIDEASTFOR	Middle East Force
MILCON	Military Construction
MIO	Maritime Interdiction Operations
MIUW	Mobile Inshore Undersea Warfare
MOU	Memorandum of Understanding
MSB	Mobile Sea Base
MWR	Morale, Welfare, and Recreation
NATO	North Atlantic Treaty Organization
NAVCENT	U.S. Naval Forces, Central Command
NAVFAC	Naval Facilities Engineering Command
NRCC	Naval Regional Contracting Center
NSC	National Security Council
OPLAN	Operations Plan
OPMSANG	Office of Program Management Saudi Arabia National Guard
OPNAV	Office of the Chief of Naval Operations
PCS	Permanent Change of Station
PWC	Public Works Center
RDF	Rapid Deployment Force
RDJTF	Rapid Deployment Joint Task Force
SECDEF	Secretary of Defense
SOCAL	Standard Oil of California
TAD	Temporary Active Duty

UAE	United Arab Emirates
UN	United Nations
UNMOVIC	United Nations Monitoring, Verification and Inspection Commission
UNSCOM	United Nations Special Commission
USCENTCOM	U.S. Central Command
USCINCCENT	U.S. Commander in Chief, Central Command
USNS	United States Naval Ship
USS	United States Ship
VBSS	Visit Boarding Search and Seizure
XO	Executive Officer

Selected Bibliography

Books

Adams, Michael, ed. *The Middle East: A Handbook*. Westport, Conn.: Praeger Publishers, 1971.

———, ed. *The Middle East*. Handbooks to the Modern World. New York: Facts on File Publications, 1987.

Al Hamad, Tawfeeq. *Khalifa bin Salman: A Man and the Rise of the State*. Bahrain: Scientific Creativity Centre, 1997.

Al Khalifa, Hamad Bin Isa. *First Light: Modern Bahrain and its Heritage*. London and New York: Kegan Paul International, 1994.

Amin, S. H. *Political and Strategic Issues in the Persian–Arabian Gulf*. Glasgow, Scotland: Royston Limited, 1984.

Armerding, Paul. "The American Mission Hospital: A Century of Progress in Medicine," in *The American Bahraini Relationship: A Special Report*. Washington, D.C.: National Council on US-Arab Relations, no date.

Badeau, John S. *The American Approach to the Arab World*. Council on Foreign Relations. New York: Harper & Row, 1968.

Belgrave, Charles. *Personal Column*. London: Hutchinson, 1960.

Bensen, Lawrence R. "A Survey of Bases and Forces," *The United States Military in North Africa and Southwest Asia Since World War II*. Tampa, Fla.: U.S. Central Command History Office, 1988.

Brown, Carl L. *International Politics and the Middle East: Old Rules, Dangerous Game*. Princeton, N.J.: Princeton University Press, 1984.

Burrell, R. M. *The Persian Gulf*. The Washington Papers. No. 1. The Center for Strategic and International Studies. New York: The Library Press, 1972.

Burrell, R. M., and Alvin J. Cottrell. *Iran, The Arabian Peninsula, and the Indian Ocean*. New York: National Strategy Information Center, 1972.

Carus, W. Seth, Barry McCoy, and John R. Hafey. *From MIDEASTFOR to Fifth Fleet: Forward Naval Presence in Southwest Asia*. Alexandria, Va.: Center for Naval Analyses, 1995.

Center for Strategic and International Studies. *The Gulf: Implications of British Withdrawal*. Special Report No. 8. Washington, D.C.: Georgetown University, February 1969.

Clarke, Angela. *Bahrain Oil and Development, 1929–1989*. London: Immel Publishing, 1990.

——. *Bahrain: A Heritage Explored*. Bahrain: Public Relations Group, 1991.

——. *The American Mission Hospital: Through the Changing Scenes of Life, 1893–1993*. Bahrain: American Mission Hospital Society, 1993.

Clancy, Tom, with General Tony Zinni and Tony Koltz. *Battle Ready*. New York: G. P. Putnam's Sons, 2004.

Cole, Ronald H., Walter S. Poole, James F. Schnabel, Robert J. Watson, and Willard J. Webb. *The History of the Unified Command Plan, 1946–1993*. Washington, D.C.: Joint History Office, 1995.

Cordesman, Anthony H. *Bahrain, Oman, Qatar and the UAE: Challenges of Security*. Boulder, Colo.: Westview Press, 1997.

Cottrell, Alvin J., gen. ed. *The Persian Gulf States: A General Survey*. Baltimore: Johns Hopkins University Press, 1980.

Crowe, Adm. William J. Jr., with David Chanoff. *The Line of Fire: From Washington to the Gulf, the Politics and Battles of the New Military*. New York: Simon and Schuster, 1993.

Department of State. *U.S. Policy in the Middle East: November 1974–February 1976*. Selected Documents No. 4. Washington, D.C.: Government Printing Office, 1976.

Friedman, Norman. *Desert Victory: The War for Kuwait*. Annapolis, Md.: Naval Institute Press, 1991.

Gaddis, John Lewis. *Strategies of Containment: A Critical Appraisal of Postwar American National Security Policy*. New York: Oxford, 1982.

Gordon, Michael, and Bernard Trainer. *The Generals' War: The Inside Story of the Conflict in the Gulf*. New York: Little, Brown, and Company, 1995.

Grayson, Benson Lee. *Soviet Intentions and American Options in the Middle East*. National Security Affairs Monography Series 82-3. Washington, D.C: National Defense University Press, 1982.

Hana, Sami A. *A Modern Cultural History of Bahrain*. Bahrain: Ministry of Information, 1991.

Harkavy, Robert E. *Great Power Competition for Overseas Bases*. New York: Pergamon Press, 1982.

Hay, Sir Rupert. *The Persian Gulf States*. Washington, D.C: The Middle East Institute, 1959.

Helms, Robert F., and Robert H. Dorff. *The Persian Gulf Crisis: Power in the Post-Cold War World*. Westport, Ct.: Praeger Publishers, 1993.

Hepburn, Donald. "BAPCO-CALTEX: Oil Pioneers in the Arabian Gulf," in *The American Bahraini Relationship: A Special Report*. Washington, D.C.: National Council on U.S.-Arab Relations, no date.

Hines, Jay E. "Forged in the Desert: United States Central Command from Desert Shield to Today," *Desert Shield, Desert Storm: The 10th Anniversary of the Gulf War.* Tampa, Fla.: Faircourt LLC, 2001.

Hurewitz, J. C. *Middle East Politics: The Military Dimension.* New York: Frederick A. Praeger Publishers, 1969.

———. *Soviet-American Rivalry in the Middle East.* New York: Frederick A. Praeger Publishers, 1969.

Jentleson, Bruce W. *With Friends Like These: Reagan, Bush, and Saddam, 1982–1990.* New York: W. W. Norton and Company, 1994.

Johnson, Maxwell Orme. *The Military as an Instrument of National Policy in Southwest Asia: The Rapid Deployment Joint Task Force, 1979–1982.* Boulder, Colo.: Westview Press, 1983.

Kalb, Marvin, and Bernard Kalb. *Kissinger.* Boston: Little and Brown, 1974.

Kelly, J. B. *Britain and the Persian Gulf, 1795–1880.* London: Oxford University Press, 1968.

———. *Arabia, the Gulf and the West.* New York: Basic Books, 1980.

Kissinger, Henry A. *White House Years.* Boston: Little, Brown and Co., 1979.

Klieman, Aaron S. *Soviet Russia and the Middle East.* The Washington Center of Foreign Policy Research. Baltimore: Johns Hopkins University Press, 1970.

Kuniholm, Bruce R. *The Persian Gulf and United States Policy.* Claremont, Calif.: Regina Books, 1984.

LeFeber, Walter F. *America, Russia, and the Cold War*, 6th ed. New York: McGraw Hill, 1991.

Lehman Jr., John F. *Command of the Seas.* New York: Charles Scribner's Sons, 1988.

Lenczowski, George. *The Middle East in World Affairs,* 3rd ed. Ithaca, N.Y.: Cornell University Press, 1962.

Lengyel, Emil. *The Changing Middle East.* New York: The John Day Co., 1960.

Levinson, Jeffrey L., and Randy L. Edwards. *Missile Inbound: The Attack on the Stark in the Persian Gulf.* Annapolis, Md.: Naval Institute Press, 1997.

Mansfield, Peter, ed. *The Middle East: A Political and Economic Survey,* 4th ed. London: Oxford University Press, 1973.

———. *A History of the Middle East.* New York: Viking, 1991.

Marlowe, John. *Arab Nationalism and British Imperialism: A Study in Power Politics.* New York: Frederick A. Praeger Publishers, 1961.

———. *The Persian Gulf in the Twentieth Century.* New York: Frederick A. Praeger Publishers, 1962.

Marolda, Edward J., and Robert J. Schneller Jr. *Shield and Sword: The United States Navy and the Persian Gulf War*. Washington, D.C.: Naval Historical Center, 1999.

Merlin, Samuel, ed. *The Big Powers and the Present Crisis in the Middle East: A Colloquium*. Rutherford, N.J.: Fairleigh Dickinson University Press, 1968.

Metz, Helen Chapin, ed. *Persian Gulf States: Country Studies*. Washington, D.C.: Library of Congress, 1994.

Middle East: U.S. Policy, Israel, Oil and the Arabs. Washington, D.C.: Congressional Quarterly, April 1974.

Motter, T. H. Vail. *The Persian Corridor and Aid to Russia: The United States Army in World War II*. Washington, D.C.: Center for Military History, 1952.

Naff, Thomas, ed. *Gulf Security and the Iran-Iraq War*. Washington, D.C.: National Defense University Press, 1985.

Noyes, James H. *The Clouded Lens: Persian Gulf Security and U.S. Policy,* 2nd ed. Stanford, Calif.: Hoover Institution Press, 1982.

Palmer, Michael A. *On Course to Desert Storm: The United States Navy and the Persian Gulf.* Washington, D.C.: Naval Historical Center, 1992.

———. *Guardians of the Gulf: A History of America's Expanding Role in the Persian Gulf, 1833–1992*. New York: The Free Press, 1992.

Partin, John W. *Special Operations Forces in Operation Earnest Will / Prime Chance I*. Tampa, Fla.: U.S. Special Operations Command History and Research Office, April 1988.

Paterson, Thomas G. *Meeting the Communist Threat: Truman to Reagan*. New York: Oxford University Press, 1988.

Pokant, Marvin. *Desert Shield at Sea: What the Navy Really Did*. Westport, Conn.: Greenwood Press, 1998.

Polk, William R. *The United States and the Arab World*. Cambridge, Mass.: Harvard University Press, 1965.

Price, David Lynn. *Oil and Middle East Security*. Center for Strategic and International Studies, the Washington Papers, vol. 4., no. 41. Beverly Hills, Calif.: SAGE Publications, 1976.

Royal Institute of International Affairs. *The Middle East: A Political and Economic Survey,* 2nd ed. London: Royal Institute of International Affairs, 1954.

Schwarzkopf, Gen. H. Norman. *It Doesn't Take a Hero*. New York: Bantam, 1992.

Speiser, E. A. *The United States and the Near East.*, rev. ed. Cambridge, Mass.: Harvard University Press, 1950.

Teicher, Howard, and Gayle Radley Teicher. *Twin Pillars to Desert Storm: America's Flawed Vision in the Middle East, from Nixon to Bush.* New York: Morrow, 1993.

The American-Bahraini Relationship: A Special Report. Washington, D.C.: National Council on U.S.-Arab Relations, 2003.

Weinberger, Caspar W. *Fighting for Peace: Seven Critical Years in the Pentagon.* Warner Books, 1990.

Wheatcroft, Andrew. *Bahrain in Original Photographs: 1880–1961.* London: Kegan Paul International, 1988.

DISSERTATION, UNPUBLISHED MONOGRAPH, AND SPEECH

Crist, David B. *Operation Earnest Will: The United States in the Persian Gulf, 1986–1989.* Ph.D. dissertation, Florida State University, 1998.

Hanks, Robert. *Middle East Journal.* 1994.

Less, Rear Adm. Anthony A. Speech to Manama Rotary Club, 5 March 1989.

ARTICLES

Allison, Fred H. "Midnight in Baghdad." U.S. Naval Institute *Proceedings* (February 2002): 32–35.

Bosco, Lee. "Making Things Happen in the Persian Gulf: Logistic Command Proves No Desert Storm Puzzle Is Too Tough." *All Hands* 891 (June 1991): 32–35.

———. "Port Harbor Security: Interservice Coalition Kept Ships Safe." *All Hands* 891 (June 1991): 25–27.

Burgess, Richard R. "Air Strikes Hit Afghan Front Lines." *Seapower* (December 2001): 25.

Burlage, John. "Paddling above Water." *Navy Times,* 26 Nov. 1990, 4.

Crowe, VADM William J. "The Persian Gulf: Central or Peripheral to the United States Strategy?" U.S. Naval Institute *Proceedings* (Naval Review 1978): 184–209.

Cushman, Jack. "This . . . Is the Gulf." U.S. Naval Institute *Proceedings* (Naval Review 1988): 50.

Daly, Captain Thomas, "The Enduring Gulf War." U.S. Naval Institute *Proceedings* (May 1985): 151–54.

DeForth, Peter W. "U.S. Naval Presence in the Persian Gulf: The Mideast Force since World War II." *Naval War College Review* 28:1 (Summer 1975): 28–37.

Dur, Philip A. "Presence: Forward, Ready, Engaged." U.S. Naval Institute *Proceedings* (June 1994): 41–44.

Ehteshami, Anoushiravan. "Strategic Survey of the Near East 1988/89." *Middle East Strategic Studies Quarterly* (Spring/Summer 1989): 3–6.

Freedman, Robert O. "Soviet Policy Toward the Middle East Since the October 1973 Arab-Israeli War." *Naval War College Review* 29:2 (Fall 1976): 61–103.

Gresham, John D. "Forces Fighting for Enduring Freedom." U.S. Naval Institute *Proceedings* (November 2001): 45–46.

Hines, Jay E. "American Eagle in the Sand: The Story of the United States Central Command." *The Political Chronicle* (Spring/Summer 1996): 1–2.

Houlihan, Bob. "Policing the Gulf." *All Hands* (March 2003): 22–26.

Jehl, Douglas. "Sheik Isa, 65, Emir of Bahrain Who Built Non-Oil Economy." *New York Times,* 7 March 1999, A49.

Kelly, Capt. James F. Jr. "Naval Deployments in the Indian Ocean." U.S. Naval Institute *Proceedings* (May 1983): 174–89.

McDonald, Wesley L. "The Convoy Mission." U.S. Naval Institute *Proceedings* (Naval Review 1988): 36–44.

MacFarquhar, Neil. "In Bahrain, Women Run, Women Vote, Women Lose." *New York Times,* 22 May 2002, A3.

———. "Bahrain Tries to Fill Potholes on Road to New Government." *New York Times,* 18 June 2002, A6.

———. "Arab Protesters Focus Ire on U.S." *New York Times,* 6 April 2002, A1, A9.

———. "Death in Bahrain Brings Demand That U.S. Leave." *New York Times,* 8 April 2002, A9.

Mussi, 1st Class Petty Officer Chuck. "Desert Ducks: Deliverymen of the Persian Gulf." *All Hands* (March 1988): 14–15.

Nakhleh, Emile. "Bahrain and the Persian Gulf Security," in *The Impart of the Iranian Events upon Persian Gulf and United States Security* (Washington, D.C.: American Foreign Policy Institute Studies on Middle East Problems, 1979): 111–27.

Nathman, Vice Adm. John B. "We Were Great: Navy Air in Afghanistan." U.S. Naval Institute *Proceedings* (March 2002): 94–95.

O'Rourke, Ronald. "The Tanker War." U.S. Naval Institute *Proceedings* (May 1988): 30–34.

Peay, J. H. Binford, III. "The Five Pillars of Peace in the Central Region." *Joint Force Quarterly* (Autumn 1995): 32–39.

Pittman, Hal. "In the Presence of Heroes." *All Hands* (May 2001): 24–42.

Rosenberg, David Alan. "The U.S. Navy and the Problem of Oil in a Future War: The Outline of a Strategic Dilemma, 1945–1950." *Naval War College Review* 29:1 (Summer 1976): 53–64.

Semmes, Katharine Ainsworth. ""Bahrain: Pearl of the Persian Gulf." U.S. Naval Institute *Proceedings* (May 1966): 93.

Shanker, Thom. "Rumsfeld Says Iraq Has Chemical Arms Ready." *New York Times*, 11 June 2002.

Stewart, James. "East of Suez." U.S. Naval Institute *Proceedings* (March 1966): 41–51.

"Strategic Survey of the Middle East." *Middle East Strategic Studies Quarterly* 1:2 (Summer/Spring 1989): 1–59, 51–75.

Thomas, Joseph. "Fifth Fleet Stands Up." *Pull Together* (Spring/Summer 1997): 6–9.

Truver, Scott. "U.S. Navy Year in Review." U.S. Naval Institute *Proceedings* (May 1999): 79.

———. "U.S. Navy Year in Review." U.S. Naval Institute *Proceedings* (May 2001): 84.

———. "U.S. Navy Year in Review." U.S. Naval Institute *Proceedings* (May 2002): 74–75.

Wisecup, Capt. Phil, and Lt. Tom Williams. "Making Coalition Naval Warfare Work." U.S. Naval Institute *Proceedings* (September 2002): 52–55.

Withrow, John E. Jr. "Needed: A Credible Presence." U.S. Naval Institute *Proceedings* (March 1966): 52–61.

CRUISEBOOKS

LOCATED AT THE NAVY DEPARTMENT LIBRARY, WASHINGTON NAVY YARD, WASHINGTON, D.C.

USS *Duxbury Bay*, 1960, 1961, 1965.
USS *Greenwich*, 1950.
USS *La Salle*, 1984–88.
USS *Valcour*, 1953, 1955.

PRIMARY SOURCE DOCUMENTS

THE FOLLOWING DOCUMENTS WERE REVIEWED FROM THE MIDEASTFOR COMMAND FILE, OPERATIONAL ARCHIVES, NAVAL HISTORICAL CENTER, WASHINGTON NAVY YARD.

ASU Bahrain command history, 1979; 1980; 1981; 1982; 1983; 1988; 1989; 1990; 1991.

ASU-SWA command history, 1992; 1994; 1995; 1996; 1997.

COMIDEASTFOR command history, 1958–1959; 1960; 1961; 1962; 1963; 1966; 1967; 1968; 1969; 1970; 1971; 1972; 1973; 1974; 1975; 1976; 1977; 1985; 1986.

COMIDEASTFOR, Report of Operations and Conditions of Command, 1 July 1959–18 February 1960.

Middle East Force Admin. Correspondence, 1967–1987, files.

USCINCNELM command history, 1 April–1 July 1947; 1 October 1947–31 March 1948; 1 April–30 September 1948; 1 October 1948–31 March 1949; 1 November 1950–1 July 1951.

USCINCNELM, Report of Operations and Conditions of Command, 1 July 1948–30 July 1949; 1 July 1949–1 July 1950; 1 November 1950–1 July 1951; 1 July 1951–14 June 1952; 14 June 1952–1 July 1953.

USS *Rendova* Round the World Cruise Report.

THE FOLLOWING DOCUMENTS WERE REVIEWED FROM THE SHIPS HISTORY BRANCH, NAVAL HISTORICAL CENTER, WASHINGTON NAVY YARD.

USS *Duxbury Bay* command history, 1 July–31 December 1951; 1 January–30 June 1952; 1963; 1964; 1965.

USS *Greenwich Bay* command history, 1956; 1957; 1958; 1959; 1961; 1962; 1963; 1964.

USS *La Salle* command history, 1972; 1973; 1974; 1975; 1976; 1977; 1978; 1981; 1982; 1983; 1987; 1988; 1989; 1990; 1991; 1992; 1993; 1995.

USS *Valcour* command history, 1 July–31 December 1951; 1956; 1957; 1958; 1959; 1964; 1966; 1967; 1968; 1969; 1971; 1972.

THE FOLLOWING DOCUMENTS WERE REVIEWED FROM THE NAVCENT PUBLIC AFFAIRS OFFICE.

Change of Command Speech files; Press Release files; Newspaper Clippings files; PAO Award Nomination packages.

INTERVIEWS AND ORAL HISTORIES

INTERVIEWS WITH DAVID WINKLER AND/OR JAMES WOMBWELL

Addams, Rear Admiral John F. 2 March 1999.

Al Khalifa, H.H. Shaikh Salman bin Hamad. 23 August 2000.

Almoayed, Tariq A. 25 November 1998.

Al Shirawi, Yousuf Ahmed. 24 November 1998.

Bernsen, Rear Admiral Harold J. 22 March 1999.

Bigley, Vice Admiral Thomas J. 26 October 1998, 12 September 2000.

Bowie, Lieutenant Commander John. 28 November 1998.

Brandran, Framarz. 13 November 1998.

Chandonnet, Commander Charles. 22 August 2000.

Fargo, Vice Admiral Thomas B. 20 July 1999.

Fitzgerald, Rear Admiral Mark. 18 June 2003.

Fulham, Captain Marcia. 11 April 1999.

Gerringer, Charles Allen. 16 November 1998.

Gilbert, Lieutenant Jason A. 11 November 1998.

Hawkins, Commander Norman G. 12 November 1998.

Hepburn, Donald. 1 February 2001.

Holbrook, Captain Lee. 8 September 2003.

Jeffords, Senator James M. 26 July 2003.

Kaedi, Hamza A. M. 12 November 1998.

Katz, Vice Admiral Douglas. 25 February 1999.

Lyons, Admiral James "Ace." 8 March 1999.

Merkel, Dennis. 18 November 1998.

Mohammed, R.M.V.K. 16 November 1998.

Moore, Vice Admiral Charles W. 27 August 2000.

O'Donnell, Captain Gerald J. 16 November 1998.

Packer, Rear Admiral Samuel. 26 February 1999, 8 August 2000.

Pelletreau, Ambassador Robert H. 13 September 2000.

Robinson, Captain Evan. 17 March 1999.

Secord, First Class Petty Officer Kevin. 13 December 1998.

Sheek, Lieutenant Commander Gordon. 18 August 2000.

Smith, QM1 Timothy E. 17 November 1998.

Smith, Commander Victoria M. 18 November 1998.

Steele, Captain John G. 17 August 2000, 19 June 2003.

Vann, Joseph W. 18 November 1998.

Vostock, Barabara. 23 November 1998.

Walters, Senior Chief Timothy. 13 December 1998.

Wycoff, Daniel W. 17 November 1998.

NAVAL HISTORICAL CENTER, ORAL HISTORY COLLECTION, WASHINGTON, D.C.

Stanik, Lieutenant Commander Joseph T. Interview by Robert Schneller, 1994.

NAVAL HISTORICAL FOUNDATION, ORAL HISTORY COLLECTION, WASHINGTON, D.C.

Bayne, Vice Admiral Marmaduke G. Interview by David F. Winkler, 1998.
Mustin, Vice Admiral Henry C. Interview by David F. Winkler, 2001.
Plackett, William. Interview by David F. Winkler, 1997.

UNITED STATES NAVAL INSTITUTE, ORAL HISTORY COLLECTION, ANNAPOLIS, MD.

Eller, Rear Admiral Ernest M. Interview by John T. Mason, 1979.
Felt, Admiral Harry D. Interview by John T. Mason, 1974.
Gayler, Admiral Noel A. M. Interview by Paul Stillwell, 1984.
Jackson, Jr., Vice Admiral Andrew McB. Interview by John T. Mason, 1972.
Mack, Vice Admiral William P. Interview by John T. Mason, 1980.
Moorer, Admiral Thomas H. Interview by Paul Stillwell, 1984.
Peet, Vice Admiral Raymond E. Interview by Paul Stillwell, 1984.
Semmes, Vice Admiral Benedict J. Interview by Paul Stillwell, 1988.

COLUMBIA UNIVERSITY, ORAL HISTORY RESEARCH OFFICE, NEW YORK, N.Y.

Conolly, Admiral Richard L. Interview by Donald F. Shaughnessy, 1960.

Index

About the Author

DAVID F. WINKLER is the Capital Campaign Director for the National Museum of the United States Navy Cold War Gallery, Washington Navy Yard, Washington, D.C. A historian with the Naval Historical Foundation, Winkler is the author of *Cold War at Sea: High Seas Confrontation Between the United States and the Soviet Union* (Naval Institute Press, 2000); he has contributed articles to leading naval magazines and journals. He holds a bachelor's degree in political science from Penn State, a master's in international affairs from Washington University, and a Ph.D. in history from American University. A surface warfare officer and Naval War College graduate, Winkler served on active duty for ten years and is currently a commander in the Navy Reserve. He, his wife Mary, and newborn daughter Katherine Anne reside in Alexandria, Virginia.